For Richard —

cher maître
&
dear friend

LCD
Oct 2007

Charles Eliot Norton

Becoming Modern: New Nineteenth-Century Studies

SERIES EDITORS

Sarah Way Sherman
Department of English
University of New Hampshire

Janet Aikins
Department of English
University of New Hampshire

Rohan McWilliam
Anglia Ruskin University
Cambridge, England

Janet Polasky
Department of History
University of New Hampshire

This book series maps the complexity of historical change and assesses the formation of ideas, movements, and institutions crucial to our own time by publishing books that examine the emergence of modernity in North America and Europe. Set primarily but not exclusively in the nineteenth century, the series shifts attention from modernity's twentieth-century forms to its earlier moments of uncertain and often disputed construction. Seeking books of interest to scholars on both sides of the Atlantic, it thereby encourages the expansion of nineteenth-century studies and the exploration of more global patterns of development.

Linda Dowling, *Charles Eliot Norton: The Art of Reform in Nineteenth-Century America*

William C. Dowling, *Oliver Wendell Holmes in Paris: Medicine, Theology, and the Autocrat of the Breakfast Table*

Betsy Klimasmith, *At Home in the City: Urban Domesticity in American Literature and Culture, 1850–1930*

Sarah Luria, *Capital Speculations: Writing and Building Washington, D.C.*

David L. Richards, *Poland Spring: A Tale of the Gilded Age, 1860–1900*

Angela Sorby, *Schoolroom Poets: Childhood, Performance, and the Place of American Poetry, 1865–1917*

William M. Morgan, *Philanthropists in Disguise: Gender, Humanitarianism, and Complicity in U.S. Literary Realism*

Piya Pal-Lapinski, *The Exotic Woman in Nineteenth-Century British Fiction and Culture: A Reconsideration*

Patrick H. Vincent, *The Romantic Poetess: European Culture, Politics, and Gender, 1820–1840*

Edward S. Cutler, *Recovering the New: Transatlantic Roots of Modernism*

Margaret M. Mulrooney, *Black Powder, White Lace: The du Pont Irish and Cultural Identity in Nineteenth-Century America*

Stephen Carl Arch, *After Franklin: The Emergence of Autobiography in Post-Revolutionary America, 1780–1830*

Justin D. Edwards, *Exotic Journeys: Exploring the Erotics of U.S. Travel Literature, 1840–1930*

For a complete list of books in this series, see www.upne.com

Charles Eliot Norton

The Art of Reform in Nineteenth-Century America

Linda Dowling

University of New Hampshire
Durham, New Hampshire

PUBLISHED BY
UNIVERSITY PRESS OF NEW ENGLAND
HANOVER AND LONDON

University of New Hampshire Press
Published by University Press of New England,
One Court Street, Lebanon, NH 03766
www.upne.com

© 2007 by University of New Hampshire Press
Printed in the United States of America
5 4 3 2 1

Library of Congress Cataloging-in-Publication Data

Dowling, Linda C., 1944–
Charles Eliot Norton : the art of reform in nineteenth-
century America / Linda Dowling.
p.   cm. — (Becoming modern : new nineteenth-century studies)
Includes bibliographical references and index.
ISBN-13: 978–1–58465–646–3 (cloth : alk. paper)
ISBN-10: 1–58465–646–8 (cloth : alk. paper)
1. Norton, Charles Eliot, 1827–1908. I. Title.
PS2478.D69   2007
818'.409—dc22
[B]   2007021089

Edith Wharton's "High Pasture" first published in *Letters of Charles Eliot Norton*, ed. Sara Norton and M. A. DeWolfe Howe. 2 vols. Boston and NY: Houghton Mifflin, 1913. 2:387.

For WCD

Come up—come up: in the dim vale below
The autumn mist muffles the fading trees,
But on this keen hill-pasture, though the breeze
Has stretched the thwart boughs bare to meet the snow,
Night is not, autumn is not—but the flow
Of vast, ethereal and irradiate seas,
Poured from the far world's flaming boundaries
In waxing tides of unimagined glow.

And to that height illumined of the mind
He calls us still by the familiar way,
Leaving the sodden tracks of life behind,
Befogged in failure, chilled with love's decay—
Showing us, as the night-mists upward wind,
How on the heights is day and still more day.

—EDITH WHARTON, "High Pasture,"
a poem written for Norton's
80th birthday in 1907

Contents

Preface: The Ghost of Shady Hill

On a thunderous afternoon in late August 1902, G. Stanley Hall, the president of Clark University, rose from a crowded banquet table to denounce an elderly gentleman sitting nearby. The gentleman was Charles Eliot Norton, an eminent scholar and professor of art history at Harvard, and a figure widely regarded as the most cultured man in America. Hall castigated Norton for a speech he had delivered just minutes before, condemning the Spanish-American War as the expression of an arrogant and dangerous United States imperialism. The occasion was the celebrated Sanderson Academy Dinner, an annual event first organized under Norton's leadership some two decades earlier. The place was Ashfield, a little town in the western hills of Massachusetts, where Norton had been spending summers with his family since 1864.

Officially, the Spanish-American War was over, concluded by the Treaty of Paris almost four years before. Norton in his speech, however, denounced an ongoing conflict, a "needless and criminal war" that seemingly had no end. First begun by President William McKinley ostensibly to end Spanish despotism in Cuba, the conflict had swiftly shifted to another hemisphere, to the Philippines. Now it was being carried on by McKinley's successor Theodore Roosevelt in a brutal attempt to put down indigenous resistance to U.S. annexation of the vast archipelago. In the end, nearly 300,000 Filipinos would die in the struggle, a savage jungle conflict in which U.S. soldiers found themselves ordered quite literally to take no prisoners, to burn hundreds of Filipino villages, and in dealing with unwilling informants, to engage in notorious tortures like "the water cure," in which gallons of water were poured down the throats of peasants until they "confessed" or drowned. What service could Roosevelt ever conceivably render America, Norton asked witheringly, to compensate "for the evil which he renders it by his exaltation of war?"[1]

When Stanley Hall rose to respond, he set about chastising the seventy-four-year-old Norton as if he were an errant college boy, and deploring what he was pleased to call Norton's epithets, his vituperation and, especially, his "aspersions of public men whom this community respects." Speaking as someone who had grown up in Ashfield, Hall referred ominously to the way "summer visitors from near and far" with their "alien views" had in recent years come to dominate the Academy dinners. The townspeople of Ashfield, Hall declared, designating himself spokesman for villagers sympathetic to Roosevelt's Philippine adventure, "have at least a right to hear the expression of their own sentiments here."[2]

A complex personal relationship lay in the immediate background of Hall's denunciation of Norton. He had been one of Norton's youthful protégés, an Ashfield farmer's son who had gone on to become a well-known German-trained psychologist. He had attended Sanderson Academy, the town's common school for which Norton had originally organized the Ashfield dinners to raise money. Still, though this may have been the moment Hall chose for a declaration of personal independence from his one-time mentor, his account of Norton's relation to Ashfield sentiment got things essentially right. For despite his nearly forty years as a summer resident, Norton's outspoken and fearless opposition to the Spanish-American War had indeed made him an alien, no less in Ashfield than in America itself.

Norton had immediately and fervently denounced the Spanish-American War as an expression of a newborn American imperialism. When war was declared in April 1898, Norton, a legendary teacher at Harvard, told his students that their patriotic duty lay in working to improve the conditions of those less fortunate than themselves, not dying uselessly in an imperialist war. Speaking to hundreds of young men seated in a Harvard lecture hall, Norton explicitly urged them to spurn McKinley's appeal for patriotic volunteers. Then, along with a tiny band of other men and women dauntless enough to protest the immensely popular war—this "splendid little war," as John Hay would later famously describe it to Roosevelt—Norton had held to his lonely course in the face of outraged national opinion. Denounced as a "Tory," an "Unpatriotic Harvard Don," and a "Menace to Our Youth," Norton would for many months be held up to contumely and crude sarcasm in the national press. "Nortonism," declared the *Los Angeles Times*, was plainly "another name for treason"; an editorial urged that Norton be "ducked into a swill barrel, as he deserves." The *Chicago Tribune*, anticipating the "America—Love It or Leave It" slogan used against critics of U.S. policy in Southeast Asia later in the twentieth century, concluded that if people like Norton "do not like the way the government is conducting our foreign affairs," they should "change their allegiance to some other government." "[L]et them," said a *Tribune* editorial, "migrate to Spain."[3]

Whether or not he was motivated by some purely personal grievance,

Hall was also quite right about Norton's having made the Academy Dinners into a national forum on the Spanish-American War. To be sure, the Dinners had drawn national attention from the very start, for Norton and his magnetic co-founder, the liberal editor and orator George William Curtis, had been exceptionally successful in attracting distinguished speakers on important national topics to Ashfield in the otherwise empty third week in August. But in the absence of the genial Curtis, who had died in 1892, and the outbreak of the Spanish war, the tone of the Dinners had abruptly changed. In his rage and anguish at the disastrous policy thrust upon the nation by McKinley and those who favored a new American imperialism, Norton as master of ceremonies made certain that the Academy speakers would be disproportionately chosen from among those who opposed the administration side.

Moorfield Storey, Charles Dudley Warner and Daniel Chamberlain would all give ringing and memorable anti-war speeches. Even Booker T. Washington, invited by Norton to Ashfield with the express purpose of turning a national spotlight onto the plight of the Southern Negro, made a point of voicing his opposition to administration policy. In the five Augusts following the declaration of war, this small group of impassioned speakers mounted a lonely resistance to the advocates of U.S. imperialist policy who, elsewhere in the country, were greeted with tumultuous cheers as they promised coaling stations for the U.S. Navy, expanded markets for American manufacturers, new converts for Christian missionaries and worldwide hegemony for "the Anglo-Saxon race."[4]

What the Ashfield speakers against the Spanish-American War shared with Norton was a tragic sense that an ominous national milestone had been passed in the nation's reckless rush to war. Amidst the swaggering vaunts of glory and conquest that dominated the national discourse, Norton's band of fellow dissenters believed that the war was a mindless and brutal betrayal not only of the democratic ideals on which the American republic had been founded but of the more than 350,000 Union soldiers who had died to preserve these ideals in the Civil War. "We are committing this carnage for the sake of dominion, in order to compel the submission of freemen who owe us no submission," Norton had angrily told the Ashfield audience three years earlier, "to deprive them of their independence, to enforce moral slavery upon men who have as good a right to freedom as we ourselves." Minutes before Stanley Hall rose to issue his bitter rebuke of Norton, Edwin Burritt Smith, moved by a similar sense of national betrayal, denounced the administration as, in effect, traitors to the deepest ideals of the American republic. "Let us not deceive ourselves. We have not merely set up despotic government in the Philippines. We see there only instruments and its first victims. The thing itself is intrenched at Washington. The capital of the republic has been made the seat of government without consent."[5]

The incident at the Academy Dinner of August 1902 is not remembered today. American scholarship in the period since Charles Beard and Vernon Parrington and the Progressive historians associated with them has had no place for a Charles Eliot Norton who was recognized by his contemporaries as a fierce critic of national policy, a radical in the deepest sense of that often misapplied word. Bred in a family tradition of Unitarian resistance to orthodox religious dogma, Norton's dissent drew as well on the rooted moral and political principles that in an earlier century had motivated such New England radicals as John Adams and James Otis, and that in the nineteenth century would move such abolitionists as Elijah Lovejoy, Charles Sumner and John Brown to the point of physical martyrdom, their bloody fates avenged only by the wholesale bloodshed of the Civil War. The powerful dissenting strain in Norton's thought is nowhere more clearly revealed than in his resistance to the Spanish-American War, an embattled last stand that came at the end of a long life of writing and speaking and organizing on behalf of an ethically grounded vision of the American polity as it might, and deserved to, exist.

It scarcely needs saying that any notion of Norton as a radical or dissenting intellectual bears little resemblance to the Charles Eliot Norton who appears as a stock figure in most subsequent writing about nineteenth-century American culture. For as early as George Santayana's first influential essay on the "genteel tradition" (1911), there has been an unremitting tendency to identify Norton with a conservative, Anglophile, "nostalgic" position in American thought. The distortion has come about, one suspects, simply as a matter of what might be called an irresistible narrative logic. For some such character— Anglophiliac, "aristocratic," despairing—was clearly necessary to the story about art and democracy repeated by American commentators virtually since the earliest days of Jeffersonian democracy. Given certain inevitable tensions between democratic ideology—what have been called the "inhibitions of democracy" as regards recognizing differences in talent or ability—and the order implied by art and the aesthetic realm—the evident superiority of genius in a Michelangelo or a Shakespeare, the authority of the taste that comes only from education or cultural knowledge—a kind of resolution of contradictions has been achieved by imagining Norton as a certain type of symbolic opponent, the hidebound and pessimistic voice of a false and un-American aesthetic.[6]

In the 1920s and 1930s, the Progressive historians, as Ernest Breisach has shown, set out to redeem the unlovely America that had emerged from the Gilded Age—a brawling, expansive society driven by crude economic forces and shaken by the cacophonous politics of an indiscriminate populism—partly by reconsecrating it in what they took to be Jacksonian terms as a paradise of the "common man." As in the earliest days of Jeffersonian democracy, when such publications as William Duane's *Aurora* ceaselessly denounced an imaginary conspiracy of "aristocrats," "monarchists" and Anglophiles, their analysis could not do without a symbolic antagonist to structure the contrast between democratic good and "aristocratic" evil. The Norton of Santayana's so-called genteel tradition—pallid, Puritan, sapless, moribund—could not have been better suited to their purpose.

Soon afterward, Van Wyck Brooks's widely popular studies of New England literary culture would fill out Santayana's abstract character type with personally observed and sharply edged details. In Brooks's vivid and elegantly malicious pages, Norton would appear as "an autocrat in aesthetic matters," moving amidst his hushed Harvard acolytes, imperturbable as an "elegant priest discoursing of the sacred mysteries of which he had scarcely felt the inner fire." Finally, Brooks's Norton, the very embodiment of aesthetic sclerosis and patrician disdain, would be given a major role in the curious sociological melodrama scripted by Richard Hofstadter and his followers in the 1950s and the 1960s, in which Gilded Age reformers like Norton and Curtis and Charles Francis Adams, Jr., would be portrayed not as battling plutocracy and political corruption so much as "status anxiety." Whatever they consciously took their own motives to be, the "genteel reformers" in this view were seen as fighting the decline of their own elite class of educated, Protestant Northeasterners, which had been thrust aside by the surging energies of corporate magnates, Catholic and Jewish immigrants and the raw populism of the trans-Mississippi West. Even so a fair-minded and insightful study as Kermit Vanderbilt's *Charles Eliot Norton: Apostle of Culture in a Democracy* (1959) would allow its essentially sympathetic portrayal of Norton to be colored by Hofstadter's unrelenting reduction of civic idealism to a bewildered anxiety about status and social dominance.[7]

In recent years, the established portrait of Norton as neurasthenic culture snob and ineffectual political prig has, as though pursuing the logic of melodrama to its roots in the caricature of the sneering, moustache-twirling villain, been pushed to its crudest extreme. Writing in the ideological tradition of Progressivism that runs from Beard and Parrington through F. O. Matthiessen and his heirs, some contemporary literary critics and historians have attempted to demonstrate that Norton was a lifelong anti-democrat. Selectively quoting from the same small handful of Norton letters and essays, these writers have repeatedly sought to expose him as an "elitist" who not only favored coercion and "social control" but also sought limits on suffrage and restrictions on immigration—a reactionary and despairing "pessimist" who, even if he might not be an overt anti-Semite or racist, was nevertheless someone who utterly failed to measure up to recent standards of acceptability on ethnic and racial equality. Their Charles Eliot Norton is a caricature that would hardly have been recognizable not simply to his friends, but even to his foes—certainly not to the Harvard student who told him in 1898, "I will fight for you! I will try to prove by my life that the statements about your influence are utterly false," nor even to George Frisbie Hoar, the U.S. senator and former Harvard classmate who publicly castigated Norton for his "habit of bitter and sneering speech about persons and public affairs" when opposing U.S. policy in the Spanish-American War.[8]

Yet the problem posed by the twentieth- and twenty-first-century caricatures of Norton is not simply that they are explicitly false or tendentiously partial, patched together out of unrepresentative materials to answer contemporary ideological needs. The problem is that in treating Norton as a stock character or necessary villain in the progressivist melodrama of American nineteenth-century life and thought, his genuine significance has been utterly lost. For Norton was himself a progressive. The story of his actual career is one of a committed social reformer and political liberal who in witnessing the triumph of the Union cause in the Civil War believed he had lived to see, as he said, that "at last, the doctrine of human progress is proved true, and a limitless vista of peaceful advance opens to the eyes of men." It was his misfortune—shared with others of his generation—to watch the golden sunrise of 1865 fade into the tawdry daylight of the Gilded Age. It was his tragedy, experienced with a penetrating shock shared by few other leading Americans, to live long enough to see his early dreams for the American republic actually undone.[9]

As a young man in the 1850s, Norton thought he saw in the revolutionary neo-Gothic art and architecture championed by John Ruskin and the Pre-Raphaelite painters of England a means of developing the imagination as a social power, a cultural means of building greater sympathy between persons, classes and nations. As a tireless worker on behalf of the Union cause in the 1860s, he would emerge from the war believing that the dedicated war efforts of Northern soldiers and civilians had produced a new American character and with it the hope of a regenerated national community, or what he called a "moral commonwealth." When, in the years that followed, these hopes were not immediately realized, Norton's confidence in them was not destroyed but simply chastened. His Unitarian religious heritage and his liberal education told him that in human history radical social transformation occurred only over long periods of time.

This explains why Norton, during the 1870s, was able to commit himself so fully to "culture" as a way of life and an educational ideal. For Norton believed that in some historical circumstances the ideal of culture—of human development in its richest diversity—must at the outset appear in the lives and thoughts of a scattered band of highly developed individuals through whose presence there might then become visible to ordinary citizens a richer range of human possibility. Expanding their higher capacities in a country otherwise given over to a crude economic individualism, these "best men" (the phrase retains its classical associations with the *optimates* of Roman political theory) would create an atmosphere that would in time become general, raining down its intellectual, moral and aesthetic influences upon society as a whole. Even when it became clear in the 1880s that American moral and intellectual progress was lagging far behind the nation's material progress, that democratic standards were being irresistibly drawn, as Norton quaintly put it, "to the level of those whose moral sense is in their trowsers and not their breast pocket," his hopes were deferred but not significantly discouraged. It was only with the violent foreign crises of the 1890s that Norton saw that his hopes would remain unfulfilled, as the Spanish-American War and the Venezuelan emergency of 1895–96 brought unmistakably to light a brutal arrogance and indifference in the public as well as a cringing cowardice in its leaders that seemed flatly and permanently to deny the nation's foundational belief in the natural freedom and equality of all human beings.[10]

At the end, Norton would find himself in the isolated position of a liberal who had been unwittingly driven by events into a shattering collision with the previously unglimpsed limits of liberalism. In a land supposedly proud of its free speech, he would become a speaker physically threatened for daring to voice unpopular opinions. Among a people convinced of their own superiority, he was a critic who would be reviled for saying that the nation could be a great deal better than it was. In recent years, historians and philosophers of political thought have begun to pay a good deal of attention to the tensions and instabilities inherent in liberal thought. One problem in particular has drawn their attention: a large, historically demonstrable disparity between the civic virtues—courage, integrity, disinterestedness, self-sacrifice—necessary to the citizens and officeholders of a liberal state, and the willingness of liberal regimes to promote and defend those same virtues—what Peter Berkowitz has called the dilemma of liberalism having to depend "on virtues that it does not readily summon and which it may even stunt or stifle."[11]

Norton was among the first American liberals fully to experience the liberal dilemma. His reward would be to be denounced and disparaged during his own time and after his death for what his critics were pleased to call his "carping," by which they meant an unvarying insistence upon virtue and high character in both public and private life. There were not fewer good people than ever before, Norton bemusedly said to one correspondent, but for some reason "their goodness does not tell in the commonwealth." "Democracy, ideally, means universal public spirit," he would say to another friend, but "practically it exhibits itself in its actual phase as general selfishness and private spirit." The problems in liberalism that political theorists today debate in books and seminars were those that Norton at the end of his life would be fated to experience in personal terms in the form of baffling political disappointments and sickening defeats.[12]

This is not to say that Norton's exemplary position within nineteenth-century democratic liberalism is, once the fog of contemptuous misprision has been cleared away, easy to understand. Even without distortion by his ideological critics, Norton's views are no longer immediately intelligible in terms of our contemporary social and political categories. At times, this occurs because his opinions arose from specific nineteenth-century controversies whose larger historical contexts have now slipped out of common memory. More often, however, it happens because Norton belonged to a generation in which the sanctity of private or domestic affairs was a widely shared value, and the glare of sensationalism or intrusive public curiosity the mark of a coarsened civic culture. Tracing the private sources and personal significance of Norton's public views can be, accordingly, a daunting task.

"I [am] the one man in America who have kept myself private, who have hated the publicity & advertisement, and notoriety which, in these days even our poets have sought," Norton protested—to no avail—when his friend, the great English art critic John Ruskin, announced that he was going to describe their first meeting in his autobiography. But Norton did more than protest. He ruthlessly acted on his detestation of publicity, shunning would-be biographers and requests for personal information, burning enormous quantities of his own letters as well as those of his intimate friends and relations, and seeing to it that his many far-flung correspondents either returned his letters or safely disposed of them. Having arranged that his papers should be bequeathed to Harvard, Norton spent the last years of his life combing through this vast archive, reading, annotating, and emending its thousands of pages, and asking his literary executor, his daughter Sally, to go over them again after his death.[13]

In a few scattered instances, scholars have been drawn by specialized research to consult the rich trove of Norton Papers now preserved in Harvard's Houghton Library. Yet only recently, with the publication of James Turner's massive documentary biography, has it become possible to grasp the full dimensions of Norton's activity. Turner's *The Liberal Education of Charles Eliot Norton*, the result of fifteen years' labor in the Norton Papers as well as in more than a hundred other archival repositories, provides an indispensable roadmap to an enormous range of materials that would otherwise be overwhelming in their voluminousness and bewildering in their reticence and omissions. In Turner's enormously detailed treatment, there may be glimpsed the faint outlines of what might be called "the other Norton"—the young, ardent, hopeful scholar and friend of such artistic geniuses as Dante Gabriel Rossetti and Edward Burne-Jones, Norton the tireless social reformer, arts radical, abolitionist and advocate of women's rights. This other Norton, a largely hidden personality deeply committed to liberalism, enlightenment, progress and anti-imperialism, is my subject in the pages that follow.

Norton's life, a perceptive younger observer once noted, was one "of great usefulness and great unhappiness." It was characteristic of Charles Norton that he took measures to conceal evidences as much of his usefulness as of his unhappiness. At the core of Norton's passion for privacy lay his passion for his wife, who died in childbirth in 1872 after ten years of marriage and six children. Her death was the silent hinge on which his existence would turn. Her memory would become, as he would say, the secret treasure of his life. After 1872, Norton would struggle to maintain the even course of his days over the chasm of her loss. "I am the nearest to a real ghost of any man you have ever seen," he told Henry James in 1873, "leading one real life, and another unreal but visible one." Then he added a telling phrase, "But a ghost's life is not without its good."[14]

He was to succeed so well in living his unreal life that the death of Susan Norton would later seem to most observers merely another biographical datum about that minor Mugwump and man of letters, Charles Eliot Norton. Through an effort as valiant as it was invisible to the outside world, Norton would shape his outward life into a smooth routine of teaching, writing and presiding over a wide range of meetings and organizations both civic and scholarly. By the time of his own death in 1908, Norton would be regarded—and at times resented—as the confidential friend of transatlantic genius and the supreme arbiter of American cultural achievement. "The way that man gets his name stuck to every greatness is fabulous," William James stormed in comic exasperation to his sister Alice, "—Dante, Goethe, Carlyle, Ruskin, Fitzgerald, Chauncey Wright, and now Lowell! His name will dominate all the literary history of this epoch. 100 years hence, the *Revue des deux mondes* will publish an article entitled 'La Vie de l'esprit aux États-Unis vers la fin du XIXème siècle; étude sur Charles Norton.'"[15]

This book is not the study William James predicted. It proposes that Charles Norton deserves to be known for himself, not his extraordinary friends. It argues that Norton is best understood as standing in the direct line of the great New England reformers—with figures like Samuel Howe, Horace Mann and Dorothea Dix. Early and late, Norton would devote his energies to working for a total reconstitution of the social imagination, an expansion of Americans' imaginative powers that would come about only when literature and art, permitting a common participation in worlds alternative to the formless actuality of ordinary life, assumed a central importance in American culture. For Norton regarded imagination as the principal source not simply of the personal but also of the civic virtues. Imagination, he would write, "determines the aims of men, it supplies the permanent motives of action, it is the source and quickener of their sympathies, it is the inspiration of love, even of that love which is the fulfillment of the law." In the same way, he argued, the fine arts "are the most direct means by which those sympathies on which virtue depends are quickened, enlarged, and made constant."[16]

In the years after 1873, the civic landscape inhabited by Norton and other American liberals would be desolated by scandal and political cynicism, and riven by seething dissension along ethnic and religious faultlines. American politics, remarked one visiting British diplomat, was nothing more than "dullness relieved by rascality." Neither the Republicans nor the Democrats retained any of their traditional principles, declared another observer: "All has been lost, except office or the hope of it." In the political gloom of the Gilded Age, George Curtis, speaking to the graduating class of Union College, brought into view the independent ideal of civic life that Norton claimed as his own. Always remember, said Curtis, "it is not that bad men are brave, but that good men are infidels and cowards." The degradation of American politics is not due to the victory of the slums, as some have claimed, it is due to the surrender of schools like Union College. You will misunderstand your own citizenship, Curtis told the young men, if you take it to mean nothing more than casting your vote. The first obligation of genuine citizenship is "to help shape the alternative"—not by grandly official duty but by all the small, unremembered acts of civic participation: "attendance at meetings, service upon committees, care and trouble and expense of many kinds." Norton's own favorite formulation of this constant, active, practical view of civic life was a sentence written eighteen centuries earlier by the Stoic philosopher Seneca. The work of a good citizen is never useless, said Seneca, for by listening, by a glance, an expression, a nod, by steadfast silence, by the very way he enters a room, he does good.[17]

Norton's later career as a critic and a professor of art history at Harvard demands to be understood as part of this civic labor. "[H]ow much I have owed . . . to your father's whole personal influence," the philosopher Josiah Royce would tell Sally Norton after her father's death, "an influence that, as you well know, he could embody afresh, at any moment, in a word, a phrase, a tone of voice." Despising flattery as a "mortal poison" that corrupted both giver and receiver, Norton held with thinkers from Aristotle to Edmund Burke that a democratic people had more to fear from their false flatterers than did kings or despots. In an America notorious among other nations for its shameless self-promotion and self-praise—"spreading the eagle," in the phrase of the time—in an age when publishers' puffs were routinely reproduced in American periodicals "under the guise of an original criticism," Norton's incisive essays and reviews asserted a disinterested standard of genuine distinction against a tawdry critical practice of "log-rolling" and flaccid—or tainted—adulation.[18]

Norton's uncompromising standards of judgment determined the criticism he gave to individuals as well. "He never pretended to approve us without reserve," recalled Barrett Wendell, who was Norton's student and colleague at Harvard, "but he understood that we were trying to be real." As Ruskin remembered it, Norton's praise was witty and infinitely varied, becoming "a constant motive to exertion, and aid in effort." Burne-Jones confessed he needed Norton "to say to me ten times a day 'never mind' 'stick to it' 'don't give in' 'peg away' 'it's worth the while.'" Norton's blame was no less stimulating. "I've often said & oftener felt," declared Bertram Grosvenor Goodhue, the young architect who designed the neo-Gothic citadel at West Point, "that I'd rather have you damn my stuff than to have anyone else praise it."[19]

Towards the end of his 1844 essay "New England Reformers," Ralph Waldo Emerson lays down a remarkable teaching. It is a saying that might be engraved in stone as a memorial of Charles Eliot Norton's steadfast commitment to a core of civic and cultural values in American democracy. Those who love us are dear to us, says Emerson, because they enlarge our life. But dearer still, he insists, "are those who reject us as unworthy," for in so doing they "urge us to new and unattempted performances." Only such souls as these, says Emerson, can supply us with new powers out of the recesses of the spirit. Only they can "add another life," opening "a heaven before us, whereof we had not dreamed."[20]

⚘

In working on *Charles Eliot Norton: The Art of Reform* I've accumulated numerous debts of help and support. A fellowship from the John Simon Guggenheim Memorial Foundation underwrote an essential year of research and travel to archives. Over a series of summers, Tom and Vera Kreilkamp provided a home away from home while I was at work on the Norton Papers at Houghton Library. Prof. James Turner of Notre Dame generously let me read the original version of his landmark biography of Norton subsequently published by the Johns Hopkins University Press.

At the very beginning of my work, Richard Howard gave me both helpful advice and the unforgettable gift of one of Norton's key works. Conversations with Rochelle Gurstein, one of the few contemporary scholars who shares my own sense of Norton's crucial importance for any true understanding of nineteenth-century American culture, were a constant source of encouragement. The late John Bicknell unhesitatingly shared with me his immense knowledge of Leslie Stephen's life and work, and in the course of doing so became a cherished friend.

A number of scholars and archivists were generous in helping me solve specific problems related to Norton. I want especially to thank Peter Accardo, of Houghton Library, for his help with the Ruskin-Norton relationship; Fred Bauman, Jr., of the Library of Congress, for his assistance with the Norton–E. G. Squier correspondence; Janice Chadbourne, Curator of Fine Arts, Boston Public Library, for help with Norton's relations with the Society of Arts and Crafts and the younger Boston artists of the 1890s; Mark Samuels Lasner of the University of Delaware Library for assistance with Norton's literary relations; Pauline Pierce, retired curator of the Historical Room of the Stockbridge (MA) Library Assoc., for her help in clarifying Norton-Sedgwick relations; the late Rev. Mr. Harold Bend Sedgwick of Lexington, Massachusetts, for information concerning his cousins, Sally, Lily and Margaret Norton; Nicholas B. Scheetz, Manuscripts Librarian of the Georgetown Univ. Library, for allowing me to see some valuable items in his personal collection of Norton materials; Mark Stirling, of Up-Country Letters, South Lake Tahoe, California, for helping me untangle the publication history of Norton's works; Christopher Stray of Swansea, U.K., for valuable aid with the British repositories containing Norton's letters and information on Norton's dealings with British classicists; Meg Winslow, of the Mount Auburn Cemetery archives, for help with documentation regarding the Norton family's burial arrangements; and Philip Weimerskirch of the Providence Public Library for information about Norton's relations with Daniel Berkeley Updike and the younger Boston artists of the 1890s.

In South Carolina, Robert Cuthbert of Summerville assisted me with information about Henry A. Middleton, Jr., killed at First Bull Run, Francis Kinloch Middleton, mortally wounded at Haw's Shop, as well as about Frank's garden at Weehaw Plantation; Barbara Doyle, Historian of the Middleton Place Foundation, gave me much valuable information regarding the Norton-Middleton connection; Miss Elise R. Pinckney of Charleston kindly made available information about her kinswoman Sarah Henrietta Rutledge Pinckney and the Pinckney family heirloom, a Gilbert Stuart replica portrait of George Washington, which the Pinckneys sought to sell after the Civil War through Norton's auspices (it was purchased in 1869 by Judge Horace Gray of the Mass. Supreme Judicial Court and is now held in the National Portrait Gallery, London); nearer home, Eliza Cope Harrison of Philadelphia provided me with details concerning her relative Susan Matilda Middleton.

I'm grateful as well to the librarians of the many libraries and collections I have consulted over the years, most especially to the staff of Houghton Library, Harvard University, the Massachusetts Historical Society, the Princeton University Libraries and the South Carolina Historical Society.

My greatest debt is, once again, inexpressible in words, so initials must suffice.

Princeton, N.J.
Thanksgiving Day, 2006

Charles Eliot Norton

CHAPTER ONE

The Art of Reform

*I*n July 1857, Charles Eliot Norton was a well-connected but essentially unknown young man of twenty-nine who was making a final round of visits in England before returning home to America. Two years before, in poor health, he had arrived in Liverpool with his mother and two sisters, staying on in Europe a year after their departure in order to assure his recovered strength. Now, like tens of thousands of other people in England that summer, Norton wanted to see the great "Art Treasures" exhibition in Manchester, where the novelist Elizabeth Gaskell had invited him to visit her. With thousands of *objets d'art* and more than 2000 paintings by Old Master and modern artists gathered into one vast exhibition hall—it covered nine acres—the Manchester show was attracting 9000 visitors a day. By the end of its run in October, over 1.3 million people would see it, from Queen Victoria, Alfred Tennyson, Nathaniel Hawthorne and Harriet Beecher Stowe to thousands of working-class people, who thronged the hall on Sundays when admission was lowered to half price.

Much later, the Art Treasures show would be recognized as the ancestor of all mammoth public art exhibitions. Even at the time, however, visitors were aware that they were seeing art works arranged on a revolutionary new plan of chronological order. At the urging of Prince Albert, the Queen's husband, the exhibition organizers had adopted a chronological arrangement to make the show more educational. For the first time, visitors were able to survey the entire course of European painting, viewing individual art works in their historical relations to one another, from Giotto to John Everett Millais. The Manchester Art Treasures show was thus not simply a display of art open to the nation as a whole, but the public unveiling of a distinctively modern notion of art history.

Norton's first important writing about art would be a review of the

1

Manchester exhibition he published that fall in the first number of the *Atlantic Monthly*, the magazine that would become a major force in nineteenth-century American intellectual culture. To those contemporaries who would later know Norton as a celebrated Harvard professor of art history, it would be natural enough to see in the *Atlantic* review an early sign of the famous career to come—Norton as teacher and critic of art, "the American Ruskin," lecturing Harvard undergraduates and Americans at large about art and refinement, vulgarity and taste. Those modern readers who are aware of his role in nineteenth-century American culture are similarly disposed to view this younger Norton through the lens of his later fame—as an elderly figure, a personage always already eminent, whatever his chronological age. This Norton is the weary old man made familiar in the earlier twentieth century by Van Wyck Brooks's popular literary histories—Norton the captious pessimist, the critic with a "Ruskin-haunted mind," at home "only in the age of Giotto" and imaginatively open "only to the Pre-Raphaelite world."[1]

But at Manchester in 1857, Charles Norton had not yet become that old man. At twenty-nine, he was an eager social reformer and publicist, an activist who had not hesitated to alienate his own uncle, the stately and patrician George Ticknor, by voicing such opinions as "whatever be the rights of property, they weigh nothing against the rights of humanity." By the time he visited Manchester in 1857, Norton, harrowed by the sight of homeless children, had already set about organizing architectural plans and private financing for two model lodging houses to be built for poor families in Osborn Place, Boston. Deeply committed to helping the poor, he had established a night school for working men and poor boys in nearby Cambridge, his native town. Norton's was the first night school in all Massachusetts, itself the pioneer in reforms among the American states. Unlike the wildly utopian schemes—vegetarianism, homeopathy, hydropathy, mesmerism—of New England's Transcendentalist reformers, Norton's reformist zeal was hard-headed and practical. He belonged to the "North End Eliots," the mercantile branch of the Eliot family. Much later a New York friend was to reflect that Norton would have made "an excellent 'operator' on the Stock Exchange." Norton's model houses, initially envisioned as yielding a 4 percent return to investors, in fact would generate 6 percent. At his night school he insisted each boy pay a small fee, a requirement meant to take away the sting of charity and make the lessons more valuable because the children did not get them for free. No benevolent institution whatever its good intentions, he believed, should diminish the self-reliance and self-respect of those receiving its aid.[2]

One of these night school students was a bright Irish boy, orphaned with his six brothers after both parents died in Boston's Deer Island quarantine aboard the ship that had brought them from Ireland. Driving a milk cart and tending cows in the open fields of neighboring Somerville, Patrick McCarthy was to remember Norton as "a kind, generous, fatherly friend," who even offered "to provide for my support and [further] education if I was allowed to go to school and reside where he chose." His aunt, needing the boy's labor, was unwilling to release him. But Norton's firm encouragement of high aspiration left its mark. Sixty years later, after serving in the Rhode Island legislature and completing two terms as mayor of Providence, McCarthy would acquire one of Norton's books and write on the flyleaf, "I procured this book through regard for the author. I revere his memory."[3]

Militant idealism would characterize Norton's work for the rest of his life, separating him from the mass of his contemporaries and estranging him from a condescending posterity. "Charley Norton is a very noble youth," Longfellow's wife Fanny noted in a letter of 1852. He "interests me much," she continued, because he is "so full of sympathy for the unfortunate, and not like so many of our youths sneering at all misfortune." Fashionable cynicism about social reform was common enough among dandiacal younger Americans. "[S]pending a year or two in Paris, and a month or two in the rest of Europe," a sharp-eyed satirist of New York's "best society" noted in 1853, "they endure society at home, with a smile, and a shrug, and a graceful superciliousness, which is very engaging." The satirist was the Byronically handsome but uncynical George William Curtis who, first becoming acquainted with Norton in Paris in 1850, was to become one of his closest friends.[4]

Paris in the 1850s was a touchstone for the two friends, the sociopolitical symbol of an impulse to reform gone horribly awry. The Paris of Louis Napoleon—proclaimed Napoleon III, Emperor of the French in 1852—supplied the key, not simply to Curtis' satire of 1853, *The Potiphar Papers*, but to a remarkable little book Norton published in the same year, *Considerations on Some Recent Social Theories*. Frequently mistaken for a commentary on conditions in the U.S., Norton's essay in fact surveys the tragicomic outcome in Europe of the revolutionary ideas of 1848—"associationism," socialism, communism, *vox populi/vox dei*—as these glowing slogans were played out in actual history. For by 1853 it seemed clear that a summary judgment had been passed on such radical schemes of reform. Louis Kossuth's conviction that "the people is everywhere highly honorable, noble, and good," Guiseppe Mazzini's faith in "the instinct of the multitudes" and the efficacy of "the spontaneous, sudden, electrical association of the public square," Louis Blanc's trust that the formula "from every one according his aptitudes, to every one according to his needs" supplied an adequate basis for the economic reorganization of society—all these buoyant "theoretical

The Art of Reform

fancies," as Norton called them, had been tested and found wanting in France.[5]

For in France, through an adroit combination of flattery, manipulation of French revolutionary abstractions and the deployment of some 60,000 troops in the heart of Paris, Louis Napoleon had at a stroke turned the liberal dreams of the 1848 reformers into a nightmare of political despotism. With his coup d'état of December 1851, this ominous new Napoleon—the nephew of the first terrible Bonaparte—"has riveted chains," as Norton was quick to say, "on the neck of an unresisting nation." Within two months of the coup, 27,000 persons—Alexis de Tocqueville was one of them—were being arrested by "mixed committees" of the police, the army and the public prosecutor's office. Of these persons, nearly 10,000 would be forcibly deported, condemned to slow death by disease and hard labor in Algeria or in Cayenne—the French penal colony in Guiana notorious as "Devil's Island." Three months after the coup, martial law would be enforced and all liberty of the press revoked. To Norton and Curtis alike, the crucial point was that Louis Napoleon had first been elected President of France and then been confirmed as Emperor by huge majorities of voters. "It was the act of the majority," Norton emphasized, "which has established the present arbitrary ruler in France." He said it with the same grim chagrin that twentieth-century people would feel when they acknowledged that Adolf Hitler came to power in Germany in 1933 through democratic means.[6]

Duped by Napoleon's skillful appeal to the sacred name of "Liberty," trusting in his bona fides as the propagandist who in 1844 had promised *L'Extinction du paupérisme*, the French soon discovered, said Norton, that "[t]he name of Liberty is one of the disguises of tyranny." But political repression and the replacement of the Second Republic by the Second Empire did not mark the full extent of the Napoleonic tyranny. For by returning French education to the control of the Catholic Church, the Emperor would subjugate the mind and spirit of the rising generation in France (or so the fervently Unitarian Norton believed). This miserable spectacle of the French people bravely marching out "under a banner upon which Liberty was inscribed," only to find themselves, as Norton said, "serving in the army of oppression" supplied the darker background to questions of reform as they arose in America.[7]

Even so enthusiastic a reformer as George Curtis had taken the point of this recent French history. Curtis had been a Brook Farmer. He had helped to raise Thoreau's cabin at Walden. But when he came to satirize the luxury and vapidity of Francophiliac New York, he pointed to the fate that lay in store for republics that settled too softly into their velvet *fauteuils*. Curtis' *Potiphar Papers*, a witty adaptation of Montesquieu's premise in the *Persian Letters* (an Oriental diplomat writes home about the "barbarous" customs of the West), depicts the dissipated young fop Mr. Gauche Boosey. Preening himself on having been presented to the French Emperor, Boosey declares with unconscious penetration, "I have a great respect for Louis Napoleon. Those Frenchmen didn't know what they wanted; but he knew well enough what he wanted: they didn't want him, perhaps, but he did want them, *and now he has them*."[8]

The actuality of Napoleon's coup d'état and its aftermath explains why even the patent absurdities and failures among the recent social theories Norton surveys in his *Considerations* always retain for him an ominous edge. What, a modern reader might reasonably ask, could be less menacing than the ideas of Pierre Leroux, who delivered his solution to the "tyranny" of family and private property in an impenetrably mystical prose? But Norton recognized in such abstract theorizings a will to remake individual characters and individual interests so ruthless as in itself to constitute a form of tyranny. Or again, what could be less threatening than the hare-brained scheme for a worker's communistic utopia sketched out by Étienne Cabet in his social romance of 1842, *Voyage en Icarie*? But Norton knew that after an "Icarian" community was actually founded in Texas' Red River valley in 1848 (Cabet himself prudently remained in Paris), one of its survivors declared, "there is no slavery so hard as communism in action."[9]

Modern readers, who know how the story of nineteenth-century America "turned out," tend to dismiss the fears Norton expressed in *Considerations on Some Recent Social Theories* as the symptom of elite class anxiety or a case of filiopietistic Federalism or simply the apprehensions of an overly sheltered and scholarly young man. But in 1853 that reassuring outcome of the American experiment was by no means so clear. The dangers posed by a volatile, uneducated public with an appetite for flattery and "theoretical fancies" seemed to be growing, if only because the post-1848 repressions on the Continent were forcing revolutionaries and their sympathizers across the Atlantic, bringing with them all their fierce grievances. Nearly one million Germans would emigrate to America during the 1850s. Already, tens of thousands of impoverished Irish had been coming yearly since the mid-1840s—in 1847, the year before Patrick McCarthy's family of nine arrived in Boston, 37,000 Irish landed in that city alone, then a municipality of less than 100,000 persons. Kossuth himself, the Hungarian patriot whose inflammatory appeals to Magyar racial pride had risked civil war in his own country and briefly raised him to virtual dictatorship there, arrived for a U.S. tour in 1851–52. His glamorous career and towering eloquence assured he was rapturously received by Americans. "He is an inspired man," declared Senator Charles Sumner, himself no mean orator. Had not Kossuth fatally mismanaged his appeal to the Senate by calling upon the all-powerful Southerners to oppose the "enslavement" of Hungary, he might well have flattered Americans into entangling themselves in precisely the kind of the foreign affairs and alliances George Washington had warned against in his Farewell Address as president.[10]

By the time the twenty-nine-year-old Charles Norton found himself standing at the door of the Manchester Art Treasures hall in 1857, then, he knew that neither supercilious detachment from human misery nor headlong allegiance to brave new theories promising to end it utterly were of any help in the crisis facing social reformers. Looking out at "the great workshop city, already stretching its begrimed arms in the direction of the Exhibition," he confronted the frightful new powers wrenching hundreds of thousands of families like Patrick McCarthy's out of their known worlds. He recognized what English reformers since the 1840s had been calling the "Two Nations"—the appalling, widening gulf between rich and poor. In Manchester he was seeing what Charles Dickens in *Hard Times* had described just three years earlier as "Coketown," a place of roaring machinery and towering chimneys, with "a river that ran purple with ill-smelling dye and vast piles of building full of windows where there was a rattling and a trembling all day long." Norton saw in the reverberation of Manchester's ceaseless trip-hammers and the grimness of its coal-blackened factories what he declared "was never to be seen in the world before this century": a city built entirely by trade and worked for profit, the home of machines and the hellish dwelling-place for human beings forced to live like machines.[11]

Yet the tendency to view the young Norton at Manchester as if he were already the celebrated old professor at Harvard is not in the end wholly mistaken. The day after Norton died in November 1908, William Dean Howells was sitting on a sunny bench in the Boston Public Garden. Beside him, he was astonished to hear an ordinary working man speak with "passionate regret" about Norton's death. "I wish I could remember the words," Howells continues, for "they implied and revealed a brotherly relation to such men which I had not imagined of him." Yet the fraternal tie between Norton and "such men" may be traced back to his earliest youth, when, in the scrupulously neat account books he kept for expenses, cold cream and gloves alternate with "charities (to workmen)." Another story, this one told by his younger relative, the historian Samuel Eliot Morison, reveals Norton's deft touch and sympathetic interest in others unlike himself. In the smoking room of a ship bound for England in 1900, Morison's father was talking to a shoe salesman. Norton joined them. Morison continues:

> On being introduced, Norton put the salesman at his ease, with the question, "Do they still make those boots with elastic gussets let into the-

sides?" "You mean 'Congress boots' don't you?"—"Yes."—"Oh, no, they went out long ago."—"I never thought they were very good style, did you?"—"No, completely second-rate"; and so on. After Norton excused himself and left the group, the shoe salesman turned to my father and exclaimed, "What a delightful old gentleman! Interested in everything and everybody."[12]

Common to both Nortons, early and late, is a single overriding concern with "imagination." Norton was convinced that imagination was above all a social power, at once the vital principle of sympathy between individuals, and the durable force for cohesion between groups or classes or nations. During the course of a long life that was to witness brutal social dislocations and tragic personal change, Norton would persist in this belief. It would dominate his thought, uniting his early social activism with his later cultural teaching, and illuminating the enduring love of Gothic art and the age of Giotto that was to seem so unaccountable—so "nostalgic" or perverse—to Van Wyck Brooks and his twentieth-century heirs.

To understand how an ardent social reformer of the 1850s could become what has seemed to later generations the despairing "Ruskin-haunted mind" of the 1890s is in part to trace the fate of imagination as a social power in later nineteenth-century America. The relation between the two Nortons, young and old, however, becomes fully intelligible only when we see that the central importance that imagination possessed for him—as it did for Dickens, Stowe, J. S. Mill and others in the great transatlantic generation of humanitarian reformers to which he belonged—arises from the new theory of sympathy put forward almost 100 years earlier by Adam Smith in his *Theory of Moral Sentiments*.

⚘

Before he ever wrote his famous treatise on *The Wealth of Nations*, Adam Smith, lecturing as professor of moral philosophy at the University of Glasgow, made a profoundly original suggestion about the psychology of sympathetic response. If our neighbor is in distress, Smith said, as long as we ourselves are at our ease, our five physical senses will never tell us what he suffers, because "[t]hey never did, and never can, carry us beyond our own person." It is only by bringing home our neighbor's situation to our own consciousness by representing it mentally as if it were happening to ourselves that his agonies "begin at last to affect us, and we then tremble and shudder at the thought of what he feels." Taken alone, the outward signs of our neighbor's passion may appear grotesque or incomprehensible. It is only by conceiving through imagination the situation which has provoked his cries or wild gesticulations

that our sympathy begins to awaken: "By the imagination we place ourselves in his situation, we conceive ourselves enduring the same tor-
ments, we enter as it were into his body, and become in some measure
the same person with him, and thence form some idea of his sensations,
and even feel something which, though weaker in degree, is not altogether unlike them."[13]

Even though our own feelings of compassion will differ in degree
and kind from our neighbor's feelings of distress, the approximation
of his original sorrow that we achieve through imaginative sympathy
is, Smith declares, close enough for the purposes of social harmony.
"Though they will never be unisons," as he says, referring to the correspondence between the two sentiments, "they may be concords, and
this is all that is wanted or required." Nor is our sympathetic response a
disguised mode of selfishness, as the followers of Thomas Hobbes and
Bernard de Mandeville were too apt to assume. For "[h]ow can that be
regarded as a selfish passion," Smith demands, "which does not arise
even from the imagination of any thing that has befallen, or that relates
to myself, in my own proper person and character, but which is entirely
occupied about what relates to you?"[14]

Instead, the crucial element in sympathetic response, on Smith's account, is our power to picture another's situation mentally in all its distinct specificity, for our sympathy will vary "in proportion to the vivacity
or dullness of the conception." If we do not "take the time to picture
out in our imagination the different circumstances of distress" which attend our neighbor's sorrow, we are likely to feel little concern for him.
This is why Smith insists the witness to suffering must continually struggle "to bring home to himself every little circumstance of distress which
can possibly occur to the sufferer," entering into "the whole case of his
companion with all its minutest incidents." Sympathy, quite simply, lives
in the details.[15]

One man who heard Smith's Glasgow lectures said they seemed like
"a very ingenious attempt to account for the principal phenomena in
the moral world from this one general principle, like that of gravity in
the natural world." Smith's master principle of sympathy with its correl-
ative notion of imagination would become just that in the century that
followed, as it quickly permeated philosophy, theology, aesthetics, social analysis and conduct, and literature of all kinds. It would help John
Stuart Mill liberate himself from the arid theory of his great Utilitarian mentor Jeremy Bentham. For despite his extraordinary gifts and un-
doubted contributions to the nation, Bentham was critically impaired,
as Mill said in 1838, by his signal "deficiency of Imagination," defined
by the younger man as "the faculty by which one mind understands a
mind different from itself, and throws itself into the feelings of that

Charles Eliot Norton

other mind." In the same way, a writer for the *Westminister Review*, struggling in 1856 to express her dissent from the conventionalized art of the day, seized upon sympathy as the crucial point of difference, declaring, "[t]he greatest benefit we owe to the artist, whether painter, poet, or novelist, is the extension of our sympathies." A few years later, writing as "George Eliot," this writer would make an expansive notion of sympathy the gravitational principle of her own novels, saying, "the only effect I ardently long to produce by my writings is, that those who read them should be better able to *imagine* and to *feel* the pains and the joys of those who differ from themselves in everything but the broad fact of being struggling, erring, human creatures."[16]

In America, Adam Smith's theory of sympathy would become part of the larger inheritance of Scottish Enlightenment ideas from such figures as Thomas Reid, Adam Ferguson and John Millar, serving the nation as its "official metaphysic," in Perry Miller's phrase, until the Civil War. This body of progressive and optimistic thought penetrated the consciousness of Americans through sermons, lectures, self-improvement texts and college curricula, entering with the help of such popularizers as Archibald Alison, Hugh Blair and Dugald Stewart. Stewart's *Elements of the Philosophy of the Human Mind*, for instance, was a required text at Harvard during Norton's undergraduate years in the 1840s. In it, Norton read the Scottish Enlightenment's explanation of the coldness and selfishness of mankind—faults that were traceable, as Stewart declared, "*to a want of attention and a want of imagination.*"[17]

It was, however, through literature, above all through novels, that Smith's theory of the moral sentiments achieved its most pervasive diffusion in England and America. By the earlier years of the nineteenth century, literary sentimentalism with its notions of the "power of sympathy," the "man of feeling" and its signature motif of reconciling tears had been remolded by the pressures of Romanticism and the evangelical religious revival to become the dominant mode in fiction in both countries. In recent years, much valuable commentary has been devoted to the cultural impact of literary sentimentalism, especially upon nineteenth-century social reform and reformers. What has drawn less attention, perhaps, is the way in which Smith's theory of sympathy came to pose a serious and unforeseen problem for those writers who sought to advance social reform through literary art.

By the 1850s, Smith's moral psychology of sympathy and imagination had come to serve as the implicit philosophical charter for the humanitarian realism then being produced by such socially conscious novelists as Dickens, Stowe, Eliot, Charles Kingsley and Elizabeth Gaskell. Together with journalistic writers like Henry Mayhew and Charlotte Elizabeth Tonna, the humanitarian realists operated on the literary frontier where fiction meets journalism, incorporating eyewitness accounts as well as detailed testimony given to commissions of inquiry, in order to accurately portray for their readers the dreadful conditions endured by factory workers or field slaves or the unemployed poor. Dickens, for example, went to Yorkshire in 1838, where reports were circulating about certain notorious proprietary schools mistreating their students. He published what he saw in *Nicholas Nickleby*: "Pale and haggard faces, lank and bony figures, children with the countenances of old men, deformities with irons upon their limbs." In her novel of 1848, *Mary Barton: A Tale of Manchester Life*, Mrs. Gaskell drew upon her own experiences in aiding the poor as a Unitarian minister's wife. In addition, she took over verbatim testimony gathered by the Manchester Mission to the Poor for her description of the poorest class of dispossessed workers in that city, starving in unheated cellars, "three or four little children rolling on the damp, nay wet brick floor, through which the stagnant, filthy moisture of the street oozed up."[18]

In picturing so concretely for their audiences the lives lived by their suffering fellow men and women—making visible what Smith called "every little circumstance of distress"—humanitarian writers sought to prompt their readers' imagination, their sympathy and as quickly as possible, their acts of benevolent intervention. Conventional images of jocund farmers and contented operatives must be discarded, George Eliot declared, to be replaced by realistic pictures of "the peasant in all his coarse apathy and the artisan in all his suspicious selfishness." Only such true pictures, she insisted, were capable of surprising "even the trivial and the selfish into that attention to what is apart from themselves, which may be called the raw material of moral sentiment."[19]

Without such prompting, it could be a formidably difficult task for charitable, well-disposed people to imagine the struggles and sorrows of people remote from them on the social scale. In 1852, Frederick Law Olmsted, during one of the investigative forays into American South that would later be published in *The Cotton Kingdom*, watched slaves laboring in Virginia. "As they are seen at work, under overseers, in the fields," Olmsted wrote in his journal, the slaves appeared "very dull, idiotic, and brute-like." It required an effort, he reflected, "to appreciate that they are, very much more than the beasts they drive, our brethren—a part of ourselves." In the same year, Mrs. Stowe published *Uncle Tom's Cabin, or Life Among the Lowly*, the book that would do more than any other work except the Bible to move white readers towards precisely this appreciation of black humanity. For Mrs. Stowe does not *tell* us about slavery, declared one American reviewer, "but *shows* us what it is. She does not analyze, or demonstrate, or describe, but, by a skilful manner of indirection, takes us over the plantation, into the fields."[20]

Charles Eliot Norton

In *Mary Barton*, Mrs. Gaskell achieved for English factory workers what Mrs. Stowe accomplished for American slaves: she made readers see them for the first time as fully human, not merely as passively suffering human beings but as autonomous moral agents, capable of the acts of moral recognition that the readers themselves were being implicitly asked to perform. A famous scene from *Mary Barton* depicts the flash of moral acknowledgment the humanitarian novelists were constantly seeking to ignite. John Barton, an embittered mill-worker, whose sick young son has died from a lack of nourishing food and who in an act of class revenge has killed the son of Mr. Carson, a factory owner, recognizes upon hearing the details of Carson's desperate grief that here is "the very anguish he had felt for little Tom." In this moment of imaginative sympathy, Barton perceives the figure before him no longer as an employer, a rich man, an oppressor but simply as "a very poor and desolate old man." For this moment at least, the gulf between the "Two Nations" has been bridged.[21]

Yet there always lurked a danger in following Adam Smith's advice about activating sympathy by picturing "every little circumstance of distress." As the scale of human misery grew with the spread of the industrial revolution, graphic descriptions of suffering and degradation could overwhelm readers, engulfing them in impressions of hopelessness and vice, and in effect plunging them into the very conditions the reformers wanted to abolish for the poor. As Mrs. Stowe herself declared in 1844, "The descriptions given by Dickens are almost the same to all intents and purposes to a young mind as would be actual contact with such scenes and company." She may have been referring to the sadistic school world pictured in *Nicholas Nickleby*. Or perhaps she meant the scarifying account Dickens had just published in *American Notes* of New York City's notorious "Five Points" slum, with its "leprous houses," its alleys "knee-deep" in mud that reeked of human and animal excrement and its "coarse and bloated faces at the doors." Mrs. Stowe deprecated Dickens because she wanted to gain American readers for another English reform writer, Charlotte Elizabeth Tonna. Tonna's realist descriptions, Mrs. Stowe insisted, "are not so minute as to become themselves corrupting." But not everyone agreed. Andrews Norton was as convinced as Stowe that religion and humanity "demand the emancipation of the poor in England as strongly as the emancipation of the slaves in our Southern States." But when Charles Norton pressed his father to read Tonna's famous tract *The Wrongs of Women*—an account of industrial slavery and infanticide in Manchester and Leeds—Andrews quickly decided the book was, as he said, "too *terribly* true" for his wife Catharine to read without harm.[22]

Here, then, was the problem posed to Victorian humanitarian reformers by Adam Smith's theory of sympathy and imagination: how could imagination—the motive force behind sympathy and hence all effective social reform—be roused into activity by picturing "every little circumstance of distress" without as a side effect exposing the reformers themselves to psychic damage, indifference or despair? As Charles Norton pursued his own reform activities in the earlier 1850s, he felt the problem acutely. For by this time the problem of the "Two Nations" had arrived in America. When Dickens saw Five Points in 1842, the novelist thought the district equaled for squalor London's Seven Dials, that city's most notorious slum. But at that point, neither the vast Irish immigration, driven by the failure of Ireland's entire potato crop in 1845, nor the large German immigration, hard pressed by the failure of the 1848 Continental revolutions, had yet begun. By contrast, ten years later, when Norton was visiting Five Points in New York and planning model tenements for the poor in Boston, the huge influx of new immigrants had radically altered the terms of poverty in both American cities. Haplessly thrust into the fearful new conditions bred by industrialism, immigrant and native alike were deformed by its pitilessly impersonal forces. Severe overcrowding coupled with the sanitary habits of an illiterate peasantry had brought cholera, typhus, tuberculosis and other diseases. Harsh competition for jobs coupled with hostility from already established American residents had brought unemployment, malnutrition, demoralization, drunkenness and at times savage violence.

Norton knew that in both Boston and New York one person in twenty lived underground, in basements or sub-basements or even "tide-cellars"—tiny, airless chambers, where twenty or thirty Irish huddled together to sleep when the tide was out, and the cellar was barely dry. What he could not understand was how his declaredly Christian fellow citizens could allow these "cellars dark, wet, rotting, stifling" to remain "the homes of men, of our fellow-men." Still less, how could they bear to see poor children, malnourished and living in filth, being daily imprinted by inescapable images of squalor and horror. During a trip to India in 1849–50 for the Boston export-import firm he then worked for, Norton had seen "the worst part of Madras"—the desperate Black Town. How could equivalent conditions, he now demanded, be appearing in "our own most flourishing, most Christian cities"? How could more fortunate men and women, lapped in velvet ease and gourmandizing plenty, remain coldly aloof in the face of such conditions? Norton's answer to the question was the same one Dugald Stewart had given. He said, "*It is from want of thought and want of imagination.*"[23]

But by now, it seemed neither effective nor even possible to urge the comfortable classes to feel sympathy for their impoverished fellows simply by picturing every little circumstance of distress. For the "grinding, squalid misery" of the new industrial poverty, as Mrs. Gaskell had called it in *Mary Barton*, increasingly defeated one's imaginative power to bring home all its minutest incidents. As Norton warned, "No imaginary picture can, drawn equal in horror to the realities which the dwellings of the poor present." Even if they could, such mental pictures carried their own dangers—not simply the "corruption" Mrs. Stowe had feared but the depletion or exhaustion of sympathy—what a later century would call compassion fatigue. This is why, when Norton reported on Five Points for *Putnam's Magazine* in 1853, he refused to detail all the particular horrors of this urban abyss. "I distrust descriptions where horrors are heaped together," he told his readers. "As most people turn away from them as exaggerations, they often serve the bad end of blunting the keen edge of sympathy. I will not describe here." Adam Smith's deep insight into moral psychology still held true: imagination was indeed the highway to sympathy. But graphic descriptions of distress as given in humanitarian realist writing, it now seemed to Norton, were no longer the best way to imagination.[24]

As he stared out from the door of the Art Treasures Palace at the dead vista of Manchester's industrial brick and smoke, then, Norton could see "no single object upon which the eye or the imagination can rest with pleasure." Instead, everywhere he looked he saw "the cold and dry elements of purely unimaginative life." It was as if the blind and ruthless processes of industrial modernity were visibly extinguishing the living sources that fed imagination and sympathy, the very powers most needed to overcome their devastating effects. In this moment, as Norton tells his *Atlantic* readers, he turned back to enter the Palace of Art. Though he does not say so directly, by July of 1857 Norton had come to see that the path to social reform must necessarily lead in an unlooked-for new direction, beckoning reformers onward, precisely through "the age of Giotto and the Pre-Raphaelite world."[25]

⚹ ⚹

Norton's immediate aim in writing his essay about the Manchester exhibition was to tell Americans why a dissident group of medievalizing English painters known as the Pre-Raphaelites was poised to remake the future of modern art. On reading it in the *Atlantic*, Fanny Longfellow found Norton's essay "a little à la Ruskin, not in style, but in theory." In fact, though, even stylistically this was to be the most Ruskinian piece Norton would ever write. John Ruskin's "theory" had been vital in winning for Pre-Raphaelite painters much of the critical acclaim and popular acceptance they had achieved by 1857. But he had done more than this. In the years since 1843, when he published his first book—*Modern Painters*—at the age of twenty-four, Ruskin had taught a generation to see in an entirely new way. Although Norton himself was at first slow to embrace Ruskin's theories, by July 1857 he had come to know the art critic personally and to study his ideas closely. Neither Norton's hopes for social reform nor his continuing search for the means to renew imagination as a social power can be well understood apart from them. Kindly, generous, indefatigably energetic, Ruskin, now thirty-eight, seemed to Norton entirely lovable and unspoiled by the vast praise and abuse that had come to him as a young man. But what attracted the younger man most about Ruskin and the Pre-Raphaelites, as someone who knew Norton intimately would later remember, was their dream of a marriage between morality and art.[26]

From the first volume of *Modern Painters* onwards, Ruskin's great project had been "teaching Sight"—showing artists as well as untrained viewers how to develop their moral acuity of vision. He did this by teaching his readers to look for the "facts" of external nature, as he called them, by which he meant the individualizing details and structures of the natural world. Ruskin's theory held that minute study of these "unobtrusive truths" could pose no danger to human powers because the natural world, created by God and providentially fitted to human capacities, was beneficent. Moreover, as Ruskin's own practice as an amateur artist had taught him, the effort to see nature truly was morally strenuous, requiring one to set aside all egotism and self-regard. Thus a deep attention to the exquisite forms of external nature would lead men and women toward sympathizing with their human fellows. For "the habit of trying to ascertain facts, even with the bodily eye," as Ruskin told a group of art school students, "was the most wholesome initiation into the habit of trying to see them with the mental one."[27]

Although he rather despised Adam Smith's *Theory of Moral Sentiments* for having given merely the "mechanics of feeling," Ruskin, who was himself of Scottish descent, had silently absorbed his great countryman's teaching about sympathy, selflessness and imagination. In particular, he shared Smith's sense of the dynamic interrelations among these faculties, declaring that it is only when we forget about ourselves, that we may imaginatively "enter, like possessing spirits, into the bodies of things about us." Or insisting there is an unmistakably "reciprocal action" between the intensity of moral feeling and the power of imagination, for "on the one hand, those who have keenest sympathy are those who look closest and pierce deepest, and hold securest; and on the other, those who have so pierced and seen the melancholy deeps of things are filled with the most intense passion and gentleness of sympathy."[28]

Yet as the insistent superlatives in the preceding passage may suggest ("keenest, closest, deepest"), it was less the philosophical sources of Ruskin's thought than its recognizably religious sincerity that arrested his English and American readers so forcibly, convincing them that in "teaching sight" Ruskin had given them the visible world back again on infinitely precious new terms. For until about 1857 or 1858, Ruskin's evangelical religious faith would hold firm. His overflowingly eloquent expression of it in the earlier, generously optimistic works of the 1840s and 1850s served to reassure his many religiously earnest but aesthetically inexperienced readers that in embracing the new visual culture they would not imperil their older allegiance to faith. In these earlier works, a counterpoint of religious reference seemed always to play beneath the overt discussions of art and artistic representation, as when Ruskin said, in the richly patterned style that first made him famous, there was "that to be seen in every street and lane of every city,—that to be felt and found in every human heart and countenance,—that to be loved in every roadside weed and moss-grown wall which, in the hands of faithful men, may convey emotions of glory and sublimity continual and exalted."[29]

Ruskin's specific argument, pursued with acrimonious brilliance through the five volumes of *Modern Painters* published between 1843 and 1860, was that no one had actually seen the natural world before the English landscape artist J. M. W. Turner began to paint. Instead, artists since the sixteenth century had been blindly following the mechanical conventions of academic painting which had been viciously deduced or extrapolated by unseeing hacks from the paintings and practice of Raphael. Three hundred years of copying Raphael and then copying the copies had produced a glacial classicism, a heartless formalism and a chilled, bleached palette. It was, as Ruskin did not hesitate to say, "the old art of trick and tradition," and it had hopelessly alienated modern painters and viewers from "what was really there." The surest index to the failure of academic painters to paint the truth was their cold and muddy color. Ruskin brought about a revolution among his contemporaries in preferring color to form in art. He held that "of all God's gifts to the sight of man, colour is the holiest, the most divine, the most solemn." Preternaturally sensitive to color himself, Ruskin was gifted with powers of description that made the colors he wrote about seem to glow on the white page. He delighted in the pure, clear, luminous hues of Turner, the Italian "primitive" or medieval painters and, after 1851, the English Pre-Raphaelites.[30]

As a gifted amateur artist, Ruskin had repeatedly had the experience of discovering that when he fully concentrated his own "mental sight" upon a bit of ivy or an aspen tree in order to draw it, the lines "composed" themselves as if by hidden laws. Turner, by virtue of his great genius and his years of unremitting labor, had succeeded in wresting the secret of many of those laws from nature. The task for those who came after Turner—artists and spectators alike—was to get convention and selfishness out of the way, continue Turner's faithful study, and "go to Nature in all singleness of heart," as Ruskin said in a celebrated passage, "rejecting nothing, selecting nothing, and scorning nothing." These words were to become a sort of Pre-Raphaelite battle cry.[31]

It is difficult today, when Ruskin is more often remembered for his sexual misfortunes and tragic later madness than for anything else, to recover an adequate sense of the power of his astonishing cultural dissent and the difference this made to mid-century Anglo-Americans. "His whole heart is in his subject, isn't it?" marveled one young woman. "And it opens a new world to us, who are so ignorant of architecture and painting. It has given us quite a start in a new direction." The first volume of *Modern Painters*, recalled another reader, "fell upon the public opinion of the day like a thunderbolt from the clear sky," immediately dividing the art world into two parties, "the one embracing most of the reverent and conservative minds, and by far the larger; the other, most of the enthusiastic, the radical, and earnest." After 1851, when Ruskin undertook to defend the Pre-Raphaelite painters (at their request) from hostile critics, he was denounced by one conservative Anglican clergyman as "*a Revolutionist*" whose insistence on truth to nature in painting and honesty of construction in architecture resembled the worst excesses of "Puritanism, Fanaticism, Quakerism, Radicalism."[32]

Pre-Raphaelite painting was no less radical in its assumptions and divisive in its effects upon the public. Led by William Holman Hunt, John Everett Millais and Dante Gabriel Rossetti, the "Pre-Raphaelite Brotherhood" had been founded in the revolutionary moment of 1848. At first, in a gesture of affiliation with the anonymous medieval craftsmen they so admired, the artists signed their works with just the mysterious monogram "PRB," enraging critics. By the time of the Manchester exhibition, the group had passed out of its first notoriety, thanks in part to Ruskin's vigorous defense of their work. But Pre-Raphaelite paintings still retained their power to disturb viewers. Upon seeing such Pre-Raphaelite works at Manchester as Hunt's *The Awakened Conscience* and Millais' *Autumn Leaves*—(Rossetti, who shunned public venues, did not exhibit there)—Nathaniel Hawthorne was both repelled and attracted by their feverish naturalism. "[A]lthough every single thing represented seems to be taken directly out of life and reality, and, as it were, pasted down upon the canvas," Hawthorne noted in his journal, yet "[n]ever was anything so stiff and unnatural as they appear."[33]

Fanny Longfellow, who had seen Pre-Raphaelite works earlier, disliked them because they missed, as she complained, "all the poetry of the art in their foolish mania for detail." Reactions like these showed contemporary viewers struggling to understand these strangely dissident artists who seemed determined, as the puzzled Hawthorne put it, "to abjure all beauty, and to make their pictures disagreeable out of mere malice." How could artworks attack "beauty" or "grace" or "poetry," such viewers wondered. Wasn't that what art *was*? Why would artists deliberately flout the expectations and approval of their audiences? Weren't "the million" to be the new patrons of art in the modern age? Pre-Raphaelitism seemed intent on undermining the very ground on which people with conventional ideas of art might reasonably expect it to stand.[34]

But "conventionalism" was exactly the point. The Pre-Raphaelites, who had read Ruskin along with everyone else, had set themselves to attacking conventional expectations about art—that it should be graceful, that it should present a "poetical" subject in a dignified, idealizing way—so that they could jolt their mid-Victorian audiences out of their blind habits of seeing. Despite their self-chosen name, the group was less interested in assailing Raphael himself than in attacking what had happened to him at the hands of later academic painters—the way Raphael's work had been reduced to a set of formulas or gimmicks, ultimately to little more than a safe visual shorthand for winning patrons and placating critics.

In an age of reform, the Pre-Raphaelites wanted to effect the reform of art. In an age of gimcrack construction and adulterated food, they insisted on genuineness in artistic methods and materials. In an age of sentimental prettiness, they risked depicting ugliness and awkwardness in order to approach unconventional beauty. Instead of the unobservant, idealized forms ("slosh") purveyed by the great academic painters ("Sir Sloshua Reynolds"), the Pre-Raphaelites turned to nature with the spirit and singleness of heart they discovered in such medieval and early Renaissance Italian painters as Giotto and Fra Angelico. Theirs was thus a retrospective radicalism, summoning the example of the past as the moral measure by which to reform the present. Even long after the Pre-Raphaelites' movement had become an outmoded fashion in painting, merely one convention among others, their standard of craftsmanship and artistic dedication would remain—for Edith Wharton as for Henry James—the measure by which later and more commercial avant-gardes would be judged.

Nothing expressed the Pre-Raphaelites' zeal to reform the art of their own day more forcibly than the aggressively uncommercial and anti-academic way they set about painting nature. By the 1850s, after an explosion in amateur and professional scientific studies, "nature," had come to refer to an external non-human realm, complexly ordered, infinitely various and microscopically detailed. Charles Darwin had published his *Voyage of the H.M.S. Beagle* in 1839; his *Origin of Species* would appear in 1859. The charismatic Swiss naturalist Louis Agassiz had been lecturing in America since 1846, and like a great field marshal deployed hundreds of volunteers—Charles Norton was one of them—to collect specimens for his museum at Harvard. Philip Gosse's *The Aquarium*, published in 1854, began a craze on both sides of the Atlantic for gathering marine creatures in large glass tanks—Norton would keep one in Newport, and tell *Atlantic* readers about its entrancements. Quickened by the introduction of inexpensive microscopes, the Victorian passion for natural history and "botanizing," or collecting and arranging natural specimens with a Linnaean precision, had schooled the mid-century generation in habits of accurate observation in the field and close comparative study in the parlor or library. But even so, the Pre-Raphaelites' disciplined fidelity in recording natural "facts" amazed their contemporaries.

For in its strictest interpretation, the Ruskinian and Pre-Raphaelite ethic of painting—they called it "truth to nature"—required that the transcription of natural facts be accomplished in the physical presence of those facts. Or as one American follower of the Pre-Raphaelites would later express the principle, "Every tree or wayside flower must be the portrait of the living vegetable." Pre-Raphaelite artists went to extraordinary lengths of physical exertion and mental ingenuity to fulfill this demanding ethic. Holman Hunt, for example, had to construct a temporary hut made of straw to shelter him as he worked for eight hours each night to capture the effects of moonlight, starlight and lamplight he needed for his celebrated picture *The Light of the World*. W. S. Burton, a minor Pre-Raphaelite painter, dug a hole for his easel and himself so that he could get closer to the ferns and brambles he was painting for the foreground of his sensation picture of 1856, *The Wounded Cavalier*. Many viewers detested the hardness and aridity—Hawthorne called it "acerbity, like unripe fruit"—that such laborious fidelity to visual "facts" could at times produce. Norton himself fretted that a too literal-minded application of the "truth to nature" principle might clog their paintings with mannerism and make the Pre-Raphaelites forget the equally essential Emersonian doctrine that "the actual is not always the real." At times, the Pre-Raphaelite "mania for detail" even seemed to approach the extreme circumstantiality of the humanitarian realists, burdening the imagination itself.[35]

This is why the Pre-Raphaelite artist to whom Norton devotes the most attention in his *Atlantic Monthly* review is precisely the one who did not exhibit at Manchester: Rossetti. For though remaining "true to nature" in the Pre-Raphaelite sense, Rossetti had managed to reach through all merely truthful details to grasp what Norton called "the higher truths of Nature." Rossetti, whom Norton had first met in mid-

October 1856, was a magnetic figure, "of slight form, and delicate look, with large, dark eyes and finely cut features, and simple, direct manners." Yet he could be as masterful as a Renaissance prince. Volunteering to teach painting at the newly founded Working Men's College in London, Rossetti had insisted Ruskin teach there too. "[H]e was the only one of our modern painters," as Ruskin would later remember, "who taught disciples for love of them." Rossetti's powers of inspiration and enthusiasm were now drawing a new circle of Pre-Raphaelite artists around him. Norton met the artist in the same moment that Rossetti was meeting William Morris and Edward Jones (later Burne-Jones) for the first time—the painter becoming energized by the younger men's admiration, and electrifying them in turn with his confidence in their untested powers. After Rossetti's wretched death years later from addiction to the sedative chloral, Burne-Jones would say in sober retrospect, "He gave me courage to commit myself to imagination without shame, a thing both good and bad for me." But in the glowing excitement of his first friendship, the younger man experienced Rossetti's historicist imagination, with its overmastering preoccupation with Dante, Giotto and other "Immortals," as a call to new life. "[N]ow that I have set aside my heroes for peculiar reverence," Jones declared in a letter written at this time, "—all such as have been highly blessed with Imagination, and have laboured nobly, and fought valiantly, hundreds of them up and down the great centuries—since then I have seen things more truly than ever before."[36]

In the month before visiting the Manchester Art Treasures exhibition, Norton had breakfasted with Rossetti twice, and gone to see the painter's work both at his Blackfriars Bridge studio and at a small semi-private exhibition of Pre-Raphaelite paintings then showing in London. He had met Rossetti's fiancee, the frailly beautiful Elizabeth Siddal, formerly a milliner's assistant and now a Ruskin-trained artist whose drawings Norton admired. At some point, conscious of his poverty ("Rossetti is very poor"), Norton had also commissioned a "grand finished delicate oil" portrait of Ruskin plus another picture at fifty guineas, the subject to be left to the painter's choosing.[37]

The Norton family was in the habit of commissioning artworks from their artist friends. But Charles was no Mæcenas. Compared to the rich English Midlands merchants and mill owners who were becoming the Pre-Raphaelites' best patrons, his means were modest enough. His own income derived from trading potentially profitable but always uncertain commodity cargoes to and from India. Even combined with the income generated by his mother's substantial fortune (held in trust since Andrews' death in 1853, and safely invested in bonds and real estate), the money available for the family's travel and residence abroad in 1855–56 was not sufficient to cover their expenses. To bridge the shortfall, Norton had had to borrow $5000, telling his brother-in-law who arranged the loan, "I do not want my Mother & the girls to go home feeling that their income will be materially less owing to the pleasures or expenses of this year abroad." This principle would guide him for the rest of his life: the best is never extravagant—only make sure that it *is* the best. As Norton liked to say, "in what pertains to culture gold is not too good for any of us."[38]

Norton had seen not only Rossetti's *Found*, his picture of the great contemporary misery of prostitution, but the many "ultra-medieval" pictures the artist was then painting on Biblical, Arthurian, Dantean and Shakespearean themes. In a letter written to his mother, now at home, Norton told Catharine, "I am not sure that Rosetti's [*sic*] imagination is always sound." But in his *Atlantic Monthly* essay Norton did not voice this misgiving. After describing some of Rossetti's medievalist pictures for his readers, Norton bestowed his highest accolade upon the artist: Rossetti, he declared, had produced "works of imagination" which ranked among the best the age had produced.[39]

In their own day and afterwards, nothing has seemed more at odds with the Pre-Raphaelites' ambition to reform modern art than the aspect that was so striking in Rossetti's work—a love of the medieval past. Norton, as if recognizing the difficulty this might present his readers, repeatedly stressed in his review that Pre-Raphaelitism involved neither antiquarianism nor revivalism nor obsolete methods. Instead, he told them, Pre-Raphaelitism meant the fostering of a progressive "spirit" that had been as modern in 1300 as it was in 1857: "the spirit which united Art with Religion." The leading Pre-Raphaelites, he noted, were all young men—Millais was 28, Hunt was 30, Rossetti was Norton's own age, 29—and they were all fully modern, Norton declared, "fully up with the day in which they live."[40]

In more recent times, Norton's own medievalism during these years—his affection for "the age of Giotto and the Pre-Raphaelite world"—has been taken as proof of the "escapism" or "nostalgia" of a man unable to cope with the predicament of modernity in which he found himself. But to assume this is to project an essentially late-Victorian attitude back upon an earlier phase of consciousness, as if the *fin de siècle* actress Lily Langtry could inhabit the same mental world as the mid-century "lady with the lamp," Florence Nightingale or as if the stolidly despairing Thomas Hardy could have written Elizabeth Barrett Browning's passionately hopeful *Aurora Leigh*. The Middle Ages, however, possessed a different cultural valence for mid-Victorians than it did for later generations, not least because Gothic art and architecture remained as yet undarkened by the failure of the hopes mid-Victorians themselves would invest in them. In this sense, Charles Norton in the 1850s was, quite simply, seeing a different Chartres than the cathedral that would become visible to Henry Adams, writing in the 1890s.

Nor was this all. For to the historically informed Victorians the past constituted an open vocabulary of politics. Invoking a historical parallel meant declaring a political allegiance—in the case of both Norton and the Pre-Raphaelites, an allegiance to republicanism, because the age of Giotto and Dante had seen the superb flowering of the Italian republics, the model for the mid-century struggle for republicanism and reform then underway in Italy and elsewhere, including Britain. Rossetti's father was an Italian emigré liberal, who had deliberately named his son Dante for the medieval poet whose name and fame had become a rallying cry among partisans of the Italian *Risorgimento*.[41]

Yet the meaning of the medieval or Gothic past lay deeper than this. By the middle of the nineteenth century, the Middle Ages had come to be regarded as the home of the imagination in a way that was as yet quite untouched by modern psychologistic notions of escapism or nostalgia. To understand how the Middle Ages came to assume this new character for Norton and his mid-Victorian generation, however, requires first glancing at a far vaster change, a historic change involving history itself.

For the generation coming to intellectual maturity in the 1850s—the generation of Charles Norton, George William Curtis, Leslie Stephen and James Anthony Froude—the time-scale of human history had been transformed, becoming, as a modern historian has said, "not merely longer, but immensely longer." During the preceding one hundred years, breakthroughs in the human and physical sciences, together with the mental revolution known as Romanticism, had brought about a dramatic alteration in notions of history and history-writing. Discoveries in astronomical and geological science were opening a view of a majestic new uniformity of operation and a vast new scale in natural phenomena. Pierre Laplace's brilliant mathematical calculations, collected in his *Mécanique céleste* (5 vols. 1799–1825), not only confirmed the regularity of the heavens earlier projected by Newton's law of gravitation. Laplace also established that this regularity and invariability extended even to the smallest apparent anomalies in planetary motion, thus banishing at a stroke the last signs of instability in the solar system. At the same time, the discovery of the planets Uranus (in 1781) and Neptune (1846) expanded the dimensions of that solar system, while William Herschel's observations of the Milky Way (during 1784–1818) conveyed a sense of the staggering immensity of the galaxy to which our solar system belonged—now reduced to a sort of insignificant celestial backwater.[42]

So too, Charles Lyell's *Principles of Geology*, first published in 1830–33, extended the earth's own temporality into a hitherto unimaginable past—natural history now stretched back millions, not merely thousands, of years. At the same time, Lyell stressed the almost inconceivably slow operation of natural forces in eroding and rebuilding the earth's surface. Reading Lyell's *Principles*, said Charles Darwin, altered the whole tone of one's mind. Even when viewing something never seen by Lyell himself, "one yet saw it partially through his eyes." Norton's generation thus saw the dimensions of the past enlarged by several orders of magnitude.[43]

During this same period, astonishing archaeological discoveries had opened a fascinating new window on the human past. Such celebrated discoveries as Pompeii and Herculaneum (systematic excavations begun in 1763), the Rosetta Stone (found in 1799), A. H. Layard's excavation of ancient Nineveh (begun in 1845) and soon, William Pengelly's discovery of paleolithic tools in Victorian Devon (in 1858)—achieved tremendous éclat with an international public. Archaeology, uncovering the ordinary domestic artifacts and life conditions of ancient peoples, made these unimaginably remote men and women seem as familiar as neighbors. Sandals, pots, children's toys—objects known to be thousands of years old were seen to differ but slightly from their nineteenth-century equivalents, for a moment at least closing the gaping crevasse of millennia. Meanwhile the quieter, less visible theoretical revolution in philology and historiography set in motion by such German scholars as C. G. Heyne, F. A. Wolf and B. G. Niebuhr promised that it would at last be possible to separate myth from fact in historical accounts, and thus to trace back the branching tree of historical causation as surely as philologists followed the etymology of Germanic or Romanic words back to their Indo-European roots.

The influence of these revolutions upon early and mid-nineteenth ideas of history was profound, transforming history into the precious vessel of what may be called a human sublime. Ancient peoples, formerly little more than vaguely grasped names of tribes, were suddenly individuated, brought forward with all their struggles, defeats and triumphs into a vital, breathing relation with nineteenth-century men and women. In the same moment, the living path connecting the ancients to the moderns was revealed to plunge backwards into an unfathomable abyss of time. The effect of this double perspective was at once thrilling and vertiginous—as if a zoom camera were suddenly to draw a bright and busy human foreground startlingly near while simultaneously thrusting the non-human background at warp speed far back into an infinitely deep distance.

Against this dramatically altered backdrop, such writers of the Romantic generation as Thomas Carlyle and Thomas Arnold began to write history. Carlyle and Arnold, both born in the same year as John Keats, both turning twenty as Napoleon I was defeated at Waterloo, both belonged, like the slightly younger Thomas Babington Macaulay and Ralph Waldo Emerson, to the supremely confident English and American generation coming into conscious power in the years after 1815—the moment, that is, when the power of masses of men and women to shape history had never seemed clearer or more hopeful. For Carlyle and Arnold and Emerson, the human advance through time was heroic in its vastness and infinitely slow conquest of adversity. This vision they conveyed to the young men and women of Norton's generation with an incomparable vividness and a high prophetic earnestness—Carlyle in *The French Revolution* (1837) and *Past and Present* (1843), Arnold in his Oxford lectures as Regius professor of modern history (1841), Emerson in his essays (read weekly by young Englishmen clubbing together for the purpose in Manchester) and his celebrated lyceum lectures (from 1833 onwards). "Consider History, with the beginnings of it stretching dimly into the remote Time," Carlyle commanded with characteristic force, "emerging darkly out of the mysterious Eternity: the ends of it enveloping us at this hour, whereof we, both as actors and relators, form part!"[44]

To read such writers was to share in their living sense of vanished precursor generations as the direct progenitors and chief (if unacknowledged) benefactors of the present day. Carlyle and Macaulay had both learned from Walter Scott's historical novels how to convey a densely detailed and imaginatively concrete sense of past scenes and personalities. Carlyle, the Ecclefechan peasant's son, felt (as Macaulay did not) the pathos of anonymity in the past. It was not just the heroes with names—the Dracos and the Hampdens—who had furnished the nineteenth-century house of life, Carlyle reminded his audiences. All that they saw around them—if they could only recognize it—was the work of nameless Phoenician mariners, Italian masons, alchemists and philosophers, laboring and vanishing in the abyss of time. History, Carlyle told them, was nothing less than "the Message, verbal or written, which all Mankind delivers to every man." Across the Atlantic, Emerson was urging his listeners to dispense with history as it had been rendered by pedants and antiquarians—the "preposterous There or Then," Emerson called it—and put in its place "the Here and the Now"—that is, history recognized simply as one's own life and thought as unnumbered others had earlier lived it and thought it. Both men agreed that there was "no use writing of things past," as Carlyle said to Emerson, "unless they can be made in fact things present."[45]

By the end of the nineteenth century when Henry Adams, eleven years younger than Norton, would be writing *Mont-Saint-Michel and Chartres*, a colder, positivist, professionalized mode of history-writing focused on impersonal forces and material evidence would banish as "unscientific" this kind of sublime Romantic narrative history. To the mid-century generation of young men, however, who read by the blazing light thrown off by such teachers as Carlyle and Emerson—especially to those like Norton and Stephen and Froude who were themselves to turn to historical writing—history would never entirely cease to be the urgent, electrifying message that mankind, leaping across the gulf of oblivion, brought to every individual man and woman in the here and now.

Ten years before he ever stood in the doorway of Manchester's Palace of Art, Norton had bought Carlyle's *Past and Present*. Written during the nadir of England's "Hungry Forties," the book contrasted the hunger and rage in contemporary Manchester—where as Carlyle said in a famous phrase "Cash-payment [is] the one nexus of man to man"—with the human interdependence and coarse plenty in the twelfth-century monastery of St. Edmondsbury. The idea of juxtaposing the two historical periods was not original with Carlyle. Both Robert Southey's *Colloquies* (1829) and A. W. N. Pugin's *Contrasts* (1836) had used the foil of medieval abundance and social cohesion to criticize modern impoverishment and social atomization. But Carlyle's 1843 "tract for the times" was witheringly effective—"as full of treason as an egg is full of meat," declared Emerson with delight, "and every lord and lordship and high form and ceremony of English conservatism tossed like a football into the air, and kept in the air with merciless rebounds and kicks."[46]

Drawing on the Latin chronicle of Jocelin of Brakelond published for the first time just two years before, Carlyle probed the twelfth-century world of Abbot Samson for its wisdom, humor and human qualities, insisting upon its lived reality. "[I]t *was* a world, and not a void infinite of grey haze with fantasms swimming in it," he declared, but a world peopled "with men of flesh and blood, made altogether as we are," whose eyes are "deep as our own, *imaging* our own." Invoking history, especially medieval history, thus became for Norton's mid-century generation neither an "aristocratic" flourish nor a "nostalgic" appeal but a fervent gesture of sympathy and solidarity with humanity—a means of conceiving humanity in the widest possible terms. "I want to teach you so much history," Ned Jones said to a younger friend at just this time, "that your sympathy may grow continually wider, and you may be able to feel and realize past generations of men just as you do the present, sorrowing for them when they failed, and triumphing with them when they prevailed."[47]

To honor one's forgotten benefactors in the past became one more way to acknowledge the mass of equally nameless benefactors still working all around one in the present—artisans, navvies, farm laborers, factory operatives. It was no accident that Rossetti should be translating thirteenth-century poets at the same time he was teaching working-class men to paint. A famous painting—*Work* by Ford Madox Brown, the patriarch of the Pre-Raphaelites—became the most forcible visual image of this mid-Victorian celebration of human fellowship in labor. Walt Whitman's *Leaves of Grass*—first edition published July 1855—became its most abundant expression in literature. Warmly welcomed by Emerson and enthusiastically taken up by the Pre-Raphaelite circle, Whitman's volume had received a generous and perceptive (and anonymous) review from Charles Norton just before he left for England in 1855.[48]

Only one aspect of the medieval St. Edmondsbury monastery lay beyond Carlyle's kindling sympathies—its architecture, identified by him with "dilettantism" and hence with the game-preserving, corn-lawing, much-consuming aristocracy whose idleness and selfishness had brought England in the 1840s so near to ruin. Here, however, John Ruskin had stepped into the breach, in the space of five years publishing four books dealing with medieval architecture, from *The Seven Lamps of Architecture* in 1849 to the final volumes of *The Stones of Venice* in 1853. Eventually, Ruskin would give away his own copy of *Past and Present*, saying, "I read [it] no more because it has become a part of myself—and my old marks in it are now useless because in my heart I mark it all." But in the decades before he gave Carlyle's book away, Ruskin carried out the older man's own work of making past things present—by showing readers how the disregarded forms of Gothic architecture were, rightly seen, "the record of thoughts, and intents, and trials, and heartbreakings" of men as real and struggling as they were.[49]

Norton would later say that Ruskin's great contribution had been to make English-speaking people understand architecture as the most trustworthy record of the life and faith of nations. In fact, this kind of expressivist interpretation of art had really begun with such writers as A. F. Rio in France and A. W. N. Pugin in England—Catholic partisans both, who liked to contrast the religious "sincerity" of imperfect medieval forms to the irreligious "degeneracy" of Renaissance works. But Ruskin in an extraordinary feat of cultural appropriation had captured Gothic for Protestantism. Beneath all the fantastic buttresses and spandrils and sprockets of actual Gothic buildings, he told his readers, there lay a "universal Gothic"—the direct expression of the Northern European peoples as they struggled to build their communities amid the harsh conditions of Northern life. As described in the famous "Nature of Gothic" chapter in the second volume of *Stones of Venice*, this paradigmatic Gothic character was Protestant in its energy, individuality, variety and love of change. His largely Protestant English and American readers eagerly hailed this "spirit" as their own.[50]

Ruskin wrote about Gothic architecture as if it were as urgently important as anything his readers might find in their morning newspapers. Gothic mattered, he told them, because it was the only architecture that was able to admit the imperfection, the aspiration and hence the real humanity of the workers who produced it. Unlike ancient Greek architecture, medieval work did not hold its artisans to soul-crushing standards of perfection. Unlike modern British industry, Gothic imposed no fatal "division of labor" so productive of mutilated men—maimed, starved creatures the capitalists' cash-nexus had reduced to little more, as Ruskin famously said, than "leathern thongs to yoke machinery with." Instead, Gothic architecture freed each individual worker both to design and to execute—to labor, taking pleasure in the labor—within an acknowledged and humane structure of varying competences. "The principal admirableness of the Gothic schools of architecture," he declared, is that "they thus receive the results of the labour of inferior minds; and out of fragments full of imperfection, and betraying that imperfection in every touch, indulgently raise up a stately and unaccusable whole."[51]

Ruskin would give an authoritative name to this principle of dynamic cooperation by which all parts contributed to make up a whole, calling it "the law of help" in the final volume of *Modern Painters*. But even unnamed, as it was depicted in his earlier books on medieval architecture, the notion of cooperative interdependence as the source of vitality and energy—in polities as well as in the architecture that expressed those polities—became the radiant core of the Anglo-American reformers' faith in Gothic. As it rose to visibility from the pages of Ruskin and Carlyle, this Gothic ideal of a moral community springing from and expressing itself as devoted, cooperative labor seemed to liberal reformers as solid as the sculpted stone portals left behind at Chartres and Orvieto as the indisputable evidence of its earlier existence.[52]

Under the electrifying influence of *The Stones of Venice*, two undergraduates in Oxford decided to found an "Order of Sir Galahad" to realize its glowing vision of the cooperative integration of art and life. In New York, a reform-minded young lawyer reading *The Stones of Venice* encountered as a revelation Ruskin's contention that in pursuing mere "finish, completeness and money-profit" modern society had forfeited "vitality and value in the work done." On both sides of the Atlantic, architects began striving to realize in bricks and mortar Ruskin's idea of Gothic architecture as the most suited to modernity because the most flexible and forgiving of human error, in the decades to come building hundreds of neo-Gothic churches, public buildings and private houses.[53]

The first of these was already rising—the Oxford University Museum of Natural Science—fulfilling on a North Oxford building plot, as Ruskin said of it, "this old faith in nature, and in the genius of the unassisted workman who gathered out of nature the materials he needed." For its architect, Benjamin Woodward, had specified that the museum's interior columns were to be left *en bloc* so as "to allow as much liberty as possible to the carver." Its chemistry laboratory was to be modeled on the great medieval kitchen of Glastonbury Abbey. Yet it was "not a copy," Norton declared, "but an original creation of thought, fancy and imagination," proving "the perfect pliancy of Gothic architecture to modern needs." Writing about Gothic architecture in the way he did in the 1850s, Ruskin convinced liberal readers like Norton that what began with the Pre-Raphaelites as a reform of art was its way to becoming a larger art of reform.[54]

Yet Norton had not been among the enthusiastic early Ruskinians. He seems to have bought *Modern Painters* relatively late, in 1848, and then been put off by its dogmatic tone. (Ruskin would later condemn his own early tone as "nasty, snappish, impatient"). In autumn 1855, arriving in England with Catharine, Jane, and Grace Norton, Charles met Ruskin briefly when he secured permission to view the critic's famous collection of Turners. Sometime afterward, Norton bought another copy of *Modern Painters*, and began to study both it and *The Stones of Venice*, apparently acquired a bit later for use as a guidebook in Italy. By the time he was touring Italy in the spring of 1856, Norton had become immersed in the critic's views about the expressive character of art, and this framed the way he saw Florence, Orvieto, Venice and Rome. When Norton came to write about these Italian experiences, Ruskin's deeply cadenced prose with its pattern of tripled phrases was to leave its mark, briefly but plainly, on Norton's own style. Above all, it would be Ruskin's gleaming vision of Gothic cathedrals as the supreme art form of medieval life that Norton would carry away—how they so richly expressed the spirit of the people who built them, how they allowed, as Norton would say, echoing Ruskin's "Nature of Gothic," "the largest scope for the play of fancy and the exercise of special ability by every workman," while at the same time integrating "the multifarious differences of parts into one harmonious whole."[55]

Ruskin himself would later say of Norton at this time that "All the sympathy, and all the critical subtlety, of his mind had been given, not only to the reading, but to the trial and following out of the whole theory of 'Modern Painters.'" In late July 1856, when Ruskin and Norton met again by chance with their families on a steamer crossing Lake Geneva, Norton seized the opportunity to follow out Ruskin's ideas more fully. In the days that followed, the two men walked together in the mountains above Sallenches in Savoy, eagerly discussing many topics—hope for the rapid progress of the working classes, Rossetti, the position of women in America. But Norton also had a very specific question for Ruskin: "I asked him about the meaning of the passage in *The Stones of Venice* in regard to the most religious men he had known being without interest in art, & this doubt whether the deepest concern in religion could consort with much interest in art." It was a crucial question for Norton, and one that would lie at the troubled heart of their relationship ever afterward.[56]

For Norton at this time was a Unitarian of confirmed and earnest faith. The English poet Arthur Hugh Clough, who had first met Charles in America in 1852, even described him as "religiose." Andrews Norton, a tenderly attentive but humorless father, had been a professor at the uniformly Unitarian Harvard Divinity School and the author of an impressive but unread work in three volumes, *Evidences of the Genuineness of the Gospels*. The central impulse of both Andrews' and Charles's reform activities had been religious in origin, rooted in the Unitarian sense of the progressive unfolding of religious truth, from patriarchal to Mosaic to Christian and beyond. Though Norton seems to have accepted the Transcendentalists' critique of Andrews, he continued to offer doubting friends to "send you my Father's book," and religious belief of a progressive and fervently anti-theological sort remained a real presence in his life. It bound him deeper in friendship with Mrs. Gaskell, the Unitarian minister's wife. It pervaded his *Atlantic* review of the Manchester exhibition, which concluded by saying that the Pre-Raphaelites promised, if they kept to their high principles, to produce "works which shall take us into regions of yet undiscovered beauty, and reveal to us more and more of the exhaustless love of God." "Exhaustless" was a Ruskinian word but the "love of God" and the forward-straining perspective ("more and more") expressed Norton's own belief.[57]

Ruskin's answer to Norton's question was scattered and equivocal. He replied that he been brought up in the Presbyterian belief that men were damned for errors in faith, that such men consequently had little time or thought for art, that he had not seen that art actually helped to a religious life, that the greatest artist he had ever known—this was Turner—had shunned religious subjects and lived what the world would count an immoral life, that in his own case the study of art had not directly conduced to a religious life, and that since writing the passage in question he had in any case changed his mind. He now believed, as Norton recorded Ruskin's words in a travel diary, "that art might be made to tend directly to religious ends, and that he certainly should not write more in regard to it did he not think that the study of art might lead to the contemplation & to the comprehension of the beauties which God has spread through the natural world & thus to a fuller knowledge of and stronger faith in God himself."[58]

At this juncture, Ruskin was feeling the first faint tremors of the upheaval in religious belief he would later call (with characteristic rhetorical heightening) his "unconversion" of 1858. In denying the connection between art and faith, he may have wished to sincerely express his doubts or perhaps to reduce the dimensions of those doubts by speaking them out. On the other hand, in reaffirming the connection between art and religion, Ruskin may have wished to leave Norton's earnest faith undisturbed or possibly to reassure himself that his own belief remained unshaken. In any case, the friendship between the two men—which properly begins in this moment in the mountains above Sallenches—would ever afterward involve the negotiation of affection across a changing terrain of belief and doubt.

In the following year, as Norton remained abroad to recruit his fading strength while his mother and sisters returned home, the ongoing conversation between the two men continued. Then, in early July of 1857, just before setting off to see the Manchester exhibition and Mrs. Gaskell, Norton spent a week with Ruskin. The critic was living in the village of Cowley three miles outside of Oxford, writing the lectures he had agreed to give at Manchester as part of the Art Treasures ceremonies. The two men saw each other daily—Ruskin reading from his lectures, Norton raising questions, Ruskin overruling the questions and proceeding as before. "In the main," as Norton was to say many years later, "I was desirous to hold him to the work of the imagination, and he was set on subordinating it to what he esteemed of more direct and practical importance."[59]

In retrospect, it would become clear that the divergent paths the two men would later take had already began to part ways at Cowley—Ruskin passing over into immediate reform activities even as Norton was coming to see the underlying limits to such activities. At the time, however, it was less evident that Ruskin really meant to withdraw from "the work of the imagination," that is, developing the social powers of human sympathy through art. Although Ruskin was in a mood to tweak Manchester's laissez-faire loyalties—provocatively entitling his lectures "The Political Economy of Art"—the lectures themselves did not seem to mark any decisive new direction for the critic. To be sure, in a moment of Shakespearean jeremiad he warned the fashionable Manchester girls that beneath the costly embroidery of their ball gowns lurked "strange dark spots, and crimson patterns that you knew not of—spots of the inextinguishable red that all the seas cannot wash away." But in Manchester, that sort of talk belonged to a recognizable grammar of traditional humanitarian reform. Charlotte Tonna had warned her lady readers about the terrible suffering that lay hidden behind their straight pins. Earlier still, English abolitionists had warned about spooning "blood sugar" into tea.[60]

Instead, when Norton went up to the Manchester exhibition a week after the art critic left, he was following Ruskin in no merely literal sense. His review of the Art Treasures show for the *Atlantic* would be as "à la Ruskin" as a Harvard graduate of cautious temper and temperate prose style could make it. At the same time, Norton had become "Ruskin-haunted" in a way Van Wyck Brooks and his heirs could never recognize. Through Ruskin, Norton had come to perceive the social power of imagination in history—of "spirit" shaping stone—with a fullness and immediacy he had not grasped before. Guiding his *Atlantic Monthly* readers room by room through the Art Treasures exhibition hall, Norton must be seen as leading them along the path of a human sublime blazed by Ruskin and Carlyle—from Giotto whose hand had, as Norton now said,"snapped the fetters of authority and tradition" in the thirteenth century, to Turner and the Pre-Raphaelites who seemed to promise so boldly to continue the reform of art forward into the twentieth. In following the chronological sequence of pictures, Norton's American readers, like the thousands of English visitors to the Manchester exhibition, were being led along the track of their own history—the sublime story of humanity laboring its way up and down the great centuries, out of the anonymous darkness into the light.[61]

⚜ ⚜ ⚜ ⚜

After Charles Norton returned to America in August 1857, Pre- Raphaelitism followed him across the Atlantic. In October, a large exhibition of modern British paintings, almost half of them Pre-Raphaelite works, opened in New York, later traveling to Philadelphia before closing in Boston in June 1858. The new paintings provoked varying responses from viewers. Expressing a common reaction among the press, one writer in the *Boston Evening Transcript* called the Pre-Raphaelites "pretentious egotists" and their art a persistently fruitless search "for truth, be it ever so hideous or disgusting." Two works in particular attracted abuse from reviewers: Elizabeth Siddal's alarmingly indecipherable drawing *Clerk Saunders* based on a gruesome Scots ballad ("'Pre-Raphaelitism' run mad") and John Ruskin's vividly cerulean *Fragment of the Alps: A Block of Gneiss* ("But such a sky! really, Mr. Ruskin, you must have had the *blues* when you painted it"). Norton made a point of rescuing both works from contempt and incomprehension by purchasing them out of the show, securing Siddal's drawing in New York and Ruskin's in Boston. Over the next few years, he would generously make these drawings, along with precious works by Rossetti, available on extended

Charles Eliot Norton

loan to younger artists seeking to enroot the Pre-Raphaelite reform in America.[62]

Yet Americans' response to Pre-Raphaelite painting was by no means all negative. "On the whole, I incline to favor Pre-Raphaelitism," remarked a New York lawyer, adding, "These pictures are hideously ugly, but new, unconventional, laborious, and faithful." Even the laborers employed to set up the exhibition in New York responded enthusiastically to the strange new pictures. Pre-Raphaelitism "takes with the working men," reported the exhibition's manager to William Michael Rossetti, the painter's brother, back in England. "They look, and they look, and they look, and they say something that the author of the picture would be pleased to hear." In Philadelphia, one young artist was so impressed by Pre-Raphaelite truth to nature that he set his own easel outside for the first time, painting a blackberry bush *en plein air*—a picture that was to prove widely influential among his American contemporaries. In Boston, a friendly reviewer from the *Atlantic Monthly* predicted this "absolutely revolutionary movement" would find a truer home in America—already the home of republicanism, non-conformity, radicalism and empirical science—than it ever had or could have done in England.[63]

Indeed this seems to have been Norton's own view. As he wrote Arthur Clough from Newport in June 1858, "It seems doubtful if the present generation of the Pre-Raphaelites will have strength enough to carry forward the reform they have begun." Perhaps Norton was thinking of his two unfulfilled commissions by the brilliant but erratic Rossetti— the Ruskin portrait was not yet even begun (in fact, it would never materialize). Or perhaps he meant the still unfinished frescoes Rossetti had so masterfully set in train upon the upper walls of the neo-Gothic Oxford Union debating hall just as Norton himself was leaving Oxford. These were richly colored Arthurian designs by Morris, Jones and other insouciant spirits, who gaily worked without fee, simply for the cost of materials (plus unlimited soda water). Whatever the case, Norton told Clough, "Art is stepping on very fast here, and I look rather to our artists to develop the good principles of Pre-Raphaelitism."[64]

The key to Norton's remark is "here." For here meant Newport, Rhode Island, then a quiet rural town, not yet encumbered by the millionaires' monstrous "cottages." By 1858, Newport's "little white hand" of land reaching into the green waters of Narragansett Bay and "that unmistakable silvery shimmer, a particular property of the local air," as Henry James was later to describe it, had made it a center for art and for artists. (Both Henry and William James would study painting there.) Earlier in the 1850s, the Norton family had built a summer house in Newport as a refuge from the harsh east winds of Massachusetts that annually wreaked havoc with Charles and Andrews' health. After returning from England in 1857, with his briefly improved strength having given way again, Charles decided to take up residence in Newport for over a year, where as in the past he could see his artist friends. These included the sculptor Benjamin Paul Akers, the Luminist landscape artist John Frederick Kensett, the portraitist Samuel Worcester Rowse and William J. Stillman, painter, photographer and editor of the first American art magazine, *The Crayon*, founded in January 1855.[65]

Stillman was just a year younger than Norton, but socially raw and racked with religious anxieties, he seemed much younger. He was the reader on whom Ruskin's *Modern Painters* had fallen "like a thunderbolt." First encountering Pre-Raphaelitism on a trip to England in 1850—in particular, Millais' fearlessly "ugly" *Christ in the House of His Parents*— Stillman was now struggling to reconcile his inherited religious beliefs with the new gospel of Pre-Raphaelite and Ruskinian "truth to nature." With generous financial and moral support from Norton, Stillman had made *The Crayon* into the chief organ of Pre-Raphaelite and Ruskinian principles in America. In 1859 he would leave again for England, where a closer acquaintance with both Rossetti and Ruskin was to produce a tortuously long process of disillusionment with their ideas about art. Stillman's disengagement from his own minutely Pre-Raphaelite paintings would be completed when an obtuse American critic mistook a photograph of one of them for a photograph of the actual landscape. "What is the use," this man demanded, "of Stillman making his pre-Raphaelite studies when we can get such photographs from nature as this!" Stillman grimly answered the criticism by pursuing only photography after that. At the end of a morbidly disappointed life, he would look back upon his time at Newport with Norton as his halcyon period, and recall "those golden dreams which I used to entertain when we were at Newport together—when we used to dream of a new art & a new American life."[66]

While in Italy, Norton had sent back travel sketches to Stillman for publication in *The Crayon*. Now, self-sequestered in Newport, he lived as an invalid whose prospects for long life as assessed by a London physician were not particularly bright. A pastel portrait taken of Norton at this time by his friend Samuel Rowse shows a dapper, delicately made young man with a moustache, curling hair and fashionable cheek whiskers—a face whose sweetness and self-possession are underlaid by weariness. Like other men of strenuous mind but weak physique, Norton sought to escape his personal situation by immersing himself in mental work. His mind was quick and exquisitely precise. He was gifted with an exceptionally retentive memory. Much later, his colleague Barrett Wendell would recall an extraordinary sort of academic parlor trick that

Charles Eliot Norton

Norton performed without apparent effort at the age of sixty-four: forty or fifty books to be awarded as prizes to Harvard students lay upon a table. Norton looked them over for ten minutes. Wendell continues:

> Then he sat down in some comfortable place from which he could not see the titles. The assignment of prizes began; one book allotted to this student, the next to that, and so on. By the time we had dealt with a half dozen, I could not have told you what was on the table, or what had never been there,—still less what had been assigned to whom, and what not. Norton, meanwhile, not only kept the whole fortuitous collection, of forty or fifty volumes, clearly and firmly in mind. From his distant chair, he reminded us with unfailing accuracy of just how we had disposed of every book already dealt with. To him, I dare say, the incident seemed commonplace, for it was only a casual example of how his mind worked. To me it was like some incredible feat of trained skill on the part of some famous player at chess or at cards.

Wendell at the time was thirty-six.[67]

Now in Newport, thinking about the conditions actually required for a new art and a new American life, Norton began to revise and expand his Italian sketches for publication as a book. Appearing at the end of 1859 as *Notes of Travel and Study in Italy*, the collection would take as its centerpiece the long section that Norton now added about the Gothic cathedral of Orvieto. Converging with this work was Norton's translation, with commentaries, of Dante's *La Vita Nuova*, another project begun in Italy and now undergoing revision. Dante and Giotto had ignited the Pre-Raphaelites' own hopes for a Victorian rebirth of the arts, just as they had fired the contemporaneous dreams of the Italian *Risorgimento*. Norton had earlier seen in London some of the designs Rossetti was drawing from the *Vita Nuova*. Even now, the poet-painter was at work on his own translations of *La Vita Nuova* and the early Italian poets. Pursuing his own Italian and Dantean projects in Newport allowed Norton to participate in the Pre-Raphaelite project of reform from a distance. Through reading and writing he could escape the constraint of his enforced inactivity by searching out the chances for "new life" in a polity. Studying the extraordinary blossoming of human and civic powers in medieval Florence and Orvieto did more than bring sunny Italy closer to a wearisome convalescent's couch in wintry Rhode Island. It made an ennervated but quietly ambitious American ask, How did such energies arise? How did they maintain their ascendancy? Why did they then wither?

Norton looked upon the Orvieto cathedral, with its superbly integrated profusion of sculpture and mosaics, as a work of democratic architecture *avant la lettre*, the "perfect monument of the past munificence and spirit of its people." When he had first visited the church in March 1856, he had seen it marooned on its abrupt hilltop above an oppressed and exhausted land. For by the mid-nineteenth century, Orvieto was a decayed city, shrunken within its ancient walls, its streets echoing and dirty, the Ruskinian heartbeat of its buildings—the "spirit of its people"—long since ebbed away. Yet once upon a time a miracle of cooperative action and high communal expression had taken place there. Like the Gothic cathedrals of northern Europe, Orvieto had sprung up, Norton told his readers, "by a great impulse of popular energy," an "expression of the popular will and the popular faith." It represented nothing less than "the prevalence of the democratic element in society." For the religious zeal and skill of the artists and artisans alone were not enough to uprear the great cathedrals. Given the enormous expense of construction carried out over generations, there must have been "a faith no less ardent among the people for whom the church is designed." No sooner did a city achieve its freedom from the feudal barons "than its people began to take thought for a cathedral." And no sooner were "the turbulent, but energetic liberties of the people suppressed" all over Europe in the fifteenth century than the building of cathedrals ceased. Only then did there appear what Norton called "the architecture of the intellect" expressive of the new despotism of Prince and Pope. Only then did such grandiosely theatrical, inertly imitative churches as St. Peter's in Rome begin to thrust aside the older Gothic "architecture of the imagination."[68]

La Vita Nuova, Dante's collection of poems about Beatrice interspersed with narrative and commentary in prose, told Norton a different but related story. Translating the title as "the new life" (instead of "the early life" preferred by some commentators), Norton stressed that the historical moment in which Dante wrote the work "might well, indeed, be called a 'new life' for Florence, as well as for Dante." For at precisely the same moment that Dante was expressing his life as changed by love, the most direct and unfalsifiable expressions of the Florentine spirit—that is, the marvelous architectural works of the Duomo, the Palazzo Vecchio, the Bargello, Santa Maria Novella and Sante Croce— were all miraculously rising, each new building, as Norton said, "at once the fruit and the seed of glorious energy." In the 1290s Florence had been a city with a population roughly the size of Boston's in the 1850s. In territory, Florence had been no larger than the smallest states in the American Union. And yet, he marveled, "The small city, of less than one hundred thousand inhabitants, the little republic, not so large as Rhode Island or Delaware, was setting an example which later and bigger and richer republics have not followed." Nor was Florence alone in

Charles Eliot Norton

striving, as Norton put it, "to build herself into beauty." For, Venice, Verona, Pisa, Siena, Orvieto—all the other little Italian republics of the day had done the same.[69]

How was such "new life" to be explained? Both in Italy and afterward, Norton had pored over medieval sources in studying Dante and the Italian Gothic cathedrals. In addition to his fluent Italian and French and passable German, his Latin and Greek were excellent, and his knowledge of Western history was highly informed. As early as 1853, the young man who would later become the brilliant historian Lord Acton had been struck by Norton's unusual breadth of historical knowledge, noting in his journal, "I was surprised at the good things he said about history." Yet as Norton surveyed the flood and ebb of cultural "energy" and popular "spirit" in Florence and Orvieto, he now applied an analytical schema that derived more from Scottish School and Unitarian notions of progressive enlightenment than from any medieval primary sources. He had felt his way towards a three-stage theory of cultural energy, and in the Orvieto chapter of *Notes of Travel and Study in Italy* he tentatively put it forward. In barest outline, it proposed that (1) intellectual awakening or reinvigoration leads to (2) a quickening of moral energy which in turn expresses itself in (3) expanded powers of artistic and other achievement.[70]

In England, the brilliantly creative Elizabethan period had been succeeded by the doggedly moralizing Puritan rebellion. In France, the dazzling lucidity of Voltaire's age was followed by the pitiless "Virtue" of Robespierre's day. So too, in medieval Europe the eleventh and twelfth-century intellectual revival led by Anselm and Bernard, as Norton pointed out, was followed by a widespread popular "outbreak of moral earnestness" which in its impassioned piety had found outward expression in cathedral-building and the Crusades. "It is at such times as this, when moral energy corresponds with and supports a condition of spiritual enthusiasm," Norton declared, "that the powers of men rise to their highest level." He continued, "It is only when men in this world are in conscious spiritual relation with another that their characters acquire dignity and strength, and their works possess enduring vitality." Norton was describing the moment in culture which moved him above all others.[71]

Norton ended his *Notes of Travel and Study in Italy,* by casting his eye over modern Rome, pointing out "the deadness of the Roman imagination, the absence of all intellectual energy in literature and in Art" and most intolerable to an American Unitarian, "the political and moral servitude under which the Romans exist" because of their domination by the Catholic Church. During the last two hundred years, he declared, "Italy has lain dead," with the French invasion to crush

Garibaldi's Roman uprising of 1849 representing simply the latest shovelful of earth on her grave. Yet "from such graves," Norton told his readers, "there is in time a resurrection." Indeed, by the time he came to write the preface to the book, dated December 5th, 1859, the wars for Italy's liberation had already reversed the tragic fortunes of the country decisively, bringing the prospect of Italian reunification near.[72]

As always when Norton wrote about Italy, however, America was not far from his thought. Just as the little republic of medieval Florence had brought Delaware and Rhode Island to his mind, so the "political and moral servitude under which the Romans exist" had another bearing much closer to home. By 1859 the political and moral servitude of the American North to the South, with all its deadening effects on mind and spirit—to speak of no worse slavery—had assumed a sharp immediacy. For when Norton wrote his preface and dated it December 5, 1859, the anti-slavery zealot and martyr John Brown was newly dead, hanged just three days before for leading the attack on Harper's Ferry. Soon, John Brown's body, in the words of the song that would immediately become famous in the North, would lie "a-mouldering in the grave." And from that grave would come a great and terrible resurrection.

CHAPTER TWO

War and Democracy

On a suffocatingly hot day in July 1865, Harvard College assembled to commemorate the end of the Civil War and the ninety-five Harvard students and graduates who had died in it. The pace of the ceremony was slow, less because of the great heat than out of consideration for the frailty of the many returning soldiers who marched in the long procession weakened by wounds, amputation or lingering illness. In all, five hundred and eighty-nine men had gone out from Harvard to serve under the Union colors, more than from any other college. Held under a vast awning behind Harvard Hall, the ceremonies lasted from morning to late afternoon. Beginning with an eloquent prayer by the Rev. Phillips Brooks, listeners heard addresses by Harvard's President Thomas Hill, General George Meade, Admiral Charles Davis, Governor John Andrew and Ralph Waldo Emerson, as well as poems by Dr. Oliver Wendell Holmes and Julia Ward Howe. By the end of the long program, when James Russell Lowell was scheduled to read his Commemoration Ode, the audience had grown distracted and weary. Even the shrilling locusts had been silenced by the heat. Exhausted by working on the poem all the night before, speaking in the open air and shaken by painful memories, Lowell was barely audible. His ode, though praised, failed to make the impact he had hoped for. Listeners that day came away more impressed with Brooks's words or with Emerson's. "We see the dawn of a new era," Emerson had said, "worth to the world the lives of all this generation of American men, if they had been demanded."[1]

Emerson was not alone in speaking this way. In the immediate postwar moment, most people in the North did. The horrendous human costs of the war—well over a third of a million Union soldiers dead, to speak of no other losses—seemed to Northerners redeemed by the "new birth of freedom" first hailed by Abraham Lincoln in his address at Gettysburg. Many years after this moment, Henry James would recall

37

its sense of limitless new life, of "such big things at last in sight, the huge national emergence, the widening assurance . . . and something strange and immense, even like the light of a new day rising above a definite rim." At war's end, Charles Norton, too, believed he was living in a new dawn. "[A]t last, the doctrine of human progress is proved true," he declared, "and a limitless vista of peaceful advance opens to the eyes of men." Like hundreds of thousands of other people, Norton felt himself to be living in a regenerated nation—"the first nation which deserves the name of commonwealth," as he said.[2]

It was Norton's distinction, however, to believe as well that the new spirit in American life—the "spirit of the people," as he called it in the phrase that held such meaning for him—would soon express itself in a regenerated art and architecture in America. All his recent experience and study combined to encourage such a belief. From his perspective at war's end, the pattern seemed unmistakable: the intellectual awakening represented by the New England Transcendentalism of the 1830s and 1840s had been followed by the outbreak of specifically moral energy constituted by the selfless actions of millions of Union soldiers and civilian volunteers during 1861–1865—"our Emersonian June," as Norton would later call the war period. The three-stage sequence of cultural development Norton had outlined in *Notes of Travel and Study in Italy*— from intellectual to moral to artistic—thus seemed about to complete itself in America. For unexpectedly and exhilaratingly, something otherwise impossible to imagine in the 1850s America of sectional hostility, moral insensibility and material self-seeking had happened: a sense of democratic community had emerged out of the war effort, a conscious spiritual relation among fellow citizens as pervasive as the impassioned religious belief that had once moved medieval men and women to build the great cathedrals. Who could doubt this new spirit would now seek expression in art? By Harvard's Commemoration Day, plans were already underway for building a memorial to honor its Civil War dead, an effort led by Norton himself.[3]

In the end, of course, the aftermath of the Civil War would see neither a morally regenerated America nor a renovated American art. Instead, the failure of the Radical Republicans' vision of Reconstruction was to constitute, as a modern historian has said, the single greatest disappointment in U.S. history. Yet the depth and meaning of Norton's later "pessimism" cannot be grasped without understanding the height of his hopes in this immediate postwar moment. Norton would later take care to eliminate from the personal papers he left to Harvard many of the traces of the faith he once felt in this Emersonian June. Some strikingly prescient lines from Lowell's Commemoration Ode, however, express the meaning that the Civil War and the sacri-

Charles Eliot Norton

fices it called forth were ever afterward to bear for Norton and others in his generation. For just three months after Appomattox, Lowell, in a remarkable feat of imaginative perspective, was able to glimpse the memory of the war and of those who died in it as if from a great distance. Lowell compared it to the persistently returning beam of a powerful lighthouse seen from afar: "a light across the sea, / Which haunts the soul and will not let it be, / Still beaconing from the height of undegenerate years." Thirty years after the hot July afternoon on which Lowell first gave out his Commemoration Ode, Norton would have come to regard the war and its stabbingly recurrent memories in precisely the same way. "[T]o us, who lived through it," he would then say, "the war is in a sense always present."[4]

❦

Charles Norton's personal Civil War would be fought with words rather than bullets. By 1863, when the military draft was first established, he was a thirty-six–year-old man with a wife and infant son, as well as two unmarried sisters and a widowed mother to look after, and like other men of his age and family responsibilities he was not called up. Instead, Norton contributed money to pay for a substitute—$575 to John Riley of Cambridge—thus helping his Cambridge district meet its draft quota. This was an unusual step for a man officially declared "not drafted" to take. But Norton contributed more than money. As an anonymous and unpaid publicist for the Union, he entered upon an indefatigable campaign in print and private letters to aid the goal of total victory over the South and slavery by strengthening civilian morale in the North. Norton would pursue this goal even to the point of repeatedly insisting that the North must be willing to undergo a longer war and more "suffering." It is because the civic language in which he uttered such pronouncements has been lost to our own generation that Norton has sometimes seemed to recent commentators a figure open to question and challenge.[5]

Even had he been younger and single, Norton would have been useless on a battlefield, given his lifelong history of ill health. When the war broke out in April 1861, he could look back on years when bouts of illness and debility had repeatedly brought him to collapse. Norton's most recent biographer has suggested that these persistent illnesses may have been the result of an undetected disease or tropical parasite he contracted during a five-month stay in India during 1849–50. Whatever may have happened in India, by late 1856 a frank assessment of his health given by Sir James Clarke, the eminent physician Norton had consulted in London, was sufficiently gloomy that the young man decided on the spot to give up his small importing business, and devote himself henceforth entirely to writing and scholarship. For as he told his brother-in-law at the time, "If my life is not to be a long one, it makes no matter what money I might gain." Alternately prostrated by summer heat and by winter cold, Norton struck onlookers as thin and shockingly pale. Frequently subject to a feeble pulse, he was occasionally prey to loss of consciousness. By 1863 he was a stooping, balding, unprepossessingly small man, hoarding his energy and looking out at the world from preternaturally large dark eyes. As one observer noted, "he could not have served a month in the field."[6]

"As I cannot go with the army," Norton told his friend George Curtis, "I must do my part at home." He threw himself into public and private-sphere activity—writing, editing, organizing and corresponding—that would help to sustain the moral unity of the North during the difficult middle years of the war. Active in the Boston branch of the U.S. Sanitary Commission, the greatest of the wartime civilian organizations, Norton joined his sister Jane in early 1862 to organize a supply depot in Cambridge for making soldiers' clothing under government contract. By January 1863, however, he was concentrating his efforts on the New England Loyal Publication Society (NELPS), a group founded by the Boston railway magnate and abolitionist John Murray Forbes to provide the small country newspapers across the North and West with strongly loyalist arguments and articles to reprint. First offered in the form of individual "slips" offprinted from the original publications and later as twice-weekly broadsides with new editorial material written by Norton, NELPS articles by the time of their widest circulation would reach over 1500 newspapers and not less than a million readers.[7]

At first glance, Norton's work as editor of NELPS seems to fit easily enough into the succession of "genteel" editorial tasks he regularly assumed throughout his life—from editing his father's papers in the 1850s to editing the *North American Review* with Lowell in the later 1860s to the editorial work for which he was perhaps to be best known, the rigorously discreet editions of the letters or works of such friends as Lowell, Curtis and Ruskin. For a sense of its true significance, however, Norton's work as NELPS editor must viewed against the desperate background of its historical moment. For the seven months following the 1st of January 1863, when Lincoln's Emancipation Proclamation came into effect, through mid-July 1863, when the savage New York draft riots broke out, were a perilous period for Northern morale. This was the moment when the danger of a "fire in the rear" of the Union armies spread by Copperheads and Peace Democrats had become acute, threatening to sabotage the entire Northern war effort.

Already, in the mid-term elections of autumn 1862, Peace Democrats had made alarming gains—gains indeed so large as to hearten many Southerners, who realized that the war could be won on the hustings as well as the battlefield. "The triumph of the Democrats is in fact a victory to the C[onfederate] S[tates]," one lady from South Carolina declared happily, "inasmuch as it is a national disapproval of the present incumbent and incumbrances." During these fall campaigns, Peace Democrats attempted to foment ill-will between the two great loyalist regions of the North by focusing on the weariness, resentment and racial fears bred in Ohio, Indiana and Illinois by the war. "It was a staple of every Democratic speech," as the governor of Indiana warned Lincoln, "that we of the North-West had no interests or sympathies in common with the people of the Northern and Eastern States; that New England is fattening at our expense; that the people of New England are cold, selfish, money-making and through the medium of tariffs and railroads are pressing us to the dust." One Ohio Democratic newspaper demanded more vehemently what many in the North-West had begun to ask themselves: "*Shall we sink down as serfs to the heartless, speculative Yankee for all time to come—swindled by his tariffs, robbed by his taxes, skinned by his railroad monopolies?*" Some went so far as to propose setting up a new North-Western confederacy that would join the South in resisting New England. Others, alarmed by the rise of such secret antiwar societies as the Knights of the Golden Circle and the Order of American Knights, feared an armed uprising in the North-West.[8]

Fed by the Union defeat at Fredericksburg on December 13 with its frightful butcher's bill of 13,000 dead and wounded men, these fears and resentments festered and grew during the dark winter of 1862–63. On January 14, two weeks after the Emancipation Proclamation became law, Indiana Democrats introduced a motion in the state legislature declaring that until Lincoln's edict was withdrawn, the state would never contribute another man or another dollar to the war. On the same day, the most effective speaker among the Peace Democrats, Ohio Congressman Clement Vallandigham, called for peace without victory. After the slaughter of Fredericksburg, after the deadly morass of Vicksburg, Vallandigham told his colleagues in the House of Representatives, "Defeat, debt, taxation, sepulchres, these are your trophies."[9]

During the winter weather-enforced lull in the fighting, a depressed, discouraged mood spread like contagion between the homefront and the Northern armies. Enlistments fell off dangerously. Absenteeism and malingering increased. In the Army of the Potomac, desertions during January 1863 were averaging more than a hundred a day. In the Army of the Tennessee, "voluntary capture" became such a problem that General Ulysses S. Grant ordered the court-martialing of any paroled man or officer who had been captured while "straggling" or wandering from the line of march. To one Wisconsin officer stationed in Virginia, the army seemed by the end of January willing to accept peace on almost any terms: "I think the *fight* is out of the men," the officer said. Napoleon Bonaparte's famous dictum held that in war, moral factors were three times as important as material ones in accounting for ultimate success or failure. By 1865, General William Tecumseh Sherman would prove Napoleon's ratio held as true for civilian morale as it did for the soldiers'. But in winter of 1863, long before Sherman's epic march through Georgia and the Carolinas broke the spirit of the South, George Curtis, sensing the deep hesitancy among Northerners, told a friend, "The fate of the country is being settled in this lull."[10]

This was the crisis of demoralization in which Norton took up his pen as editor of NELPS. His opponents were not so much Southerners as Northern Copperheads and opportunists of all stripes. Such men as Vallandigham of Ohio and Mayor Fernando Wood of New York, as Norton told readers in a NELPS editorial for March 19, 1863, "are as much the enemies of the free laboring man at the North as any Southern rebel who would like to own him and his wife and children, and sell them at his will." In such men, Norton recognized the expediency, selfishness and cynicism he had been opposing as an advocate of social reform in the 1850s—as when, in the pages of *Putnam's Magazine*, he depicted the banqueters in a lavish new Broadway hotel heedlessly feeding upon choice delicacies as their fellow human beings scavenged for scraps of food only a few steps away.[11]

Against a political party that had effectively appropriated the name "Democracy," Norton invoked "the true cause of an honest, hard-working Democracy." Against an insidious faction that played on amorphous Northern fears of racial "amalgamation," he countered with the much more immediate threat by Southern slaveowners "to bring the white laborers of their own race under the yoke of servitude." Against the regional forces working to drive a wedge between New England and the North-West, Norton deployed the expanding correspondence he now began with loyalist editors all across the Union. Nor did the editor of NELPS confine his resistance to domestic foes. When Thomas Carlyle published a satiric squib against the North, Norton like many other Americans responded sharply. For he knew that Carlyle's quips condensed "the spirit that has characterized the mass of English feeling and expression concerning our war,—a spirit of ignorance, arrogance, and inhuman indifference as to the cause of liberty and justice." Unopposed, Carlyle's jests would comfort the South, embolden the Copperheads and conceivably even unsettle the British government's disposition to remain neutral in the American conflict.[12]

The genial Emerson broke off correspondence with his friend at this time because of Carlyle's coarsely phrased contempt for the Union cause. Norton had been reading Carlyle's book about Oliver Cromwell with its vivid portrayal of the English civil war between the Cavaliers and the Roundheads—between gilded despotism and the "Good Old Cause" of political and religious freedom—precisely as a parallel to the American struggle. Now, mastering his anger by calling it "sorrow," Norton struggled to dismiss Carlyle from his admiration, declaring with a tense formality, "He who might have lived forever in the grateful remembrance not of one nation only, but of all lovers of right, by speaking earnest sympathetic words for the cause of freedom, he who might have helped on the world[,] insolently flings a scoff into the face of those fighting for the good old cause, and puts a stumbling block into the path of mankind." Carlyle, the teacher of earnestness to a generation, had been rapped with his own ferule.[13]

Norton's patriotic indignation on behalf of the North is easy to understand. More difficult to appreciate is his urgent and repeated call for a longer war and more "suffering." After the panic rout of the first battle of Bull Run, Norton told the readers of the *Atlantic* that more such Union defeats—even with more such bloodshed—were to be welcomed if the North did not learn the lesson of its first loss: that vanity and recklessness had undermined genuine preparation and sober thought. Though uncommon at the time, Norton's opinion was by no means idiosyncratic. The acerbic Southern diarist, Mary Chesnut, for example, shared it. After the Federal forces' defeat at Bull Run, she declared, "the shameful farce of their flight will wake every inch of their manhood. It was the very fillip they needed." A year later, as General Robert E. Lee's Army of Northern Virginia finished crossing the Potomac River and headed north, Norton wrote George Curtis to say, "The best thing for our cause at the present time would be, I believe, a few days' invasion of Ohio or Pennsylvania. Our people would really feel *war* then and I think the Administration would have to carry on war with vigour after that." Ten days later, the battle of Antietam claimed more than 12,000 Union casualties. Among them was the son of Dr. Oliver Wendell Holmes, left for dead on the battlefield.[14]

When Norton refers to "suffering," he has in mind a great deal more than the physical agony of the maimed and dying soldiers. For he is speaking as well of moral suffering necessary "to quicken our consciences and cleanse our hearts," the collective trial of citizens—but especially civilians—by which individual self-interest is purged away and the vital needs of the community become universally visible. To fail to see this larger context of moral experience would be to make Norton's emphasis on suffering during the American Civil War either unintelligible or repugnant. For what Norton meant by "suffering" was what the French republican historian Edgar Quinet called the power to "*souffrir moralement.*" In *Les Revolutions d'Italie*, published in 1848, Quinet had attributed the long enslavement of Italy at the hands of foreign powers precisely to its inability to endure trial or purification through shared sacrifice for an end greater than private good. Norton had singled out Quinet's phrase in his own *Notes of Travel and Study in Italy*, translating the French phrase in order to explain to American readers why Italy had collapsed in the fifteenth century. "Even trouble and misfortune failed to rouse her to energy," Norton told them, for Italy, preferring physical comfort and ease of mind, "had lost the capacity of moral suffering." The grievous consequence for the Italian republics had been centuries of oppression.[15]

On a purely personal level, Norton would always have an acute sense of the agonies being undergone by those in the field. In the tightly-knit Boston and Cambridge community—held together by a web of family connections as well as a common intellectual and religious heritage— the death of any young man was a death in the extended family of Boston relationships. Nor was it uncommon either there or elsewhere in the Union for brothers in arms to be brothers in fact. The intensely local character of military recruitment only reinforced the communal sense of immediate relation to the soldiers. The 20th Regiment of Massachusetts Volunteers, for example, was led almost entirely by men from Harvard College. Soon known as the "Harvard regiment," the 20th Mass. was the regiment of Dr. Holmes's son, two of Lowell's nephews and later, of Norton's own brother-in-law. Its lieutenant-colonel had grown up in Cambridge as Norton's next-door neighbor.[16]

The constant anxiety felt by Norton along with everyone else in Boston and Cambridge during these days is vividly caught in Dr. Holmes's half-mocking yet wholly serious essay "Bread and the Newspaper" published in the *Atlantic Monthly* for September 1861. Dr. Holmes warns his readers that a war fever fiercer even than that gripping the young men is spreading to the civilian population in the North. Its victims—those with friends or relatives in the military—present symptoms ranging from obsession with the latest news, nervous restlessness, disordered sleeping, dreamlike waking and abandonment of all settled habits. Its causes spring from the radically changed character of war in a country penetrated by "a network of iron nerves which flash sensation and volition backward and forward" and a "vast system of iron muscles which, as it were, move the limbs of the mighty organism one upon another."[17]

Holmes was referring to the thousands of miles of telegraph and rail lines that were changing not only military strategy and tactics in the war but the very experience of war on the home front. Word from the battlefield now reached hearth and parlor with electric speed, its shocking directness tempered only by an awareness that there were always frequent errors in the reporting. "Always remember," a first lieutenant in the 21st Mass. told his father on March 9, 1862, "that *any hour* or *any moment* may bring you news that I am killed or dangerously wounded." Five days later such news indeed came: the son had been killed in the capture of New Berne, North Carolina. With letters from the front uncensored by Union military authorities, constant visits by friends and relatives from home to base camp, and unexcused absences and even desertion going relatively unpunished, Northern civilians lived in closer connection to their soldiers than was ever possible before or indeed for a hundred years afterward. Under the continuous strain, Dr. Holmes declared, "We live on our emotions, as the sick man is said in the common speech to be nourished by his fever."[18]

Holmes's son would be wounded three times before resigning his commission in the 20th Mass. Norton's family would remain safe until July 30, 1864, when Arthur Sedgwick, his twenty-year-old brother-in-law, was captured on picket duty in Virginia with thirty-two of his men. Seized during the aftermath of the spectacular but tragically ineffective explosion of "the Crater" outside the fortifications of Petersburg, Sedgwick was sent to Richmond's notorious Libby Prison. His capture dramatically illustrated Dr. Holmes's point about the changed civilian relation to war in an age of telegraphs and railroads. For the family first learned of Sedgwick's capture from a newspaper. As soon as they did, Norton appealed to his friend John Murray Forbes to use his railway and banking connections to speed money, clothing and tinned meat to succor the young man in a prison known for its epidemic illness and chronic shortage of food. Released in a prisoner exchange later that September, Sedgwick would return home to Cambridge, gaunt and shaken with fever.[19]

Such relatively happy individual outcomes, however, were overshadowed by the heavy tidings that came to Norton's closest friends. "We have shared your anxieties & deeper interests," he wrote George Curtis after the desperate battle of Winchester on May 25, 1862, when news finally came that Curtis's brother-in-law, Robert Gould Shaw, had survived it. But Curtis's brother, Joe, Lieutenant-Colonel of the 4th Rhode Island, was to be killed that December at Fredericksburg. And six months after that, Shaw himself, commanding the vanguard black regiment, the 54th Mass., would be cut down leading his men over the ramparts of Fort Wagner outside of Charleston, in one of the most celebrated actions of the war. Three of James Lowell's beloved nephews were successively killed at Ball's Bluff in 1861, at Glendale in 1862 and at Cedar Creek in 1864. As the news raced across the close network of friends and relations, the shattering effect of such losses may glimpsed in the death of the last of these men. For Col. Charles Russell Lowell, the poet's nephew, was also the brother-in-law of George Curtis. "No death in the war," as Norton told a correspondent, "is felt as a greater loss, or touches more hearts in our community than this."[20]

Although he preserved Lowell's anguished letters after Ball's Bluff ("We have the worst news. Dear Willie is killed & James badly wounded") and Glendale ("All we know yet is the telegram 'mortally wounded, sensible & cheerful'"), most of Norton's own letters to Lowell about these deaths do not survive. Norton was Lowell's literary executor, and these letters touched the core of his friendship with the poet, which had begun in 1853 at a time of mutual bereavement, when Lowell had lost his first wife and Norton was mourning his father. Gifted and witty but also indolent and defensive, Lowell possessed the outward aspect of genius without its spine of discipline and self-forgetfulness. Norton, the younger man by eight years, often assumed the role of sympathetic guide towards his dilatory and easily discouraged friend, suggesting topics for poems and urging craftsmanship ("One blow must be struck, not ten"). Yet Norton would always remain the suitor in the relationship. In later years when the poet was long resident in Europe, the sight of Lowell's empty house would bring tears to Charles's eyes, and Lowell's conversation—"our unfinished, never-to-be-finished talks"— as Norton would painfully discover, was found to be irreplaceable.[21]

The emotion of Lowell's friends regarding the deaths of his cherished nephews is thus only to be glimpsed in small outward details— as when, for example, Lowell's Harvard colleague, the great philologist and ballad collector Frank Child, was ever afterward to hang the pictures of the two Lowell boys in his study beside those of the Brothers Grimm. Or when Norton, invited to present a new regimental flag memorializing Ball's Bluff with its severe losses to the 20th Mass., said in his address to the troops, "Fight in the name of your dead, & for the honoured captives whose places are vacant here, & who lie languishing in Southern jails." Read long after the day in which they were written, such words may sound merely rhetorical or emptily bellicose. But Norton knew these dead and captured men, and he was thinking of poor Willie Putnam, who died of his terrible wound the day after Ball's Bluff, and of old Col. William Raymond Lee, then threatened with execution in a Richmond jail.[22]

⚹ ⚹

Through all this suffering at the personal level, Norton's public and private calls for a longer war and more collective suffering could nonetheless be understood as a call for moral clarification through sacrifice because by now the "cause" for which the Civil War was being fought had at last been formally recognized to be the abolition of slavery. Al-

Charles Eliot Norton

though we now see the path that leads from William Lloyd Garrison's *Liberator* through Lincoln's Emancipation Proclamation to the Thirteenth Amendment abolishing slavery as part of an irresistible historical and ideological tide, a true understanding of Norton on "suffering" demands that we recall the long period of temporization and compromise, lasting from Webster's "Seventh of March" speech in 1850 to Lincoln's painfully deliberate approach to emancipation during the war, with the President blandly telling the impatiently abolitionist Senator Charles Sumner, "the only difference between you and me on this subject is a difference of a month or six weeks in time."[23]

Norton's own movement towards the Abolitionist position was only slightly more accelerated than Lincoln's. From the youth who in 1846 dubiously reported to his mother a Washington, D.C., slave trader's claim that "the slaves liked to go to the South, that they had found out that they were better treated there than at the North," he had grown into the young man who in 1855 felt oppressed by the "moral miasma" of slavery during a visit to friends in South Carolina. Only by November 1860 had Norton become so convinced in his anti-slavery sentiments that he could declare himself to be "ready that the Union should be broken up if in no other way the aggressions of the Slave power can be checked." Before the war, he had questioned the efficacy of immediate abolition as a policy, favoring instead—as Lincoln did—eventual repatriation for freed slaves in Africa.[24]

During the perilous "secession winter" of 1860–61, however, Norton feared specifically that a desire for peace and financial stability at any price would make Northern legislators accept the so-called Crittenden Compromise, a move which would have allowed slavery to enter all territories south of latitude 36° 30′—whenever such territories might be acquired by the United States. Such a provision, as he knew, catered to the slaveholders' cherished ambition of adding Cuba, Mexico, Central America—the "Golden Circle of the Gulf"—to the dismal realm of oppression, moral degradation and agricultural exhaustion already under their sway. During January-February 1861, in a review published in the *Atlantic Monthly*, Norton expressed his dread of the expansion of this "New Africa" through the loophole of yet another compromise. For he had seen that on the level of practical morality, slavery brought debauchery and demoralization to both masters and slaves. Through the entire process, however, Norton's religious faith in the brotherhood of humankind under God never led him to doubt the ultimate moral equality of blacks and whites.[25]

After the war began in April 1861, Norton, frustrated at Lincoln's slower progress toward emancipating the slaves, permitted himself to hope for a longer war in the conviction that "the longer the war continues the weaker does Slavery become." With Union armies penetrating Tennessee and the Virginia Peninsula by April 1862, as Norton wrote a friend, "our whole army, as it sees the South, is turned into an army of abolitionists." "The most pro-slavery 'hunker' in the ranks," he continued, using a common term for conservative Democrat, "is educated by his new life in an incredibly short time, & brought into the college of the Anti-slavery [sic]." When Lincoln at last issued his preliminary announcement of emancipation on September 22, 1862, Norton wept with relief and gratitude. "God be praised! I can hardly see to write," he confessed to Curtis. "I think to-day that this world is glorified by the spirit of Christ," Norton told his friend. "The war is paid for." A week later in another letter to Curtis, he declared, "The 22nd September will be one of our memorable days forever."[26]

Norton's call for a longer struggle and more "suffering," then, must always be understood in terms of a single-minded demand for abolition as the very essence of a war being fought for a selfless purpose. Simply to preserve the Union was, however generously interpreted, to answer certain demands of pure expediency. But to abolish slavery—to fight and die on behalf of a powerless and despised people—was to regenerate the commonwealth at the deepest level of its founding principles. Nothing, not even restoring peace, seemed more important to Norton than the achievement of this goal. During the difficult middle years of the war, he constantly identified the danger of a premature peace with the destruction of hopes for complete black freedom. In April 1863, after the failure of the Federal naval attack on Charleston, he told Curtis, "The harder the war [is] for us, the better it is for the negro. We are not yet worthy of peace." Here, if nowhere else, Norton was at one with Charles Sumner who regarded even Gettysburg as insufficient expiation for the nation's crimes against an entire race. "There must be more delay and more suffering," declared Sumner, "—yet another 'plague' before all will agree to 'let my people go'; and the war cannot, must not, end till then."[27]

In May 1863, after the terrible four-days' battle of Chancellorsville ended in Union defeat, Norton wrote a friend abroad, "There is still, & this is perhaps the most dangerous element in our present condition, a strong belief in a peace to be concluded with the rebels, & a considerable hankering after [it]." In December 1863, as the Northern armies were withdrawing to their winter quarters, Norton told John Murray Forbes about a long conversation he had just had with Major George L. Stearns. Stearns, originally a Garrisonian abolitionist who abandoned his pacifism after experiencing "Bloody Kansas" in 1856, was commissioned by Gov. John Albion Andrew to raise black troops in Kentucky and Tennessee for service in the Massachusetts "Colored" regiments.[28]

"He & you & I agree essentially," Norton told Forbes, "differing only in our estimates of some minor matters of policy. It is fighting that is to *kill* slavery. The Proclamation strangles it but the armies pull the noose so tight as to make the strangling effectual." Even in late July 1864, after the horrifying bloodletting of Grant's campaigns against Richmond and Petersburg, Norton rejected peace. "I do not want peace," he told Curtis, "till there is certainty of our carrying the Amendment to the Constitution." This was the Thirteenth Amendment abolishing slavery. Already approved by the Senate, the Amendment would not be passed by the House of Representatives and sent to the states for ratification until January 31, 1865. The next day Sherman and his army would leave Pocotaligo to draw the noose tighter still, as he told Grant, around "Columbia and the heart of South Carolina."[29]

Viewed from our own perspective, through the radically alienating history of twentieth-century mechanized warfare, with its reduction of the individual soldier into a faceless unit within anonymous, interchangeable formations, Norton's opposition to a premature peace may seem strangely heartless. One contrast in particular might seem so: Norton the older, physically debilitated Union publicist rejecting peace at precisely the same moment in July 1864 that the twenty-three-year-old thrice-wounded combat soldier Oliver Wendell Holmes, Jr., was emphatically rejecting all further participation in war. In fact, however, Norton's sentiments were shared by a very large percentage of the Union soldiers whose patriotic and ideological motivation for volunteering and continuing to fight was paramount. As James McPherson has shown through a detailed analysis of over 500 letters written by Union soldiers, more than 60 percent of them expressed strongly patriotic reasons for fighting, while 40 percent of them explained their purpose for remaining in arms as being to defend liberty, democracy, the Constitution and the rule of law. Nor were these merely the easy beliefs of untested men. The assertion of faith made by a veteran Iowan soldier named James Bradd may be taken as typical, as Earl Hess has shown, of a large segment of the Federal army: "if it is my fate to fall in defence of Country So be it. I will die a true man." Perhaps nothing in the American Civil War seems more remote from modernity than the frank idealism of its soldiers.[30]

Far from exposing the ideals motivating the Union effort as empty slogans, a more protracted war, Norton was convinced, could only work to expose the truth of those ideals more fully while purging the nation's founding principles—liberty and justice for all—of their tainted compromise with slavery. "The delays of the war, its cost & its suffering, are to be counted as blessings," Norton told a friend in April 1864, for "they have tempered enthusiasms into principles, & moral sentiments into convictions." James Lowell meant the same thing when he wrote in the *North American Review* for July 1864 that after four years of earnest thought and discussion at every Northern fireside and meeting-place "the great principles of humanity and politics" have been wrested back from "the distance of abstraction and history."[31]

July 1864 represented one of the last dark moments of the war, when the Union armies of both east and west seemed to be bogged down in disastrously inconclusive operations—Grant before Richmond and Petersburg, Sherman before Atlanta—and Lincoln seemed on the verge of losing the Presidency. Yet even amidst these crushing uncertainties, it could appear to Lowell as if the nation's great core principles "have again become living and operative in the heart and mind of the nation." For beyond the disheartening pattern of Union victories followed by inertia or defeat, Lowell and Norton saw clearly the possibility of a brighter national future—not the *status quo ante bellum* but that new birth of freedom about which Lincoln had spoken so eloquently at Gettysburg. All three men were glimpsing the possibility for America of moral regeneration.[32]

Looking across the Atlantic from England, John Stuart Mill had seen this same possibility of total moral transformation as early as the first year of the war. In "The Contest in America," published in *Fraser's Magazine* in February 1862, Mill assured English readers of that "a war to protect other human beings against tyrannical injustice; a war to give victory to their own ideas of right and good, and which is their own war, carried on for an honest purpose by their free choice—is often the means of [a people's] regeneration." Published immediately after the resolution of the *Trent* affair, Mill's article—"the magnificent essay in *Fraser's Magazine* by the acknowledged chief of English thinkers," as the American diplomat John Lothrop Motley called it—was eagerly read and widely circulated in the North. "[It] has delighted people here more than anything for a good while," Dr. Holmes reported, grateful like so many Northerners for Mill's sharp dissent from the otherwise largely sneering and unsympathetic British response to the American war.[33]

At a time when many people on both sides of the Atlantic were still assuming the conflict would be short, Mill pointed to the specifically moral advantages of a longer war, arguing from a longer-term historical perspective that "parties in a protracted civil war almost invariably end by taking more extreme, not to say higher grounds of principle than they began with." By February 1862, the London *Times*'s famed war correspondent William Russell was already predicting that if the war were not terminated by the end of the coming summer, it must explicitly become a crusade for the abolition of slavery. "[I]f Mr. Russell be right," declared Mill, "Heaven forbid that the war should cease sooner, for if it lasts till then it is quite possible that it will regenerate the American people."[34]

As the war did grind inexorably on past the desolating summer of 1862, with its seemingly unstoppable succession of Confederate triumphs—Stonewall Jackson's brilliant Shenandoah Valley campaign, George McClellan's bloody withdrawal from the Virginia Peninsula, the successful arming of the Confederate cruiser *Alabama*, the second disastrous battle of Bull Run—Union loyalists like Norton were able to find solace in Mill's vision of national regeneration. For there were already important signs of social transformation. During the summer of 1862, for instance, widespread religious revivals began to be held both in the Confederate ranks and, more unexpectedly, among Union troops. Complete with open-air prayer meetings and Bible study groups, these revivals would continue until war's end, powerfully contributing to the intensifying idealism which formed such a remarkable, and to modern eyes so unexpected an aspect of the later Civil War.[35]

In their attempt to come to terms with the staggering horrors of a war that was rapidly becoming without historical precedent in the degree of its carnage, nineteenth-century men and women eagerly sought for spiritual reassurance in traditional structures of comprehensibility. So, for instance, many in both the North and the South would come to see the blood sacrifice of Jesus Christ as the only adequate parallel to the immense effusion of blood for cause and comrades taking place in their divided nation. In a poem published in the *Atlantic Monthly*, Rose Terry would depict the battlefield deaths of Union soldiers as the "New Sangréal," with Christ appearing in a vision to say "'The blood poured out for brothers is my blood; / The flesh for brothers broken is my flesh / No more in golden chalices I dwell." Jesus' last sermon in John 15:13 became the text of innumerable funeral services: "Greater love hath no man than this, that a man lay down his life for his friends."[36]

There were other parallels as well. Soldiers and civilians alike looked to literature, history and myth to express the extraordinary acts of gallantry and self-forgetful service they were witnessing. Lancelot of the Lake, the Crusaders, Bayard, the famous sixteenth-century French chevalier *sans peur et sans reproche*—all the great heroes of the past, Norton told his readers after the first battle of Bull Run, "did nothing too high for us to imitate." In the years following Bull Run, many Union soldiers lived the myths thus summoned to memory. Private Richard Wyatt of Pennsylvania, riding beside his brother just before the battle of Murfreesboro, was overheard chanting the famous lines from Tennyson's "Morte d'Arthur"—"Now I go / To the island valley of Avilion, / Where falls not hail, or rain, or any snow." An instant later he was shot dead.[37]

Today, after a dark and troubled century of mass slaughter and genocide, such episodes might seem grotesquely romantic. But Malory's Knights of the Round Table and Crusaders like Richard the Lion-Hearted provided a mythic vocabulary to men and women struggling to put an otherwise inexpressible experience into words. The story of the Crusaders is especially pertinent now, Capt. Oliver Wendell Holmes, Jr., told Norton (who had just published an article about them) "when we need all the examples of chivalry to help us bind our rebellious desires to steadfastness in the Christian Crusade of the 19th Century." At Chattanooga, when the Union troops—who were commanded to take only the first line of Confederate trenches on Missionary Ridge—instead swept on, unordered, to capture the second and third lines, and then defying all odds seized the crest, one amazed officer called their action "more like romance to me now than any I have ever read in Dumas, Scott or Cooper."[38]

¥ ¥ ¥

Such stories convinced Norton that the dark and bloody struggle for human rights, liberty and law was bringing forth something fine and entirely new: "a type of character such as has not been known before," as he put it, "a distinct moral nationality," "a national character different from any that has heretofore existed." When a memorial volume of contemporary biographies of Harvard's soldiers was published, Norton would read it as evidence of the national regeneration he had so devoutly hoped for. The young men remembered in its pages had not been exceptions to the national character, he declared, but typical examples of it. Harvard's soldiers were not "nobler or better in native qualities than the young farmer from Maine or Illinois, or the young shop-boy from New York, or the mechanic from Philadelphia"—merely more fortunate in having their characters developed by a deeper culture. The new character revealed by the war was national in its scope, erasing the regional differences between East and West that had once threatened to fracture the moral unity of the North. "The portrait of the youth from Indiana, or Ohio, or Minnesota, or California," he declared, "is the portrait of the youth from Maine, or Rhode Island, or New Jersey, or Maryland." Their stories offer proof "of what the world is to become, as well as of what it is." By war's end, Norton was able to assert that Lancelot, Saint Louis or Chevalier Bayard could not present "so good an image of what a man should be, as that drawn from the lives of these average soldiers of our war."[39]

Even the obvious objection that America might have been weakened by now having to go forward without the 360,000 devoted men who died fighting for the Union cause could not diminish Norton's optimistic sense of the nation's dawning prospects. "For the first time," he told the readers of the *North American Review*, "we find a sufficient number of instances to allow safe inductions to be drawn from them, of characters formed and lives led under the influences now at work in America." Norton's very language—instances, safe inductions, proof—suggests how completely he regarded such hopes for a regenerated America as an empirically based prediction drawn from a "scientific" examination of incontestable facts. It was another reason why his later disappointment when it came would be so sharp.[40]

Norton was convinced as well a similar process of moral regeneration was taking place in civilian life. For the Civil War, putting Northern armies in the field into a close relation to the people on the home front, had involved vast numbers of civilians in commensurate sacrifices and unselfishness. Immediately after First Bull Run, with its ignoble aftermath of drunken and demoralized behavior among the Federal troops in Washington, Norton had been alarmed lest the soldiers not live up to the level of their great cause and "the communities from which they come." By 1864, he was able to reverse the polarity of emphasis: now he urged the home communities to live up to the high level of their soldiers. At the moment his own young brother-in-law was setting off for war, Norton broke through his own habitual reserve to exclaim, "Dear friends and brothers! Your love inspires our hearts, and shall make us worthy of you!"[41]

Many had tried to be worthy of their fighting sons and brothers from the outset. From the day Fort Sumter fell, as one Northerner would later recall, "[c]hurches and schools, parlors and bed-chambers, were alive with the patriotic industry of those whose fingers could not rest while a stitch could be set or a bandage torn for the comfort or relief of the soldiers who might soon encounter the enemy in the field." These were the anonymous volunteers of the U.S. Sanitary Commission, constituting a parallel army of humanitarian support for the Union troops—a million volunteers, mostly women, standing behind the million men the Federal government would put into the field. Overcoming much early and sullen resistance from the Army Medical Bureau—for even Lincoln considered the Sanitary Commission a "fifth wheel to the wagon"—the organization, under the vigorous direction of Frederick Law Olmsted, quickly worked out innovative solutions to the desperate need for medical supplies, nursing and hygienic conditions in the camps. Influenced by a transatlantic culture of altruism, the Commission was consciously modeled on Florence Nightingale's Sanitary Commission during the Crimean War of 1854–56. Activating the kindliness, sympathy and humanity among Americans that had seemed to Norton and others to be lying dormant during the 1850s, the organization achieved victories in the prevention and relief of suffering that had eluded earlier reformers.

It was as if the very forces of social sympathy that Norton had so earnestly striven to awaken in his earlier writings as a crusader for social reform had now spontaneously leapt into existence under the pressure of actual history.[42]

To Norton and his generation, the Sanitary Commission would always represent much more than a supremely successful humanitarian organization. What moved them most was its simultaneous expression and creation of the new "spirit of the people"—"its indirect operation," as Norton put it, "in the development of national feeling and confidence, in binding the people of the remotest regions in the close cords of service for a common end." For the Sanitary Commission had brought about an extraordinary change in national sentiment. The anxious parents and wives who first hurried to Washington intent on helping their local regiments abruptly discovered the limits of purely local attachment when these units were shipped away to the front. Overcoming their dismay and local preferences, these volunteers then set to work on behalf of all Union soldiers, experiencing what the president of the Sanitary Commission, Henry W. Bellows would call "an education in national ideas,—in the principles of the government itself,—in the great federal idea for which we are contending at such cost of blood and treasure." The volunteers began working for all the soldiers, not just "their own."[43]

For the Norton who had written *Notes of Travel and Study in Italy*, there was one overwhelmingly obvious historical parallel to this display of zealous communal spirit and devoted self sacrifice: the Middle Ages with its cathedral-builders, Crusaders and compassionate orders of chivalry. In his Lowell Institute lectures, delivered in the dark winter of 1862–63, Norton consistently drew parallels between the medieval and modern worlds, pointing, for example, to the villein or serf receiving his emancipation for fighting in the Crusades in much the same way as a black soldier might seek his freedom by fighting for the Union. At war's end, Norton was describing the intense moral solidarity that had been achieved among American soldiers and civilian volunteers in precisely the same terms he had earlier used to describe medieval church-building. In the twelfth century, he had said in *Notes on Travel and Study*, the cathedrals had allowed "the largest scope for . . . the exercise of special ability by every workman" while integrating "the multifarious differences of parts into one harmonious whole." In the nineteenth century, Norton now said of the Sanitary Commission's work, "the resources of each individual are drawn upon for the production of the common end, and the infinite and complex variety of individual devices, powers, faculties, and energies is harmonized into co-operative unity."[44]

Uniting the industrial magnate and the village seamstress in a spirit

Charles Eliot Norton

of ennobling purpose, the Sanitary Commission became the modern equivalent of that celebrated moment in medieval cathedral-building when French nobles took their place alongside peasants at the ropes hauling huge blocks of stone up to Chartres. So too, the Commission, as Norton declared, "was to the America of the nineteenth century what the orders of chivalry were to Europe in their day"—its wholly popular, wholly extra-governmental, voluntary and largely anonymous company of workers becoming in effect "the descendant of the mediaeval Knights of St. Lazarus, the Hospitallers, or the Knights of the Teutonic Order." Spontaneous, devoted, harmonious, unnamed—the terms of Norton's praise reveal how dramatically the Ruskinian and Pre-Raphaelite ideals of Gothic were being fulfilled for him by this new national sense of moral community. Here, in effect, was Ruskin's "law of help"—the architectural principle of dynamic cooperation by which all parts contributed to make up a whole—embodied in acts of flesh and blood, making visible the new spirit of the people and "inspiring men to behold in the nation, not a mere conglomeration of individuals, with separate and clashing interests, but a marvellous, intricate organization."[45]

The titanic medieval energies raising up the cathedrals had dissipated, Norton had concluded in his Italy book, when popular religious enthusiasm—rooted in what he considered "superstition" and "mental twilight"—withered, opening the way to Renaissance worldliness and the despotism of a cold classical formalism. The moral regeneration brought about during the Civil War was fundamentally different, he thought, because it was rooted in principles as permanent as human nature itself. "I believe that we have really made an advance in civilization," Norton told Mrs. Gaskell's daughter Meta at war's end, "that the principles on which our political & social order rest are in harmony with the moral laws of the universe, that we have set up an ideal which may never be perfectly attained, but which is of such a nature that the mere effort to attain it makes progress in virtue & in genuine happiness certain." The same claim is made in even stronger terms in a book review Norton wrote at about this time. "No nation is doomed to decline and death from the operation of material causes, for these causes may be held in check and counteracted by the moral force of continually fresh, renewed, and everlasting human energies." With the return of peace, the moral principles defining the North's war against the South—namely, "the brotherhood of man, the unity in diversity of mankind"—could assure the perpetuity of the American republic.[46]

In politics, with the Radical Republicans now in control of Congress and putting through a program of anti-slavery legislation, the country seemed to be approaching what Norton called "transcendental statesmanship," the Emersonian ideal of establishing morality as the basis of all legislation. ("Morality," Emerson had said, "is the object of government.") Even the relative lack of personal distinction among the current legislators in Congress seemed to Norton an encouraging sign—an index to the true extent of the regenerated American democracy. For "when events have roused the moral energies and touched the conscience of a people," he thought, "great acts may be accomplished by men not great in themselves, but lifted to a noble height by the wave of popular emotion." This was the same argument he had made in the first months of the war, telling George Curtis, "It is an unexampled experience that we are having now, and a striking development of the democratic principle,—of great historic deeds being accomplished, and moral principles working out their results, without one great man to do the deeds or to manifest the principle in himself." Even Lincoln, whom Norton came to admire whole-heartedly, seemed to him less a great man in himself than, as he told Meta Gaskell, "essentially typical of the character & principles of the people." Norton had by now come to believe that at its most genuine, the expression of democratic energy was self-suppressing and anonymous: for in the first cathedrals neither architect nor artisans left behind their names.[47]

Lincoln's re-election on November 8, 1864, acted as a powerful confirmation of Norton's hopes for national regeneration. With the Constitutional machinery working smoothly even amidst bloody civil war, with the bold experiment of allowing Union soldiers to vote on continuing the very war in which they were suffering so grievously, with the unrebellious acceptance of political defeat by the Democrats, and above all, with the people's deliberate persistence in the path of righteousness and principle, Norton believed this day—like the day of the first emancipation proclamation, September 22—would be remembered as one of the great days in American history. "Never before," he told an American friend living abroad, "was a people called upon for a decision involving more vital interests not only to itself but to the progress of mankind, and never did any people show itself so worthy to be entrusted with freedom and power."[48]

In personal letters, in NELPS broadsides, in essays published in the *North American Review* (which he began editing with Lowell in January 1864) and in articles for *The Nation*, a new magazine he and Olmsted helped to found in 1865, Norton would repeatedly express his sense, shared by a great many in his generation, that the war marked a glorious climacteric in the life of the nation. In the context of their time, his confident, forward-looking remarks would have seemed unremarkable to his readers. Norton's bright hopes, like theirs, shared in the blaze of the Emersonian June. But given the tendency of twentieth-century commentators to construct a portrait of Norton drawn entirely from the darker background of his later life and his supposed "pessimism," one of these remarks is worth pausing over. In an 1867 letter to the poet Aubrey de Vere, Norton wrote as follows about the national regeneration he believed was underway:

> We see glimpses already, nay more, we already enjoy something of truly Christian manners & society. We are working out results which are impossible as yet in the old world, and what we have already gained,—imperfect as it is,—is enough to give firm ground for confidence in the progress of men in virtue and in happiness through the influence of liberty & equality under religion,—or rather as religious principles—upon their character & conduct.

"Old world," "truly Christian," "liberty & equality"—some of what Norton says here is designed to neutralize the known prejudices of his correspondent, for de Vere was Anglo-Irish and a Catholic convert who had strong reservations about democracy and dissenting sects like Unitarianism. But a concluding sentence states simply and grandly what Norton has come to feel about Lincoln's America. He says, "It is hard not to be an optimist here."[49]

⚹ ⚹ ⚹ ⚹

This, then, is the larger context of Norton's buoyant hopes for a new American life and a new American art. "I see now no limit to the vision we may indulge, no barrier to our hopes of the future for our country," he said to a friend. Redeemed from their corrupt compromise with slavery, the most fundamental principles of the nation had been tested: "They are no longer experimental," Norton declared. "Upon them the future may be & will be builded fair." It seemed only natural to a partisan of Ruskin and the Pre-Raphaelites that they should be builded neo-Gothic. Even before war's end, there were clear signs that a reform in art and architecture might already be underway." The Civil War had disturbed many things," one New York artist would later say of this period, "but strange to say, it had less effect upon art than upon many things with more stable foundations." For after an initial sharp contraction, the Northern economy had rebounded: art galleries were crowded, sales of paintings were increasing, artists' receptions were thronged. One art critic described it as "a kind of picture mania." In publishing, book sales—especially of serious books—were moving to previously unknown levels.[50]

Artists and audiences alike seemed to have been invigorated by the colossal national effort. A writer for the *Nation* declared that "the rapidly growing interest in art and artists and artistic pursuits in general

... is an important element in the present intellectual condition of the people." Civic and artistic energies converged when a succession of Northern cities—Chicago, Cincinnati, Boston, New York—vying with each other in a generous rivalry to raise ever larger sums for the Sanitary Commission, held "Sanitary fairs" and began including art galleries and art auctions as part of their fund-raising efforts. In New York's "medieval fair" of April 1864, the art gallery alone earned over $73,000—more money than Chicago's entire Sanitary fair of October 1863 brought in. The volunteers' wartime idealism, however, looked beyond mere monetary gains. They meant their Sanitary fairs to embody in their very organization and conduct the democratic ideals for which the war was being fought, enlisting, as Henry Bellows said, "all sympathies from the highest to the lowest—democratic, without being vulgar; elegant, without being exclusive, fashionable, without being frivolous; popular without being mediocre." Boston's December 1863 fair was notable, the *Boston Evening Transcript* remarked with a quiet pride, for "the universal participation in it by all classes and conditions of people, from the humblest to the most opulent."[51]

In aid of the Boston Sanitary fair, the managers of the Boston Athenaeum offered to open its private gallery of paintings—normally closed to the public—to fairgoers. "In so doing," declared the *Transcript*, "they have subserved patriotism and the fine arts at the same time." In addition, many socially prominent Boston collectors agreed to enrich the special Sanitary exhibition by lending valuable artworks to the gallery. Among these were C. R. Leslie's celebrated portrait of Sir Walter Scott and Ary Scheffer's *Christ the Consoler*. It is natural to see to see Norton's hand in all this activity. For besides working with the Boston Sanitary Commission, he was a member and a trustee of the Athenaeum. His uncle George Ticknor was persuaded to lend the portrait of Scott, and his brother-in-law William S. Bullard, who lent the Scheffer picture, had received it as a wedding gift from Norton himself.[52]

Not least of all, the Boston and New York Sanitary art exhibitions were notable because such wartime activities involving art—modest, popular, but above all civic—would provide an essential context for the founding of the great municipal art museums in the postwar period. For the Sanitary art exhibitions in both cities—constituting the largest gathering of important works of art yet seen in either place—were among the most popular displays with visitors. It was their success that would then prompt calls for the establishment of public art museums in both cities. After the war Boston's Museum of Fine Arts and New York's Metropolitan Museum of Art would be founded in the same year: 1870. Philadelphia's new art museum would be built a year later.

Against the background of this slowly accelerating movement toward

Charles Eliot Norton

a popular appreciation of serious art, there now appeared a number of smaller but potentially even more encouraging developments. For the American Pre-Raphaelitism that Norton had so vainly looked for in the later 1850s now unexpectedly appeared in New York. A group of young artists and architects, calling themselves with sublime confidence the Society for the Advancement of Truth in Art (SATA), began agitating for a neo-Gothic reform of painting and architecture, then publishing a fiercely polemical magazine, *The New Path*. Taking their title from Ruskin's 1859 lectures *The Two Paths*—one path, Ruskin had warned, led to a faithful perception of nature, the other directly to the Pit—the young men looked for guidance as well to the one American well known to be Ruskin's close friend. The aspiring architect named Russell Sturgis wrote Norton to say, "There are very few works on Art which seem to me to have any value,—those few are on that account the more precious, and I esteem more than I can now tell you the *Travels in Italy*." Norton immediately responded with advice, encouragement, an order for two subscriptions to *The New Path* and, later, extended loans of his own valuable Pre-Raphaelite pictures.[53]

It was a happy development that Norton was able to serve as the American representative of Ruskin's aesthetic theories. For Ruskin himself, after sending SATA an early letter of support, soon felt so profoundly alienated from Americans by the horrors of their fratricidal war that he was unable to write even Norton without bitterness and insult. When Norton's first son was born in July 1863, Ruskin responded, "That a child is born—even to my friend—is to me no consolation for the noble grown souls of men slaughtered daily through his follies & mine." A year later, the art critic peremptorily broke off his correspondence with Norton: "your American business is so entirely horrible to me. . . . [i]t is just as if I saw you washing your hands in blood, and whistling—and sentimentalizing to me—I know you don't know what you are about and are just as good and dear as you ever were—but I simply can't write to you while you are living peaceably in Bedlam." He would not write again until the war was over.[54]

The bloody conflict that drove Ruskin away from America drew the American Pre-Raphaelites closer to it. Founded in January 1863 just as Lincoln's Emancipation edict was taking effect, SATA absorbed and reflected the surging idealism of the moment in which it came to birth. Many of the core members of the group—in addition to Sturgis, these included the painters Thomas Farrer and Charles Moore, the architect Peter Bonnet Wight and the art critic Clarence Cook—regarded themselves as "radical thinkers," working to "emancipate the people" from "the smatter and conceit" of the connoisseurs and dilettantes who timidly preferred French Romanticist conventionalisms to Pre-Raphaelite realism and truth. Convinced that slavery and the toleration of slavery had for forty years produced a deadly atmosphere in which a truthful art became impossible, they consciously set out to "'agitate the question' of truth in Art" with exactly the same single-minded fervor that anti-slavery reformers had earlier called upon people to "Agitate the question" of emancipation.[55]

Today, there might seem to be little or nothing "radical" about American Pre-Raphaelite works. A modern viewer might reasonably ask, How could these obsessively faithful landscapes and brilliantly "photographic" transcriptions of mulleins, milkweeds and blackberry bushes possibly be taken for works expressive of, in Norton's words, "the most genuine artistic aspirations and most ardent feeling of the times"? Although recent years have seen a renewal of interest in the American Pre-Raphaelites, their characteristic mode of patient, self-suppressing botanical realism has most often struck modern critics as timorous or even regressive. For with its apparent lack of interest in the human form, their work can seem almost deliberately to be avoiding the social conflict of the Civil War years, to represent "a particular evasive strategy" or even a defensive "arrière-garde of the older virtues."[56]

But SATA's reverently faithful paintings of weeds or cedar boughs or snow shadows were very far from an evasion of the great issues of the war. The problem for modern criticism is that they engaged those issues in a visual language to which we have since lost the key, looking at this body work, as we are compelled to do, through the intervening conventions and assumptions of Aestheticism, Impressionism and Modernism. For the American Pre-Raphaelites believed with Ruskin that rightly seen, every roadside weed might open a door to "sublimity, continual and exalted." For what is a weed, as Emerson had asked, but "[a] plant whose virtues have not yet been discovered?" SATA's insistence on Ruskinian realism and truthfulness, as against the vapid conventionalism and evasive idealism of academic art, aimed at nothing less than the defeat of the American empire of lies built up by forty years of compromise with slavery. In their militantly detailed Pre-Raphaelite mimeticism, SATA artists set out to express, as a way of seeing, what Thomas Farrer called the "noble love of little things." The American Pre-Raphaelites in painting mulleins and milkweeds saw themselves as arguing in purely visual terms for that dignity of the disregarded that American abolititionism had been championing since the 1830s. They saw their own radically Pre-Raphaelite realism as an uncompromising response to their own historical moment. They regarded themselves as trying to record the "the power and beauty there is in the real" no less truthfully than the best newspaper and magazine illustrators were even then depicting battle scenes on the Chickahominy and Rappahannock.[57]

Charles Eliot Norton

Yet even more radical was SATA's conception of the relationship between artist and audience. For the young artists—living in an historical moment as yet untroubled by the Modernist consciousness of an absent public—conceived of this relation in fundamentally civic terms. The progress of American art, the *New Path* declared, "depends almost entirely upon the way in which the public do their part," specifically, in encouraging the artists by demanding their very best work from them. But no less demanding was the role required of the artists themselves who, as Norton and Sturgis wrote in the *North American Review,* "must speak a language understood by the people, and deal with things cared for by the people,—with real things." Without artists, the people would live blind and mute. But without the people, artists would create without sympathy and the quickening power of the common life. "We gather strength from sympathy," the sculptor William Wetmore Story told James Russell Lowell before the war, "we must have our sounding board to give effect to the tune we play." In the glowing moment of postwar regeneration, artist and audience could seem as closely bound to each other as soldier and civilian, defender and supporter, Volunteer and volunteer.[58]

To Norton and the members of SATA, the unmistakable symbol of the imminent civic regeneration of American art and life was a neo-Gothic building then rising in New York City at the corner of 23rd Street and 4th Avenue. This was the new National Academy of Design, the work of twenty-five-year-old SATA member Peter Bonnet Wight. Wight had served as a U.S. Sanitary Commission architect, in 1862 designing the first field hospital in Washington, D.C. His Academy building, devoted to art and funded by the citizens of New York, was rising on a site adjoining another neo-Gothic structure, Jacob Wray Mould's All Saints' Church. Originally commissioned by the tireless Unitarian minister and president of the U.S. Sanitary Commission, Henry Bellows, it was Mould's exquisitely rendered drawings for this building that first made Wight realize "what an architect was." Wight's own Venetian Gothic structure, though its foundations had been delayed by the draft riots of July 1863 and its dedication postponed by Lincoln's assassination and funeral, seemed to hopeful observers, as to Wight himself, to express the "unseen regenerative influences" released by the gigantic moral effort of the war.[59]

America had up to this point little art or architecture. The first hundred years of American life, as the art critic Roger Fry would later say, were distinguished by an artistic indigence unparalleled in Western civilization except perhaps for the crude huts and primitive stone monuments of early Rome. Norton himself said that from 1620 to 1820 no genuine poem had been written in America, and that its only sculpture had been gravestones so hideous as to deprive any hope of heaven of its charm. Fanny Kemble, the celebrated English actress who had married an American, was dismayed to discover that her new Pennsylvania neighbors seemed to have no concept whatever of natural beauty: their only idea of a garden consisted of "straight, ungraveled paths, straight rows of trees, straight strips of coarse grass, straight box borders, dividing straight narrow flower-beds." When Frederick Law Olmsted visited Natchez in 1854, he climbed to a public park on the steep bluff overlooking the Mississippi to view the river at sunset. Looking out at the great gleaming crescent of water and the vast, dim, continuous horizon, he was surprised to find himself virtually alone. Of all the town of Natchez, only five other people had come to see the magnificent sight. They were all Germans.[60]

In the years immediately before and after the Civil War, art critics in American newspapers regarded watercolor painting with suspicion and hostility, decrying it as "emigrant art," and condemning its subdued tones, modest tints and misty atmospheres as signs of "weakness" dangerous to a healthy republic. A sympathetic English newspaperman, touring the country in 1863, could find but a single virtue in the native architecture: "symmetry," he said. In the same year, Peter Wight and Russell Sturgis had ruefully concluded that they were the only journalistic advocates of architectural reform in America. In the *North American Review*, Norton told readers that from Maine to Texas, "the number of buildings which have any just claim to the title of works of art" could be "counted on the fingers."[61]

Wight's Venetian Gothic design was meant as a permanent and telling rebuke to the imaginative poverty of American architecture. Wight's plans called for statues of Michelangelo and Raphael to frame the front portal and—a highly Ruskinian touch—a glass mosaic in the lunette over the main door depicting Giotto's Campanile in Florence, with Giotto in the foreground instructing his workmen. Even though these elements were as yet unrealized (in fact the money would run out before they could ever be added), Wight's design—adorned on the outside with arches in polychromatic bands of color and on the inside with richly carved capitals to its columns—quickened the yearning in men like Norton—not simply for color, form and historical "associations"— but for a large and generous public art. For Norton sought for nothing less in buildings than an architecture "in which a characteristic and original sentiment is so embodied in a form of imaginative beauty, as to make it the expression of the noble mood of a great people, or of the genius of an artist inspired by a popular emotion." The decorative abundance in Wight's Academy seemed to promise—even amidst the dully geometric grid of New York's avenues and streets—"that our cities," as the *New Path* expressed it, "need not be the homes of ugliness that they now are."[62]

Hailed by the *Nation* as "the most beautiful work of architectural art in America," Wight's building was greeted by Norton in the *North American* as "one of the most original, interesting, and important works of architecture erected during the present generation," its completion representing an event of national significance. With a pardonable fraternal pride, the *New Path* predicted that "[t]his solidly and admirably built, richly decorated building, a noble design well carried out, will remain *for ages*, unless fire destroy it; its lesson ought not to be lost upon this generation, it will not be lost upon the next." For not least among the lessons the building taught was the lesson of Ruskin's "Nature of Gothic": that every bit of otherwise meaningless ornament could, if truthfully done, be made an object of interest to every beholder—including the carver himself. "This would come," as Wight said emphatically, "from giving the workmen an opportunity to THINK."[63]

The great practical illustration of this Ruskinian Gothic ideal of work was, as we have seen, Benjamin Woodward's Oxford Museum—a building, as the *New Path* reminded its readers, "of which all have heard and of which the details have been abundantly reproduced in photography." Woodward, seeking to heal the modern breach Ruskin had condemned between design and execution, brainwork and handwork— (with the "division of labor," stormed Ruskin, it was not the work that was divided, it was the *men*)—had allowed his stonecutters an extraordinary latitude in carving the capitals of columns for the interior courtyard. Two Irish workmen had so risen to the opportunity as to approach the genius of the great medieval carvers themselves. For the brothers John and James O'Shea varied each pattern on the capitals to express not only the individual differences in growth and structure of the flora and fauna but the differences in the materials being carved. (As an instructional motif, Woodward had used representative stones from all over the British Isles, arranging them by geological order: granitic, metamorphic, calcareous). Reviewing a book about the Museum in 1859, Norton had been enchanted with the result. "The beautiful marble of Marychurch, [England]" he told *Atlantic Monthly* readers, "has an exquisitely sculptured capital of ferns;—and so through all the range of the arcades, new designs, studied directly from Nature, and combining art with science, have been executed by the workmen employed on the building."[64]

In decorating the National Academy of Design, Wight had been less fortunate than Woodward in his stonecutters. Accustomed to doing Corinthian capitals and dart-and-egg moldings exclusively, his workmen needed help with neo-Gothic forms, and were set to modeling in clay as a precaution against mistakes. "I know that workmen *will think*," Wight insisted, "unless they are hindered from doing it." Even after this preliminary step was able to be dispensed with, there were, as the *New Path* frankly conceded, "capitals now standing in the building which had better been rejected." But Wight's admittedly imperfect building was merely a first step in what everyone agreed must necessarily be a long process of learning and rediscovery. What mattered far more to such admirers as Norton, Sturgis and the young Philadelphia architect, Frank Furness, was that the first step had at long last been taken.[65]

Even as the building opened to its first visitors, Norton was pointing to it as promising the kind of architecture that the regenerated national community deserved. Like Olmsted's designs for the Croton Water Works and Central Park in New York, such work, he declared, "is not only the expression of the large and generous spirit of the people, but also of the fidelity and competence of the agents whom it has employed." Even more dramatically than young Wight's apprentice effort, the work of Olmsted, the brilliant former executive secretary of the Sanitary Commission, seemed to promise that hopes for a civically expressive new American art might be fulfilled. For Olmsted's Water Works and Park, as Norton said, "are truly popular works, such as are befitting and honorable to an enlightened people. They suit the spirit of the times, and are monuments of our modern civilization." Then, bestowing his most treasured accolade, he added, "They are as characteristic or our age as the cathedrals were of the centuries in which they rose."[66]

The single most important challenge to American architecture in the postwar moment was, as Norton believed, to design memorials worthy of the devoted sacrifice of the "beloved dead" of the Union armies. The urgency felt about Civil War monuments was particularly acute at Harvard, where Norton himself led an alumni campaign to build a memorial hall. Within a few weeks of Appomattox, circulars were sent to thirteen architects, inviting them to submit designs. Despite strong feeling that the architect should be a Harvard alumnus, Norton made certain that invitations were also sent to the two young SATA architects, Sturgis and Wight. Though Wight was too busy to submit, the neo-Gothic design produced by Sturgis became Norton's favorite.[67]

Not everyone at Harvard wanted a memorial edifice. A large body of graduates preferred a military and triumphal monument. Led by John Ropes, whose brother Henry had served in the 20th Mass. and been killed at Gettysburg, this group was in favor of a bronze rostral column. Norton's reaction shows just how important the civic meaning of architecture had become to him. "That anyone should prefer such a memorial to a noble and monumental building to be used and adorned for

Charles Eliot Norton

commemorative ends is simply astonishing," he wrote in a private letter. "A heathen monument to Christian soldiers! A poor piece of classical pedantry in which to preserve the warm & glowing & dear memory of those whom we have loved & who have given themselves for us." As his brother-in-law Arthur Sedgwick, loyal both to Norton and to the 20th Mass., remembered the dispute, Norton argued for a memorial that "did not suggest victory or triumph in war, but the sacrifice of life for a cause wholly disconnected with ordinary warfare, and above it." As the conflict grew bitter, Norton invoked his old formula of sympathy and civic cohesion, saying, 'I take it for granted that much of the opposition to a Hall has arisen *from want of imagination and want of information.*"[68]

In the end, Norton's idea of a memorial hall won the day, but it was the neo-Gothic plans of W. R. Ware and Henry Van Brunt (Harvard '52 and '56, respectively) that were chosen, not Sturgis' design. Nonetheless Norton redoubled his efforts to advise, convinced that the memorial buildings at Harvard and Yale would ever afterward mold the young men who would live inside and within sight of them, and appeal "directly to the eye, and through the eye to the moral sensibilities." Norton's most incisive criticism appeared in the *Nation* for July 1867, at a moment when the winning designs for the two memorials had been chosen but the buildings were not yet begun. He argued in the most urgent terms that unless these structures could commemorate "the love of ideal beauty and utter devotion to the truth" of the soldiers themselves by representing these qualities in their construction and design, they would not be worthy of the dead. His real point was even more specific. If the buildings were built according to the existing plans, built by contract labor and built hastily, then quite simply "they should not be built at all." Van Brunt became his enemy for life.[69]

"It makes me sad," a Harvard friend told Jane Norton, "to believe that your brother's vision of what might be done here or at Yale will not meet a sympathetic response." We glimpse here the specter of the older Norton to come—militantly idealist, isolated, intransigent—and transformed into caricature by commentators like Van Wyck Brooks. Yet this is a younger Norton altogether immersed in a radically different historical moment. For his uncompromising remarks in the *Nation* were a pure expression of the exalted wartime and postwar mood of democratic faith, of hope for the moral regeneration of the American commonwealth. In demanding that the memorials be built "slowly, thoughtfully, lavishly," that they show "the evidences of lavish expense of money . . . *freely* spent," Norton is insisting that the spirit of a regenerated people be given permanent material form, that architectural time and expense be in proportion to the blood and spirit so freely spent in the war for national redemption. The medieval cathedrals ("with which these memorial buildings should be compared") are in his mind, especially the Duomo of medieval Florence. For when the Florentine commune first proposed to build a new church for the little city, its citizens decreed that it must be built with "supreme and lavish magnificence." No work of the commune, they said (in Norton's scrupulously literal 1859 translation), "should be undertaken unless the design be to make it correspondent with a heart which is of the greatest nature, because composed of the spirit of many citizens united together in one single will." Norton found the decree as magnificent as the cathedral that was actually built.[70]

The Duomo was the fruit and seed of glorious popular energy, the crown of Florence's republican spirit. In the postwar American moment, it was possible to hope that a greater and richer republic might in time achieve as much. Built slowly, thoughtfully, and lavishly, the Civil War memorials at Harvard and Yale would be worthy not only of the architects' own highest capacity, but "worthy of a regenerated people," said Norton. So only, "shall we build them better than we know." He was quoting an Emerson poem, "The Problem," in which Michelangelo, in designing the dome of St. Peter's in Rome, is said to have "builded better than he knew" because a divine power, greater than individual men and women, is working through him. In the moment Norton wrote, the spirit of a regenerated America seemed to him very like that power.[71]

Norton was realistic enough to recognize that postwar stresses—profiteering, expanding government, flagging energies—would be great. But so firm was his belief in the moral revolution that Lincoln had overseen that he thought even rampant prosperity and "luxury" could be managed "by the exercise of good sense." What Norton could not foresee was that the powerful energies released in wartime to mobilize vast wealth and new powers of social organization might be taken over and harnessed in the interest of that national selfishness and moral obtuseness he had fought against so valiantly in the 1850s. Still less, did he foresee that the hope for a genuine American commonwealth might dwindle into a spurious populism cynically manipulated by the corrupt forces of immense entrepreneurial wealth.[72]

Yet already, the promise of a new American art and a new American civic wholeness was beginning to fade into insubstantiality. The "mania for pictures" by American artists would turn out to be just a bubble of wartime inflation, exploded by 1870. The plenitude of serious books would prove to have been nothing more than a temporary defensive tactic adopted by publishers worried about high prices. The beautiful building that was to "remain *for ages*, unless fire destroy it"—Wight's National Academy of Design—would be razed in less than forty years, falling victim to the relentless real estate pressure driving ever north-ward in Manhattan. Even Harvard's Memorial Hall would be funded with a miserly hand, with only 20 percent of its alumni contributing to the cost. In the blazing Emersonian June, however, few of these shadows could yet be discerned.[73]

CHAPTER THREE

Culture as Virtue

On April 3, 1865, when the news first reached New York City that the Confederate citadels of Petersburg and Richmond had fallen, people cheered as if they could not stop. In Wall Street a huge crowd began singing all the patriotic songs, repeating the verses "The Land of the Free / And the Home of the Brave" over and over as if compelled by physical necessity to vent their overflowing hearts. "The merchants and bankers in Wall St. came out of their dens," reported George Curtis, "and sang Old Hundred and John Brown" beneath a sky "brilliant and festal with the innumerable flags." Said another witness, "I shall never lose the impression made by this rude, many-voiced chorale. It seemed a revelation of profound national feeling, underlying all our vulgarisms and corruptions, and vouchsafed to us in their very focus and centre, in Wall Street itself."[1]

Wall Street cheered because in no small measure Wall Street had won the war, by mobilizing vast financial and economic powers exceeding anything ever before seen in America. "[T]he resources of the country," marveled Norton, "are more surprisingly great than any of us knew." Manchester, England—where thousands of mill workers had been thrown out of work and verged on starvation due to the "cotton famine" produced by the Union blockade of Confederate ports—felt the calamity of the American war, Norton told Meta Gaskell, much more than either Manchester, New Hampshire or Manchester, Massachusetts. In fact, the U.S. Census of 1870 would show that per capita income had, astonishingly enough, doubled in just ten years. But though the war was over, the conflict had not yet ended. In the days after Lee's surrender, Mary Chesnut wrote bitterly of the victorious Yankees, "They are perfectly willing to have three killed for our one. We hear they have all grown rich, through 'shoddy,' whatever that is." Real Yankees, she added, could make a fortune out of trading jack-knives.[2]

68

Embittered remarks like these arose from decades of pre-war hostility between South and North as much as from the Civil War. Norton had argued from the beginning that the war was fundamentally a war of ideas—ideas so irreconcilable they that they had led through a kind of fatal inevitability to the deadly clash of arms. Now, with the arms laid aside, the strife of ideas remained. "[U]ntil one idea or the other has secured a settled triumph," he told readers of the *North American Review* in October 1865, "there can be no real peace between the parties to the war." Norton wrote at the precise moment that the great abolitionist orator Wendell Phillips was delivering his most popular and repeated lecture, "The South Victorious." This was the period of President Andrew Johnson's heedlessly lenient policy of "restoration" for the South, aimed at forestalling the Radical Republicans' sterner ideas of "reconstruction" by permitting the former Confederate states and citizens re-entry to the Union on easy terms. Johnson was now pardoning rich former slaveholders at the rate of 100 a day, allowing 90 percent of these "aristocratic" petitioners to regain full civic standing—a gesture plainly designed by the formerly illiterate tailor from Tennessee to salve his own raw sense of social inferiority by making the nobles beg.[3]

During the same period, white voters in the ex-Confederate states, operating under new postwar constitutions, began electing former Confederate army officers, politicians and supporters to state and national offices. Alexander Stephens—the Confederate Vice President notorious for declaring that slavery was the very "cornerstone" of Southern life—became U.S. senator from Georgia. With the denial of black suffrage and "Black Codes" beginning to reproduce the pernicious conditions of slavery under the cover of a spurious legality, it seemed to Radical Republicans no great exaggeration to call the South "victorious." Norton, always a deeply cautious man, phrased it more carefully. The South, he told his *North American* readers, "still clings to and maintains the idea for which it fought so strenuously in the field. We have secured a territorial Union, we have secured a geographical unity of the States, but we have not secured as yet a moral Union, a civil unity." From this, there could follow but one conclusion: "we have the harder part of our task before us."[4]

✢

Sullen and resistant, the South must be obliged to surrender its ideas of class privilege and state sovereignty, Norton declared, and take its pattern from the North, whose idea of the people as a moral community of equals existing prior to any state or government had just been vindicated by four years of war. The American political ideas of freedom, justice and equality, first fostered in the Puritan colonies of New England ("the mother of ideas and of states"), must now be introduced into the defeated Confederacy and put into political practice throughout the region. Without flinching at factitious charges of cruelty or vindictiveness, Norton told his readers, "we must use whatever means are necessary, not merely to subdue, but to destroy and utterly root out the hostile system." Were their own generation to fail to do everything it could to eradicate injustice and political inequality in the South, the persistence of these evils would burden future generations "even more than ours." This eradication, Norton conceded, would involve the ideological subjugation of the South, but it was subjugation of a mild, moral and supremely unselfish sort: "to reduce her from slavery to liberty, from injustice to justice, from oppressive privileges to equal rights and privileges, from barbarism to civilization."[5]

It is symptomatic of a deep postwar anxiety among such Republican partisans as Norton that he should at this moment specifically invoke "barbarism and civilization." For this polemical pair of opposites had long defined the pre-war and wartime clash of ideas between North and South—as when after First Bull Run, Norton told *Atlantic Monthly* readers the war was "essentially a war for the establishment of civilization in that immense portion of our country in which for many years barbarism has been gaining power." The persistence of this great polar opposition after war's end suggested that far from resolving the contention between the two ideas, the war had so powerfully unsettled the relations between them as to make a final resolution imperative. Ever since the ancient Greeks first scorned their non-Greek-speaking enemies as uncouth stutterers (βαρβαροι), charges of "barbarian" and "barbarism" had been hurled by Western polities at war. By contrast, "civilization" was still so new a word in 1772 that Samuel Johnson told James Boswell he would not admit it into his famous Dictionary. By the later eighteenth century, when "barbarism" came into relation with "civilization" as its mighty opposite, the terms assumed a provocative power to disparage and wound—not because either was a simple epithet but because both had become accepted terms of scientific analysis.[6]

This came about because in an immensely influential body of Scottish "four-stage" socioeconomic theory the two words had been used to denominate the lowest and the highest stages of social organization. Developed by such Scottish Enlightenment writers as Adam Smith, Adam Ferguson, William Robertson and John Millar, four-stage theory was an attempt to explain the new phenomenon of social progress then so visibly underway in London and Edinburgh. What made such countries as Britain and France, the Scots theorists asked, move from rudeness to refinement, while others, like China and India, remained stationary? Or as the Victorian political writer Walter Bagehot wickedly paraphrased

Charles Eliot Norton

the Scottish project: how did it happen that from being a savage, man rose to be a Scotchman?[7]

The answer, the Scots theorists argued, was property. Positing a succession of four stages of social development based on the varying relations to property involved in hunting, herding, farming and trading, four-stage theory held that property—especially the complex form of property characteristic of advanced commercial exchanges—constituted the progressive principle. Out of the ceaseless negotiation, trading and "higgling" required in modern commercial and credit arrangements, there emerged the dense webs of human connection which made complex social relations possible. In turn, out of these mutually modifying social encounters—conceived of as minute social collisions imparting "polish" to each participant—there arose a sphere of sociability, in the words of J. G. A Pocock, in which "the passions were refined, the sympathies developed, and human beings became increasingly capable of supporting the edifice of culture and the necessity of government."[8]

By contrast, men and women occupying the rudest social stage, lacking commerce or stable property relations, lacked as well the fundamental impetus to progress. In his *Essay on Civil Society*, Adam Ferguson distinguished two phases within this rudimentary social state: "that of the savage, who is not yet acquainted with property; and that of the barbarian, to whom it is, although not ascertained by laws, a principal object of care and desire." But in Ferguson and the other Scottish theorists, "barbarism" and "savagery" had no poisonous sting. The terms were merely neutral analytical tools for examining the common human features underlying more superficial—and ultimately temporary—social variations. After 1830, however, when Scottish four-stage theory began to be invoked for polemical purposes by both sides in the American debate over slavery, the tone of scientific neutrality would abruptly vanish.[9]

Published in his widely-read pamphlet of 1847 *Barbarism the First Danger*, for example, Horace Bushnell's attack on the extension of slavery into the new settlements of the West gained its force not from its rhetorical denunciations of "the bowie-knife style of civilization" but from its socioeconomic argument that the slaveholding system made any genuine civilization impossible. Drawing upon the tenets of four-stage theory, Bushnell insisted that the South, with a pattern of dispersed settlement dictated by the slave system, was too thinly populated to sustain the complex social institutions and relations required for the higher stages of human life. Incapable even of supporting the simple but vital node of institutions characteristic of the New England village—school, church and sawmill—the South betrayed "that sign, which is the perpetual distinction of barbarism, that it has no law of progress." Bushnell then proceeded to show that Southern masters were as deeply imbued with barbarous unprogressiveness as their unhappy slaves. Among Southern slaveholders, he declared, it was impossible to find a man "in any department of knowledge or excellence" who was not "a full century behind his time."[10]

Bushnell's *Barbarism* was a major influence on Frederick Law Olmsted in the series of 1850s newspaper articles published in 1861 as *The Cotton Kingdom*. With the keen observation and cool detachment of an anthropologist, Olmsted assembled a devastating empirical picture of Southern socioeconomic stagnation and cultural crudity. What was the much-vaunted "Southern hospitality"? Olmsted asked. Merely a euphemism for the custom—necessary in a region too thinly populated and traveled to support any inns—of opening private residences to travelers, who thereby obtained accommodations that were usually verminous and never free of charge (here Olmsted spoke from painful personal experience). What did their riches bring the overwhelming majority of slaveowners in the South and Southwest? The same dubious pleasures that their poorer neighbors enjoyed: "the same bacon and corn, the same slough of a waggon channel through the forest, the same bare walls in their dwellings, the same absence of taste and art and literature, the same distance from schools and churches and educated advisers."[11]

In Olmsted's book, which he dedicated to John Stuart Mill, Scottish four-stage assumptions operated at a largely implicit level. Yet even as the nineteenth-century economic, ethnographic and historical sciences were leaving the Scottish conjectural historians behind, the Scots categories continued to exert their power over the Anglo-American imagination. When the utilitarian economist John Elliott Cairnes, for example, offered a sophisticated materialist analysis of the Southern slaveholding system in his 1862 book *The Slave Power*, he invoked the four-stage terms Bushnell had employed years before. The South's slave economy, said Cairnes, was "the most formidable antagonist to civilized progress which has appeared for many centuries," a system "containing within it no germs from which improvement can spring" and which therefore "gravitates inevitably towards barbarism." To Mill himself, the South was the most "barbarous and barbarizing Power" to "rise up in the midst of our civilization."[12]

This kind of judgment upon Southern backwardness embittered sectional grievance beyond endurance, helping to create the climate of hostility and estrangement in which fratricidal war first became thinkable and then, as New York Senator William Seward famously predicted, "irrepressible." For all that Southerners might be able to dismiss the abolitionists' denunciations of slavery as fanatical raving, Scottish socio-economic theory added a new and serious element to the sectional quarrel. For Southerners hearing or reading even so deliberately rhetorical a performance as Charles Sumner's famous Senate speech of June 1860, "The Barbarism of Slavery," could feel within its rolling periods the sting of a consciously scientific superiority:

> Barbarous in origin, barbarous in law, barbarous in all its pretensions, barbarous in the instruments it employs, barbarous in consequences, barbarous in spirit, barbarous wherever it shows itself, Slavery must breed Barbarians, while it develops everywhere, alike in the individual and the society to which he belongs, the essential elements of Barbarism.

As everyone present was aware, Sumner delivered his heavy indictment while bearing the psychic and physical scars from the savage caning he had received four years earlier in the same chamber at the hands of a "chivalrous Southron."[13]

The furious attack upon the seated and unsuspecting Sumner by South Carolina Congressman Preston Brooks vividly symbolized to most Northerners the contradiction between Southern pretensions to high civilization and the savage behavior of actual Southerners, with their habits of dueling, feuding, flogging women and summary revenge. "The words 'gentleman' and 'Southern gentleman,' a New York lawyer noted, "signify things different in genre." Both kinds could be found in both regions. The trouble was, the Southern gentleman—"ready to fight duels, slow to pay debts"—set the tone for all Southern society. "[A]ll the gentlemen one meets at the South are so civil," John W. De Forest has a Southern belle remark in his novel *Miss Ravenel's Conversion*. This was so, the girl adds demurely, "because the uncivil ones are shot as fast as they are discovered."[14]

Such contradictions were so stark because Southern apologists had unwisely chosen to defend slavery within the same framework of Scottish four-stage assumptions invoked in anti-slavery literature, much as they had sought to counter the abolitionists' appeal to Christian teaching by assembling their own pro-slavery collection of Biblical texts. Employing the same Scottish School vocabulary of "cultivation," "politeness," "benevolence" and "civilization," Southern partisans tried to combat the Northern polemic not by denying its assumptions but by using them to construct an alternative account of social reality. In this opposing view, the South became the home of chivalry, honor, social grace and hospitality because its system of forced labor, "exempting so large a portion of our citizens from the necessity of bodily labor," released "a greater proportion than any other people" into the leisure that made true "civilization" possible. It was thus slavery that freed them from the "barbarism" represented by Northern wage slavery and ruthless commercial competition.[15]

When Professor Thomas R. Dew of the College of William and Mary undertook to defend slavery in 1832, for example, he argued it "changes the hunting to the shepherd and agricultural states." As the slave system propelled social groups up the four-rung ladder of social progress, it showered its beneficent effects on woman, who now had leisure for "the cultivation of all those mild and fascinating virtues which throw a charm and delight around our homes and firesides" as well as on hitherto uncouth man, who "finds his habits changed, his temper moderated, his kindness and benevolence increased." Similarly in 1852, when the popular South Carolina novelist and man of letters William Gilmore Simms sought to make the case for *The Morals of Slavery*, he appealed to Scottish School assumptions in order to establish the "superior refinement" of Southerners, known for "their grace of manner, courteous bearing, gentleness of deportment, studious forbearance and unobtrusiveness." Only within the context of Scottish four-stage theory does Simms's notable remark—otherwise so incoherent and self-canceling to modern ears—become intelligible: "I look upon Negro Slavery as the destined agent for the civilization of all the states of Mexico, and all the American states beyond."[16]

The difficulty for Republican partisans like Norton after the war was that such a picture of Southern grace and courtesy was not altogether false. For years, "plantation manners" had conferred social ascendancy upon the slaveholders, and sustained the South's political power in Congress (where, as Horace Bushnell admitted, "so much depends on manners and social address"). No less had the ease and audacity of "aristocratic" Southerners long overawed rural and socially inexperienced people in the North, many of whom would become Copperheads at least partly because of their idealization of Southern manners. The great problem was that, at its best, the Southern form of life—considered apart from its material and moral basis in slavery—could make a genuine claim to be called civilized, as Norton himself was aware from direct experience.[17]

At Harvard in the 1840s and in Newport in the earlier 1850s, Norton had gotten to know many Southerners, especially South Carolinians. Newport, then the great social crossroads and marriage mart for patrician families from both North and South, was an especially important venue for such meetings. A group photograph of Norton, his sister Grace and the brilliant Boston wit Thomas Gold Appleton taken with members of the Pringle family of Charleston suggests how easily such families intermingled there. Norton's intimate friend Edward Jenkins Pringle, who graduated third in his class at Harvard, would escape the Golgotha of the Civil War by moving to San Francisco in 1853. Another Charleston friend, William Porcher Miles, would become one of the signers of South Carolina's Ordinance of Secession and a Confederate congressman. Yet even amidst the increasing agitation over the effects of the Fugitive Slave Law in the earlier 1850s, Norton was able to discuss the nature and future of slavery frankly with these men, suggesting that, if Pringle felt his pro-slavery convictions so strongly, he ought to write a Southerner's response to *Uncle Tom's Cabin* and asking Miles to read his own *Considerations on Some Recent Social Theories* despite its "Anti-Slavery notions." (Miles was unconvinced by Norton's arguments: "You were born where there is no slavery and where it would only encumber you—I, where it seems as inevitable and necessary as any, the most ordinary, political division into governors and governed.")[18]

Newport was privileged territory, a neutral zone exempt from political broils and the workaday routines of the colder months. Located on the island the Narragansetts had named Aquidneck—"Isle of Peace"— it formed part of the American summer circuit of *Lotus Eating*, as Norton's friend George Curtis called it: Saratoga, Niagara, Newport, Nahant. "Life dreams itself away here," Norton told Arthur Clough, "as if a colony from Southern Italy" had detached itself from the mainland and floated west. In a letter to a friend, Curtis gives a vivid picture of Newport's social charm at this period:

> Time goes I knew not where, I care not how. Upon cool morning piazzas I sit talking with the Muses, in warm evening parlors I rush dancing with the Graces. Two hundred carriages with the dust of eight hundred wheels throng to Bateman's [Point] in the afternoon, or, dustless and delicious, prance along the hard bottom of the sea, or far out upon the island, driving the genial [John] Kensett. We look back across woods, and meadows white to the harvest, and see the picture of peace and plenty framed in the soft sapphire of the sea.

There were no end of pretty women, Curtis reported, including lovely Southern girls "all wrong upon the great Question!!!—wronger and more unreasonable, but more courteous, than the men." Among these were Matilda and Eleanor Middleton, daughters of the distinguished Oliver Middleton family of Charleston and "Midway," a valuable long-staple cotton plantation on the sea island of Edisto worked by between 200 and 300 slaves.[19]

The Middleton sisters were so attractive that on one occasion Norton tempted Tom Appleton to visit Newport by telling him, "The Middletons have arrived, and you & I may have a talk with Miss Matilda any morning in the Atlantic [House] parlor such as we had two years ago, and admire no less now than then. Or if you like you can talk with her beautiful younger sister, whose eyes & brow are more splendid than Clytie's," said Norton, referring to a celebrated (and lightly draped) Roman statue in the British Museum. Her father considered Matilda the cleverest of his family, and the very clever diarist Mary Chesnut called her "brilliant and accomplished." Charles and his sisters Jane and Grace befriended the entire Middleton family, from its stately parents down to its only son and heir, ten-year-old Oliver, Jr., little "Noll."[20]

The Middleton sisters visited the Nortons at their Cambridge home, Shady Hill, in November 1854. The following spring, Charles and Jane accepted an invitation to visit the Middletons in South Carolina for six weeks. Norton, who detested winter and sickened in the cold, delighted in the camellias and picturesque decay of Charleston and the soft sea air of Edisto. At the Middletons', he wrote Clough, we have been experiencing "all the grace and kindness of Southern hospitality." So hearty was their welcome in Charleston, Norton told Frank Child, that he experienced "a certain indescribable feeling of its being a hitherto unvisited home,—not a strange place, but a familiar place with unfamiliar aspects." One might imagine Edisto, he wrote James Lowell, "the genuine, original Lotus island." To his mother, he said, "If one could only forget that the slaves have souls to be saved, that they too are born not only for this world, but for immortality, that they, low as they now are, have capacities for infinite improvement, . . . there would be little that is not charming in this life."[21]

So long as she lived in "innocent slumbrous old Charleston," Mary Chesnut would later say, "like other inhabitants I saw no wrong." Only a residence in Mississippi could open her eyes to the horrors of slavery, its unbridled cruelty and the loathsomeness of what Dr. Holmes called its "seductive privileges." Living among the planter elite of South Carolina, Mrs. Chesnut would always feel torn, knowing both the grateful relief from care bestowed by "those old, gray-haired darkies and their noiseless, automatic service [who] . . . think for you [and] . . . save you all responsibility" and then "the awful effect of that stillness & torpor" in a slave-owning household. When Norton visited William Porcher Miles at Charleston College, he sensed that "in this soft air & under the deadening influences of social life here, ambition & independence of thought are considerably stifled." Earlier, Miles had complained about the vapidity of Charleston social life ("'boys, girls, dancing' compose the meager catalogue of what we call 'society'") and the "utter isolation of a man who has any real love for books" who chose to live there. Norton, always a believer in the influence of physical and social environment upon character, was now able to see in the mists and fever-bearing mi-

Charles Eliot Norton

asmas of the Southern summer "the emblem of the invisible, unrecognized, blindly guessed at moral miasma that rests over the lands where slavery exists."[22]

Yet on Mr. Middleton's well-managed properties, there were no outward signs of misery or ill-treatment among the slaves. Far from the stormy North, on the shore of a warm sea, Norton passed his days in a luxury of content, "almost as in a second home," he told Clough. On Edisto, where they spent a month, Norton was awakened by mockingbirds pouring their song in at the open window. "As long as one can live on the outside of things, & check all obstinate questionings, choke all irresistible doubts & suggestion," he wrote his mother, "—one may pass a very happy time." He read to Matilda and Ella as they worked at their sewing, saying of the experience, "It is the height of enjoyment just now to be indolent without being positively unemployed." This was meant to reassure his mother, who knew that Charles found it so irksome to remain inactive that he sometimes threw himself into activity and overtaxed his strength. But the new novel he was reading to the young ladies was deeply engaging—so much so that Norton was already planning to read it over again by himself. Just out in volume form, it was Mrs. Gaskell's tale of English regional mistrust and romantic reconciliation: *North and South*.[23]

From De Forest's *Miss Ravenel's Conversion* to Owen Wister's *Lady Baltimore*, the theme of regional reconciliation through marriage treated in Mrs. Gaskell's book would become common in post-Civil War American novels. In the lives of the Nortons and the Middletons, there would be neither romance nor reconciliation but a painful breach. "Every year I feel that the love between us grows stronger," Jane Norton had been able to say of her friendship with Matilda in 1855, "and that whether we meet or not that [it] is fixed and permanent." It did not survive the war. Despite their early efforts to maintain their affection through letters, it was shattered by the differential impact of the war on North and South. For the Middletons lost everything: their Charleston house—in a city-wide fire unconnected to the war—and their Edisto plantation—house and cotton alike burned by themselves to keep it out of Yankee hands ("We will make a Moscow of it," declared Mary Chesnut when news of these widespread self-inflicted fires first came). The Middleton family scattered, and in the last months of the war verged on starvation. Matilda took to "dining in imagination," keeping a cookery book on the mantelpiece of their rented house, she lightly told Mrs. Chesnut, "and when our dinner is deficient we just read a pudding or a crême."[24]

As Mary Chesnut noted in her diary, all this was as nothing to the one dreadful blow: their only son and brother killed in Virginia. Oliver, Jr.,—the "Noll" with whom Norton had gone crabbing at Edisto years before—by then a nineteen-year-old private in the kid-glove Charleston Light Dragoons, was mortally wounded at Matadequin Creek. It was his second day under fire. The handsomely clad and mounted Dragoons, who contrasted strangely with Lee's tattered veterans of Spottsylvania, belonged to one of the regiments newly transferred to the Army of Northern Virginia at Lee's urgent request from home defense in South Carolina. The combat at Matadequin Creek, ending in the Dragoons' rout, formed part of Lee's ultimately successful resistance to Grant's Overland campaign which ended a few days later in the terrible slaughter of Cold Harbor. The minié ball that pierced Noll's shoulder, angled downward, ploughing into his lungs, before exiting through his back. He died in Union hands.[25]

⚜ ⚜

After the war, William Gilmore Simms was heard to say that Charleston had once had "the highest culture of any people of any country on the globe." In such words the myth of the "Lost Cause" of the South had its beginnings. In fact, Simms's opinion of Charleston before the war had been much less favorable. He considered life there "a mere drowse in the lap of vanity." In Charleston, he told a friend, "a literary man is obnoxious—he is decidedly a nuisance & were it not for the outrageous indecency of the thing they would legislate upon him as such." But in defeat, the pre-war polemical image of the South as the home of hospitality, chivalry and "civilization" now became invested with the tragic glamor of heroic sacrifice and early death. Amidst the smoking ruins of actuality, the myth of the ante-bellum South sprang into existence as psychological compensation. But in addition, it would become an ideological resource to Southern whites, imparting to them a fierce sense of solidarity and common destiny. After his release from prison, Jefferson Davis would begin telling Southern audiences that the "Lost Cause" was not lost and would triumph yet. His speeches were rapturously received.[26]

As Appomattox receded, some Northerners began to sense that they lacked an equivalently sustaining and identifying ideal. At the time of the Emancipation Proclamation, the North's crusade against the barbarism of slavery had provided an idealism lofty enough to counter the relatively feeble Southern attempt to claim that it was slave-holding society that represented "civilization." Fighting a righteous war, Northerners could march into battle, Norton declared, just as Cromwell's soldiers once did, with "*Religion*" as their watchword. It had not mattered particularly—indeed, it had been useful polemically—that the North's defining war ideals were essentially negative. As a publicist for the NELPS broadsides, Norton had mobilized such Union rallying cries

Charles Eliot Norton

as "free labor" and "true democracy." But their real meaning had always been "Not Slavery" and "Not Oligarchy." Once the crusade had been won and the two grand armies of the republic—soldier and civilian—disbanded, however, the North suddenly found itself without ideological resources in relation to the growing myth of Southern chivalry and "civilization," now threatening to rise from the ashes of military defeat as the chimera of a noble "Lost Cause." Without the war to sustain its sense of idealism, there was a new vulnerability in the North. "When slavery was abolished, and the war was over," as one agitator admitted, "my occupation, in a certain sense, was gone," the half-conscious echo of Shakespeare's poignant "Othello's occupation's gone!" only heightening this man's sharp sense of his own displacement.[27]

Worse, the very conduct of the war had raised the contentious issue of Northern "barbarism." Even before actual hostilities broke out, the ideological antagonism between North and South disposed Southerners to view Yankees as ruthless barbarians like the Goths or Norsemen of old. At the time of the general secession in February 1861, the South Carolina poet Henry Timrod called upon the God of battles to smite the "Northmen" and lay waste their insolent headquarters: "There, where some rotting ships and crumbling quays / Shall one day mark the Port which ruled the Western seas." He meant New York City. To the gilded youth of Virginia and South Carolina, Union soldiers were "mudsills," the lowest of the low, fit only to wipe one's boots on. To the Confederate General P. T. Beauregard they were a rabble intent on plunder and rape, marching into battle with "Booty and Beauty" on their banners. But as the conflict unfolded, the actual barbarism of war gave these Southern insults a seeming plausibility.[28]

In the demoralized aftermath of First Bull Run, Sherman himself foresaw what would happen. "No curse could be greater than invasion by a volunteer army," he declared, speaking of his own as yet undisciplined troops. "No Goths or Vandals ever had less respect for the lives and property of friends and foes." In December 1862, during the sack of Fredericksburg, some members of the 19th Mass. Volunteers avenged the deaths of their fellow soldiers by carrying out (in addition to ordinary looting) a malicious destruction of private property. One soldier admitted their ruining work had been "done in a manner worthy of the Gothic [sic] of the Goths or the hungrish of the Huns." They had replaced the water in their canteens with molasses and poured it all over the furniture of a house. Six months later, Robert Gould Shaw was called upon by another officer to join in the burning of Darien, Georgia, an undefended town. "We are outlawed, and therefore not bound by the rules of regular warfare," the officer told him—aware that the Confederate government had declared Union officers of black troops to be "criminals engaged in inciting servile insurrection" and therefore punishable by the death penalty. Shaw declined to participate. "I do not like to degenerate into a plunderer and robber," he told his wife. "Besides my own distaste for this barbarous sort of warfare," he said, "I am not sure that it will not harm very much the reputation of black troops and of those connected with them." Sixteen months later, the mounting spiral of assault and reprisal had so intensified that Charles Russell Lowell—the very model of a Union cavalry officer—found his opinion altered about punishing Virginia civilians for the acts of rebel guerrillas by burning their houses and other property. "[I]f it will help end bushwhacking," Lowell told his wife, "I approve it, and I would *cheerfully* assist in making this whole [Shenandoah] Valley a desert from Staunton northward."[29]

Yet most such actions of plunder and despoliation by Union soldiers still belonged to war as it had been always been waged in Western civilization. It was only with Sherman's explicit policy of carrying the war home to the South's civilian population that charges of Northern "barbarism" assumed an ominous new validity. "This war differs from European wars," Sherman told the Army Chief of Staff Henry Halleck, "in this particular: we are not only fighting hostile armies but a hostile people, and must make old and young, rich and poor, feel the hard hand of war as well as their organised armies." Culminating in his March to the Sea and through the Carolinas, Sherman's policy was undertaken as a deliberate campaign to crush the civilian morale to resist, and to enforce the deliberate humiliation of the slave-holding class—especially in South Carolina, which was widely blamed for having started the war. As Sherman told Halleck, "the whole army is burning with an insatiable desire to wreak vengeance on South Carolina." Crossing the line into that state, Sherman's soldiers, having already been given permission to punish the rich and spare the poor, directed a particular ferocity against the visible signs of Southern "civilization." Family portraits were slashed, silk dresses torn up, pianos eviscerated, carpets sliced into small squares, leather-bound volumes destroyed, and ancient trees cut down.[30]

During the sack and burning of the state's capital, Columbia, the magnificent library and scientific collections of Dr. R. W. Gibbes were deliberately burned before their owner's face by jeering soldiers. William Gilmore Simms, whose own library of 10,000 books had been burned by stragglers from Sherman's army, vainly sought shelter in Columbia only to witness its destruction:

> It was in vain that the mother appealed for the garments of her children. They were torn from her grasp and hurled into the flames. The young

girl striving to save a single frock, had it rent to fibres in her grasp. . . .
You might see the ruined owner, standing woe-begone, aghast, gazing at
his tumbling dwelling, his scattered property, with a dumb agony in his
face that was inexpressibly touching.

Harriott Middleton, trapped in Columbia when the Union soldiers
came, told her cousin Matilda of "a night of horrors": "Bands of men
constantly rushed into the yard, after the first had broken the gate and
attempted to fire the house and to enter in. Parties of marauders gal-
loped about the streets." Other soldiers told Harriott "it was the most
appalling night in their experience of war. The better men and officers
were alarmed and ashamed of themselves before morning. They said,
'This is a perfect hell!' 'What a fiendish piece of work,' and such like expressions." Shortly afterwards, Sherman himself remarked, "Columbia!
pretty much all burned; and burned good." Said Harriott Middleton, "I
think that that night's work will be a . . . curse to them all their lives."[31]

The vandalism and barbarism of Sherman's March were largely in-
apparent to Northerners. Sherman detested reporters and the few of
them who accompanied the epic journey were as cut off from commu-
nications as the army itself. Thus at first, details of its horrific onslaught
upon eastern Georgia and South Carolina went largely unreported. As
Sherman completed his March to the Sea, it was a quite different form
of "barbarism" that had begun to preoccupy Radical Republicans like
Charles Norton and George Curtis: the North's own fierce delight in
extravagance and display, made possible by the astonishing prosperity
from the war. This "Oriental barbarism of our tastes," as Norton told
readers of the *Nation* in 1866, showed itself in "the white satin hang-
ings of the silly 'bridal apartments'" in steamboats and hotels and the
"wearisome excess at our public and private entertainments." "We have
grown rich for what?" Dr. Holmes had demanded during the war. "To
put gilt bands on coachmen's hats? To sweep the foul sidewalks with the
heaviest silks which the toiling artisans of France can send us? . . . [T]o
dredge our maidens' hair with gold-dust?" In the South, oranges were
selling at five dollars apiece, and people were starving. In the North,
peaches were twenty-four dollars a dozen, and people were buying.[32]

The astounding material prosperity bred in the North by the gigantic energies of the Union war effort had changed the scale of money.
"Prior to the rebellion," a writer for the *Ladies' Repository* noted, "we were
a comparatively economical people living within our means, and hus-
banding our individual resources." But as a wartime economy undermined these habits of carefulness and thrift, "we became familiarized
to enormous expenditures by the government." "The truth is," as Senator John Sherman told his brother at war's end, leading capitalists now

"talk of millions as confidently as formerly of thousands." Railroads, meat-packing, manufacturing—many of the great Gilded Age fortunes began amid the free-wheeling improvisations of wartime. At times the genuinely innovative and the shamelessly fraudulent would be strangely mixed, as when the inferior felt-like material called "shoddy" was made into Federal Army uniforms on the superior new invention patented by the Singer Sewing Machine Co. As Colonel Woodburn of Virginia, an ex-Confederate soldier in William Dean Howells' novel *A Hazard of New Fortunes*, would later remark, "Now the curse [of commercialism] is on the whole country; the dollar is the measure of every value, the stamp of every success. What does not sell is a failure; and what sells succeeds." But as the fever of wartime profiteering gave way to a postwar mania for speculation and then peculation, the barbarism of Yankee "dollar-chasing" began to seem less like a purely gratuitous Southern slur.[33]

Jay Gould would use his profits from army contracts, for instance, to launch "the Erie war," his successful assault on both the ownership of the Erie Railroad and the integrity of the New York legislature and judiciary. By the winter of 1867–68, the Crédit Mobilier began buying up influential members of Congress with gifts of railroad stock. By January 1869, the Tweed Ring began its fleecing of New York City. By 1873, one observer would wonder if the very possession of great wealth might not be taken as presumptive evidence against the character of its owner. An inflated money supply, an expanding Federal bureaucracy, a massive national debt incurred in fighting the war (more than two billion dollars) and an increasingly frenzied atmosphere of stock-market speculation further contributed to an uneasy sense among many Northerners of old landmarks dropping rapidly astern with no new ones yet visible.[34]

Yet the foreboding of observers like Norton and Holmes had another, deeper source. Despite the triumphant chorusing of "The Battle Hymn of the Republic" at war's end, it was precisely because America *was* a republic that there stirred a subliminal uneasiness among educated persons raised on Greek and Roman history. In classical republican political theory from Polybius to John Adams, the transition between victory and peace was always taken to mark the critical point of vulnerability in the life cycle of republics. This was the crucial "Machiavellian moment," as J. G. A. Pocock calls it in the title of his classic study, the pivotal juncture when the civic excellence or "virtue" called forth in citizens by a war to defend the polity subsides, and the republic becomes exposed to the disintegrative forces of naked self-interest. For the great and insoluble paradox within classical republicanism had always been that the very energy, courage and resourcefulness that carried states to power on the field of battle then, with the return of peace, led to material prosperity and "corruption," or a descent into luxury and the sat-

Charles Eliot Norton

isfaction of merely personal wants. As Adam Ferguson expressed the paradox, "[T]he virtues of men have shone most during their struggles, not after the attainment of their ends. Those ends themselves, though attained by virtue, are frequently the causes of corruption and vice."[35]

Norton and his generation of Northern liberals, having grown up in a world still residually shaped by classical republican assumptions, could scarcely avoid perceiving national experience in terms of virtue and corruption. For though the high Federalism of Fisher Ames and the *Monthly Anthology* now lingered more as a ghostly memory in the rooms of the Boston Athenaeum than as an active political force, republican and civic humanist assumptions remained alive at deep levels of New England consciousness, the natural heritage of shared habits of reading and education. Attending Harvard or Bowdoin or Yale between the mid-1840s and the early 1860s, Norton's generation of liberal reformers was the last to be educated under the traditional humanistic curriculum in its full effect and uniformity. The aim of such teaching, as James McLachlan has said, was quite simply to train students "to an almost Renaissance notion of 'virtue.'"[36]

Submerged but retaining an independent vitality, the assumptions of civic republicanism would then reappear in moments of political crisis to express the alarm—as they had earlier expressed the highest aspirations—of these college-educated men. The ancient republican language served them as a civic shorthand or common code, expressing precise degrees of rebuke or praise. Yet its very familiarity and moral precision would at the same time work to isolate this generation of men from the swiftly growing proportion of the American population who were wholly unfamiliar, not simply with the civic import of "luxury" and "corruption," but with the stories of tragic decline to which they referred, as with the fortunes of Athenian democracy under Cleon seen in the pages of Thucydides or the fate of Cicero and the Roman commonwealth in those of Plutarch. To Italian and Russian immigrants or Tammany ward heelers or self-made millionaires glorying in never having gone to college, the ancient republican language of virtue and corruption had the ring of an alien political dialect. It would not be long before they would be attributing it to an alien political tribe—the "Mugwumps."

Just as the two great ancient republics of Greece and Rome had lost their greatness along with their republican virtue, so had Florence and Venice and France. These failed republics now lay like skulls upon the American banquet table of 1865. In the postwar period, the specific form the age-old republican anxiety would assume for Norton's generation was a deep fear that in attacking Southern claims to be the superior civilization, the North had fatally undermined the social authority

Culture as Virtue

83

of such ideas as civilization, refinement and manners as they would be urgently necessary to a regenerated postwar nation. Having exploded such notions as "Southern gentleman" and "Southern chivalry" and "Southern honor," Northern liberals now began to dread that in destroying these familiar masks of Southern "barbarism" the North may have unwittingly created a vacuum in which another, previously unrecognized mode of barbarism might assume its place.

Cruelty, waste, selfish excess—these forms of licensed barbarism had been permitted to flourish so that the North might win the war. Republican partisans had earlier convinced themselves that Union troops were unleashing the unavoidable barbarism of war only to drive out the intolerable barbarism of slavery. Norton himself on more than one occasion had called for the "extermination" of the slave-owning class. But now, at the war's end, anxious new questions arose. Sherman's soldiers had burned Southern libraries, and cheered the flames. What would now keep such jeers from menacing the treasures of the peacetime republic? Southern "chivalry" had been unhorsed and humiliated, its superior "civilization" reduced to ruins and abiding resentment. Where was an alternative pattern of manners, grace and sociability to be found? In the 1830s, an Englishman long resident in the U.S. had remarked that "in the street, on the road, or in the field, at the theatre, the coffee-house, or at home, he had never overheard Americans conversing without the word DOLLAR being pronounced between them." After 1865, what force remained to challenge the rampant career of the almighty dollar, now being talked of in "millions" instead of "thousands"?[37]

Among many Northern liberals, the covert sense of jeopardy and ideological vulnerability could not be openly discussed. Their anxiety found expression instead in seemingly minor or tangential concerns, invariably touching on questions of barbarism and civilization, but more often than not doing so in eccentric or incongruous ways. In an 1868 essay for the *Nation* for example, John De Forest proposed taking over the Southern ideal of the "high-toned gentleman." After all, he noted, when the Romans destroyed a hostile city, they carried away the pictures and statues for their own good. "We, the legionaries of modern democracy have overthrown the city of patricianism which slavery had begun to build in our Southern States, and it becomes us to save from the ruins of what can never be refashioned every idea or sentiment which may add value to our own social edifice." Without some such model, the unchivalrous Northerner would be tyrannized over by impudent servants and bullying railway conductors. But De Forest's problem— "We allow Bridget to plunder us, break her bargains with us, and sauce us"—has been reduced to the conventions of farce, while his solution—

Charles Eliot Norton

"[L]et us keep the nobler lineaments of slaveocracy"—approaches the realm of fantasy.[38]

By contrast, the war had taught Norton that there had never been any such creature as the "high-toned gentleman" in the South. By the war's end, he had come to consider Southern whites as "in fact barbarians varnished with civilization." An embittered letter from Matilda Middleton to the Nortons seemed to him an obvious demonstration that "the old spirit" of Southern arrogance and unreason remained unbroken. Most of all, Norton despised the prolonged obeisance by Northern Cotton Whigs, Copperheads and Peace Democrats to the "aristocratic manners" and "superior breeding" they imputed to the "chivalrous Southron." For he believed that such "flunkeyism" had continuously worked to lower the moral tone of society in the North. Lacking self-control and a good heart, the high-toned Southern gentleman had always lacked, as Norton believed, the true basis of good manners. Southern airs of social assurance had never been anything more than "a mere pretence"—the plausible face laid over a reality of oppression and cruelty.[39]

During the war, John Greenleaf Whittier had warned his fellow Northerners, that "No foes are conquered who the victors teach / Their vandal manners and barbaric speech." Yet where was the alternative pattern for the postwar democratic citizen to come from? Where was the counterweight to the barbarism released by the war to be found? How was the dangerous allure of the South's "Lost Cause" idealism to be opposed? Northern liberals of Norton's generation would answer "culture." Amidst the ceaseless transformations of the postwar period, they would seize upon culture as the solution to the problem of their new ideological vulnerability.[40]

⚡ ⚡ ⚡

To comprehend Norton's own hopes for culture—as well as the later tragic contraction of those hopes—requires seeing how the culture-ideal of John Stuart Mill assumed a decisive ascendancy for Norton's generation in the postwar period. Certainly, Unitarian and Emersonian notions of culture and self-development had long been familiar in New England, where such divines as Andrews Norton and Henry Ware had regularly preached sermons on "the duty of continual improvement," and Goethe's theory of *Bildung* remained a vague rumor. But Mill seemed to Norton's generation to be speaking from the very heart of their own historical moment. His theory of democratic culture represented to them nothing less than the high and strenuous path that Emersonian idealism should take in its passage, as John Lothrop Motley said, through the new "age of utilitarianism at which we have arrived."[41]

It was not merely that their generation, as Norton would later recall, "had grown up as his pupils," devouring Mill's *Logic, Political Economy, On Liberty* and the *Examination of Sir William Hamilton's Philosophy* as each work in turn appeared. It was that Mill himself embodied the moral ideal of the new age, a union, as one of his English pupils was later to say, "of stern science with infinite moral aspiration, of rigorous sense of what is real and practicable with bright and luminous hope." Earlier, it had been Emerson who pointed a generation to higher aspiration by insisting that the Ideal was the only Real and forever opposed to the passing order of the actual. But by 1865 Emerson was sixty-two. Thirty years had passed since he gave out his "American Scholar" oration, the declaration of independence for all thinking Americans.[42]

In the cooler, drier atmosphere of the postwar years, Norton now saw that America had in a sense outgrown Emerson: "He was the friend and helper of its youth," as Norton said to the rising young philosopher Chauncey Wright, "but for the difficulties and struggles of its manhood we need the wisdom of the reflective and rational understanding, not that of the intuitions." Swerving away from "intuitions," Norton sought the rationalist impetus now driving the thought of his time. Charles Francis Adams, Jr., felt the same change in the mental weather while reading Mill's essay on August Comte in 1865. "[T]hat essay of Mill's," he would later remember, "revolutionized in a single morning my whole mental attitude." For Mill did not simply offer an analysis of the new democratic age. Even more irresistibly, he summoned a generation to arduous service in it. This is why, at the end of a long life, filled with a wide acquaintance among distinguished men and women on two continents, Norton would say that Mill approached "more nearly the character of the true sage than anybody else whom I have met." This meant Mill surpassed even Emerson, Ruskin and Carlyle.[43]

We have long understood Mill to be the linchpin of what David Hall in a seminal essay has called "the Victorian connection"—Mill from the 1840s to his death in 1873 as the teacher and personal friend of a compact and intellectually potent group of mid-Victorian reformers on both sides of the Atlantic. What perhaps needs more stress is the degree to which the Millite moment of culture and civic liberalism represented a punctual event. For on both sides of the Atlantic, the years from around 1865 to 1873 marked specifically, as Walter Bagehot said of this time, "a change of the sort that generates all other changes—a change of generation." In America, as we have seen, the liberals who had passed through the furnace of civil war were now girding themselves for the perilous responsibilities of peace. In Britain, the first generation born into an England remade by the great Reform Bill of 1832 (which had expanded the electorate by 50 percent) was now stepping into political power. The men and women of the Victorian connection thus not only saw themselves as a generation, but as students of Mill, they understood that a generation was precisely the unit of historical change. This doctrine, originally Auguste Comte's, had early been adopted by Mill, and it imparted an acute sense of urgency to his political and social thought.[44]

The American Civil War had only sharpened the awareness in this Millite generation of living at a definitive historical juncture, not least because the cordial transatlantic bond between them was forged amidst the fog of contempt and mistrust spread between the two countries by the war. Mill's early prediction of national "regeneration" had been a beacon to Northerners in a stormy time. Americans who had learned to despise Britain for its unprincipled neutrality—"my love of England is now extinct," one man would bitterly declare three years after Appomattox—could approve Britons who now embraced "republicanism" and "democracy" (words previously associated in England with the worst excesses of the French Jacobins). As soon as the war was over, English liberals began to make their case for extending the franchise to urban workers specifically on the ground that during the American war such men as the mill-hands of Manchester had proven their responsibility and moral character to an extraordinary degree. "That magnificent moral spectacle," as William Ewart Gladstone described the Lancashire mill operatives going workless and hungry during the "cotton famine" so that the Union might prevail and the slaves be freed, created the political conditions for the passage of the Second Reform Act in 1867. In fact, Gladstone had himself been converted by it.[45]

Emerson once remarked that the Atlantic Ocean served the English-speaking people as "a galvanic battery," allowing the race to store "her liberals in America, and her conservatives in London." During the war and just afterward, younger English liberals were drawn to America in significant numbers: Edward Dicey, E. L. Godkin, Henry Yates Thompson, Leslie Stephen, Goldwin Smith, John Morley. All these men came to observe American democracy in its life-or-death struggle, and all of them met Norton. The intense public spirit shown in the North during the war became for English liberals, no less than for their American counterparts, an ineffaceable benchmark of the civic energy and moral power that representative democracy could truly marshall. "There is so much energy and faith in these people," Thompson marveled upon visiting Boston in September 1863, "that I believe they can in their present temper carry almost anything."[46]

The mutual sympathy, helpfulness and good will visible in American social arrangements at this time also impressed the English visitors strongly. In June 1862 Dicey watched a scene in Cambridge that he knew could never have taken place in the English Cambridge: university students and their guests dancing freely on a college green in the presence of townspeople, also dancing, with everyone as quiet and orderly "as they would have been in a London ballroom." Such examples persuaded Goldwin Smith that America was approaching, however slowly, "the realization of that ideal community, ordered and bound together by affection instead of force, the desire of which is, in fact, the spring of human progress." In the same way, the central lesson taught by the American war with figures traced in blood—the tragic futility of all temporizing and accommodation in matters of moral principle—became for Morley the standard by which British political culture was to be measured. He would title his 1874 book *On Compromise*, because to the transatlantic liberals of 1865 "compromise" had become "that hideous word," that craven notion justly "killed at Sumter."[47]

On both sides of Emerson's "galvanic" ocean, then, liberals felt the electric summons to "a democratic millennium," as Leslie Stephen would later call it. Stephen would use the phrase in 1903 to characterize what seemed by then the absurd hopes of 1865. But in the sharp exhilaration of the actual moment—experienced as "a rent in the atmosphere of the times" torn by the great cataclysm of the American Civil War—transatlantic liberals seized upon Mill's thought as the road map to the new age of representative democracy. Thirty years earlier, Alexis de Tocqueville had predicted this form of government would command the polities of the future. In 1859, Mill in *On Liberty* had exposed to view with an unsparing clarity the characteristic faults and tendencies of democratic societies: their habitual self-conceit, their decided preference for mediocrity and uniformity, their encouragement of a tyrannical public opinion. This darker potentiality in democracy would shadow the American liberals' hopes for a postwar "regeneration" as persistently as did fears of "corruption" or a resurgent "barbarism."[48]

Yet Mill had also provided an answer, one especially suited to the Unitarian and Emersonian strain in New England's intellectual culture that the Mugwumps inherited. Human societies, he noted, had hitherto been heavily dependent on purely material circumstances—natural resources, population, military power, industrial might. With material progress in the nineteenth century at an apogee never before reached in human history, the future fate of civilizations would henceforth be decided by *ideas*. Only real and vigorous thinking—discovering new truths and identifying obsolete ones, commencing new practices and setting the example of better taste and sense and conduct in human life—could assure future social progress. Only a tiny handful of the population was capable of such original thought and action. These

Charles Eliot Norton

few were the salt of the earth: "Without them," said Mill in *On Liberty*, "human life would become a stagnant pool." But in order for such geniuses to thrive, there needed to be the right conditions. Or as Mill expressed it a few lines later, tracing the idea of culture to its origins in agriculture: "in order to have them, it is necessary to preserve the soil in which they grow. Genius can only breathe freely in an *atmosphere* of freedom."[49]

Mill's italicizing of "atmosphere" suggests how new the metaphorical use of the word was when he wrote. In fact, the *Oxford English Dictionary* cites precisely this instance as the first usage of the word in this sense. Mill seems to have borrowed it (along with much else in his thought) from Tocqueville, who in his 1835 *Travels in England and Ireland* had called liberty "a holy thing . . . an atmosphere." In this metaphorical sense "atmosphere" would become one of the signature terms of liberal cultural thought during the remainder of the century. That ironic and resistant liberal, Matthew Arnold, for example, would declare in 1865 that the special gift of literary genius "lies in the faculty of being happily inspired by a certain intellectual and spiritual atmosphere, by a certain order of ideas, when it finds itself in them." Such genius, Arnold warned, "must have the atmosphere, it must find itself amidst the order of ideas, in order to work freely; and these it is not so easy to command." And ever afterward Norton himself would speak of "atmosphere" as the missing medium in America for true intellectual and creative achievement.[50]

Yet the full significance to transatlantic liberalism of Mill's notion of cultural "atmosphere" only becomes clear when the focus is pulled back from the small group of generative geniuses to the democratic polity as a whole. For Mill insisted no less emphatically that the larger goal of human betterment would remain unfulfilled so long as there were produced only a relative handful of vigorous and contributing thinkers. The conditions for human flourishing needed for the generative thinkers were exactly those required by their less gifted fellow citizens to thrive and grow towards the light. Mill made this essential premise of his cultural theory clear in a letter he wrote to an American correspondent immediately after the end of the Civil War:

> There are wanted, I do not say a class, but *a great number* of persons of the highest degree of cultivation which the accumulated acquisitions of the human race make it possible to give them. From such persons, in a community that knows no distinction of ranks, civilisation would rain down its influences upon the remainder of society, & the higher faculties having been highly cultivated in the most advanced part of the public would give forth products & create an atmosphere that would produce a high

average of the same faculties in a people so well prepared in point of general intelligence as the people of the United States.

These persons Mill, without invidiousness, called "the best men."[51]

To recover an adequate sense of the utopian promise that Anglo-American liberals glimpsed in Mill's idea of culture requires understanding the purely functional role carried out by these "best men," a social fraction or sub-group that has been too swiftly dismissed in many modern accounts of Mill as an "elite" or "aristocracy." For Mill's notion of a great number of persons of the highest degree of cultivation ("I do not say a class") was a solution to a problem internal to the structure of his own thought. The great effort of Mill's philosophical career (and personal life) had been to free the Utilitarians' founding principle of the "greatest happiness for the greatest number" from a coarse reductionism that identified the value of pleasures (or pains) with their duration and intensity, as these were measured quantitatively. (Carlyle had sardonically hailed this Utilitarian system for ranking human goods and ills as a "swine philosophy"). At the same time, Mill's continuing philosophical allegiance to empiricism made it impossible for him to appeal to an innate "moral sense" or a subjective intuition of the good, of the kind proposed in the Whig moral and aesthetic tradition that had risen in the eighteenth century with the Third Earl of Shaftesbury and sunk in the nineteenth (with a devastating push from Mill himself) with Sir William Hamilton.[52]

In liberating himself from Jeremy Bentham's narrowly quantitative hedonism, Mill had turned instead to Coleridge and the rich German tradition of *Bildung* or human "development" that Coleridge had sponsored in England. A sentence from Wilhelm von Humboldt became the motto of *On Liberty*: "The grand, leading principle, towards which every argument unfolded in these pages directly converges, is the absolute and essential importance of human development in its richest diversity." To establish an objective standard of complex and qualitatively estimated human goods, Mill appealed to the judgments of competent rational agents as founded on their own experience. These were the "best men"—male and female persons who had themselves already undergone a process of development so extensive and successful as to have become in them autonomous and self-sustaining. These highly cultivated men and women would serve as models to their less advanced neighbors, making vivid to them through living examples a range of possible human goods which might otherwise remain dim or inconceivable.

Crucial to Mill's theory of culture and "human development in its richest diversity" was his assumption that these highly cultivated agents

Charles Eliot Norton

would always prefer pleasures which exercised their higher, that is to say, their moral, intellectual and aesthetic capacities. This claim, too, Mill believed was founded in experience, not wishful thinking. As he declared in *Utilitarianism*, "[I]t is an unquestionable fact that those who are equally acquainted with, and equally capable of appreciating and enjoying, both, do give a most marked preference to the manner of existence which employs their higher faculties." Yet in his cultural theory these high-minded and highly developed agents would possess no special privileges. Working exclusively through influence and example, without any coercive powers, such men and women could not dictate the value preferences or life choices of their less developed countrymen.[53]

For to do so would be to violate the central principle of Millite and Emersonian individualism: autonomy or self-reliance. As Mill declared in *On Liberty*, the power of an aristocracy or a strong man to compel others into preferences or pursuits not chosen by them "is not only inconsistent with the freedom and development of all the rest, but corrupting to the strong man himself." Instead, the role of highly developed agents was simply to "create an atmosphere"—to make manifest a richer range of human possibilities by carrying out "experiments of living." The "best men" thus constituted a genuinely open elite, consistent with the nature and the needs of democratic polities. For the defining principle at the heart of such a group—of "human development in its richest diversity"—presumed the admission to its ranks, sooner or later, of everyone willing to undertake the rigorous moral and intellectual training of self-development. Even if people should decline the specific discipline of higher education or private study, Mill insisted, they were not to be interfered with or constrained to fit a single model of life. For the "same things which are helps to one person towards the cultivation of his higher nature, are hindrances to another." Amidst the rich diversities of human beings and their possible modes of life, there thus remained for Mill just one constant: his fundamental conception of human nature as naturally seeking to nurture, expand and use its higher capacities.[54]

☙ ☙ ☙ ☙

In the postwar moment, then, Norton and other liberals of his generation recognized in Mill's idea of culture both a conclusive answer to the emergent new Southern myth of the "Lost Cause" and a counterweight to the recrudescence of Northern "barbarism." The South had gloried in what Norton called "a base and spurious counterfeit of aristocracy"— a tiny class of men, immoderate, self-aggrandizing and theatrical, who had been set free from material constraints by the stolen labor of toiling slaves. During the war, it became clear, as Longfellow told Sumner, that "the world needs a new nobility,—not of the '*gold medal*' and old

'*Sangre azul*' order. Not the blood that is blue because it stagnates; but of the red, arterial blood that circulates, and has heart in it, and life and labor." After Appomattox, it seemed plain the South must take the likeness of the North, and choose to be guided by a civic leadership of "best men," who were politically self-denying and stylistically self-effacing, free laborers along with the rest, whose ranks were open and constantly expanding to admit new recruits.[55]

Culture—understood as an activity of mind rather than as a mere array of "prestigious" information—thus silently assumes the dynamic role in Mill's civic liberalism that "virtue" assumed in classical republicanism: it becomes the active principle which is alone capable of mastering futurity and preserving the commonwealth. Had not Mill himself argued in *On Liberty* that the bold free expansion in every direction of human potentialities, in making each person more valuable to himself, made each more capable of being valuable to others? Had he not said that when there is more "fulness of life" in individual men and women, "there is more in the mass which is composed of them"?[56]

To the Anglo-American generation of 1865, the power of Mill's civic liberalism as a solution lay precisely in its capacity to reintegrate the older civic values into the modern world of individualist and utilitarian conditions. For unquestionably, by 1865 the social basis of ancient republicanism had utterly passed away. Aristotle's *Ethics*, the grand codification of classical republican thought, seemed to Norton, who reviewed a translation of it in 1866, to get things exactly reversed: Aristotle held that the individual existed for the state, while "the American view" held that "the state is conceived as existing only in and through and for the individual." It was no accident that Mill, the defender of individualism in society, should also be the champion of nominalism in philosophy. As Chauncey Wright said of Mill's *System of Logic* to Grace Norton, "A reform in logic became necessary for the overthrow of many social and religious superstitions." If such shady abstractions as "the State" and "Society" and "the Church" were now falling on every side, it was because Mill had put his nominalist ax to the tree.[57]

Norton told his *North American* readers in the autumn of 1865, "The North is civilized, the South is uncivilized. One must take the likeness of the other." The hostile Southern ideological system had pushed one assumption to the forefront which still remained to be overthrown in the ongoing war of ideas—the idea of caste or unmerited superiority. "This war, which is now drawing to an end," as he said in another essay a full year after Appomattox, "is the war between the new ideas of New England and the old ideas of the Old World." George Curtis said much the same thing in "The Good Fight," a hugely popular lecture he gave in the autumn and winter of 1865. Let us continue the struggle, said

Charles Eliot Norton

Curtis, until we "occupy the very citadel of caste, force the old enemy to final and unconditional surrender, and bring Boston and Charleston to sing Te Deum together for the triumphant equal rights of man."[58]

Once driven from the plantation house, the idea of caste must not be permitted to take up exclusive new quarters in the lyceum or the parlor. What now must be exterminated was the old caste-bound assumption of the pro-slavery apologists that "The Creator did not intend that every individual human being should be highly cultivated, morally and intellectually," as William Harper had once phrased it, together with its corollary belief that "it is better that a part should be fully and highly cultivated, and the rest utterly ignorant." Instead, to defeat "the South Victorious" was to overthrow the false choice its ideology dictated: accept universal mediocrity or take high achievement for the few along with widespread debasement for the many. The democratic principle the North was fighting for, as Norton told one of his NELPS correspondents, must include "not merely the elevation of men, but the highest development of the individual man." This meant a democracy "liberal enough to include genius." To finish "the good fight," the postwar apostles of Millite self-development must undertake at the level of the higher culture the function which the freedmen's aid societies were already performing at a more elementary level in the South. "The mighty march of Sherman, wasting and taming the land," said Curtis, "is followed by the noiseless steps of the band of unnamed heroes and heroines who are teaching the people. The soldier drew the furrow, the teacher drops the seed." So might even the worst barbarism of war be re-enclosed and safely reabsorbed into the body politic of the republic.[59]

"[I]f any encouragement were required by those who hope the best from American institutions," Mill told E. L. Godkin in May 1865, "the New England states, as they now are, would be encouragement enough." For as Mill and Norton both estimated such things, the real war had been won by New England, "the mother of ideas and of states." To be sure, a Union army of the West led by Sherman had taken Atlanta, and a Western commander named Grant had finally forced Richmond to capitulate. But their Western soldiers marched bearing New England ideas as unmistakably as they carried salt beef or Springfield rifles. In this sense, Norton insisted, "Lincoln the Kentuckian was a genuine son of New England." This is why, as he told his *North American* readers, "It is as absurd to talk, as Mr. Sunset Cox and other silly orators sometimes do, of getting rid of New England ideas, and of leaving New England out in the cold, as it would be to talk of getting rid of Christian ideas." The ultimate victory—"to make the United States a larger, happier, completer New England"—was yet to come. But once this victory— the work of self-development and culture—was achieved, promised

Norton, "New England will drop from history. Her victory will be accomplished."[60]

Mill warned his American correspondents that time was short, that the great concussion of the Civil War had opened a window for impartial reason and right feeling which would soon close again. "This great benefit will probably last out the generation which fought in the war," he cautioned them, "and all depends on making the utmost use of it, for good purposes, before the national mind has time to get crusted over with any fresh set of prejudices as nations so quickly do." Norton was one of these correspondents. He sent Mill his *North American* essay on "American Political Ideas," and he asked Mill to write a letter to the *Nation* on the vexed topic of the virtual repudiation of the Federal war debt through repayment in "greenbacks," the inflated wartime paper that was irredeemable in gold. To Norton's insistence that the South must now "take the likeness" of the civilized North, Mill wholly assented, responding in a letter to the younger man, "[T]his will be easily done if the people of the Northern States *do but will it*."[61]

This urgency, in turn, becomes the context in which Norton's wide-ranging activities as editor of the *North American* and writer for the *Nation* and other periodicals demand to be seen as characteristic activities of Millite civic liberalism. For Norton's concern throughout this time is with "development" and creating an "atmosphere." In urging Frederick Olmsted to become a contributor to the quarterly he has just taken over with Lowell, for example, Norton tells him "[t]here is an opportunity now to make the 'North American' one of the means of developing the nation, of stimulating its better sense, of setting before it and holding up to it its own ideal." In the same spirit, Norton tells readers of the *Nation*, "It is our misfortune to have no body of educated men competent to pass correct judgment, and forming a court of final appeal in matters of learning; not an academy, not an organized body, but a scattered band of men of learning and cultivated critics who would leaven the whole mass of popular ignorance." Norton has shifted the focus to criticism and scholarship, but the accent is Millite and the emphasis centers upon the transformative influence of a certain quantum ("I do not say a class") of highly cultivated people.[62]

Norton's concern for a select audience within the larger public would guide his practice as author and editor for the rest of his life. As he told an unsuccessful contributor to the *North American* in 1868, "If I print an article on such a subject" as Chinese philosophy, "I print it not for the mass but for Professor Whitney, Mr Marsh, and two or three others." Seen from a modern perspective, this sort of narrow-spectrum editorial ideal tends to be identified with such later developments as the rise of the professionalized specialist or the emergence of an alienated in-

Charles Eliot Norton

telligentsia. But for Norton in the postwar moment—as for John Morley editing the *Fortnightly Review* across the galvanic ocean—this particular editorial practice was sustained by an implicitly Millite ethic (deriving ultimately from Auguste Comte) which held that communicative exchanges among a select group need not involve the public directly in order to benefit the public ultimately. As Norton was to say to Chauncey Wright in 1870, even though "'best' men" were not numerous in either America or England, "their influence is very strong on great numbers, and frames a temper which by degrees becomes national."[63]

Yet all the while there lurked within Mill's culture-ideal an underlying flaw. Invisible now in the optimistic solstice of Millite rationalism and "our Emersonian June," it would later rise above the rim of a darker day to trouble the hopes of civic liberalism. For in vesting their faith in Millite culture, such men as Norton and Morley were committing themselves to a principle that rested upon an unstable foundation. Mill had made an empirical observation—that some persons have preferred to lead an existence which developed their higher capacities—serve as an *a priori* assumption, namely, that all human beings will by nature seek to expand and use their higher capacities. Even as Mill was making this argument in *Utilitarianism*, however, he betrayed his own anxiety about the slipperiness of the move from observation to axiom. For there he insisted with uncharacteristic heat that "it is an unquestionable fact" that those who have experienced many kinds of existence certainly prefer an existence which expands their higher faculties to an existence which does not.

Mill's "unquestionable fact," however, could not bear the weight of the hopes that civic liberalism was to rest upon it. For it remained only contingently true—true of certain moral agents living in northwestern Europe and northeastern America during the zenith of the reform decades of the mid-nineteenth century—true, in short, of a cohort that found itself living in a particular time and place under unusually favorable and, it may be, unrepeatable historical circumstances. Beneath all the optimistic assumptions about "best men" and "developing the nation," there always lurked the possibility that Mill had been unconsciously constructing a foundational premise from what might be nothing more than a wishful contingency.

Mill's generous mistake flourished in postwar New England. Emerson's influential notion of culture had preserved at its core a faith that nations would produce aristocracies "in some form, however we name the lords," just as surely as races produced women. Even more optimistically, Emerson now maintained (in the face of traditional doubts) that democratic envy would pose no threat to any aristocracy of merit that might arise in America. The doubts about mass democracy to which he was responding had been given voice in widely read books by such foreign visitors as Tocqueville and Mrs. Trollope. The English art critic, Anna Jameson, reported that the painter George Washington Allston had scribbled a bitter aphorism on the wall of his Cambridgeport studio: "The most common disguise of envy is in the praise of what is subordinate." So too, the American sculptor Horatio Greenough, assessing his countrymen's reaction to greatness, framed another apothegm: "If a man say to other men that he is great, [Americans] will laugh him to scorn—if he say that he is God, they will take it into consideration." But in an 1867 essay in the *Atlantic* Emerson generously attributed his own strength and confidence to his fellow citizens. He assumed they paid homage to distinguished men and women for the same reasons he did, out of "sympathy, love of the same things, effort to reach them,—the expression of their hope of what they shall become when the obstructions of their mal-formation and mal-education shall be trained away." Emerson believed Americans knew what he knew: "Great men shall not impoverish, but enrich us."[64]

After New England won the Civil War, Mill was prepared to believe that if Tocqueville "had lived to know what these States have become thirty years after he saw them, he would, I think, have acknowledged that much of the unfavorable part of his anticipation had not been realized." For as Mill said of New England in May 1865, "Democracy has been no leveller there, as to intellect and education, or respect for true personal superiority." Mrs. Trollope had objected that American democracy "would make of mankind an unamalgamated mass of grating atoms, where the darling 'I'm as good as you,' would soon take place of the law and the gospel." But New England believed that the essential disposition of democracy, as Theodore Parker expressed it, was to be found—not in "I'm as good as you are"—but in "You're as good as I am." At once political and cultural, the gospel of New England was a gospel of leveling *up*. Even as late as 1884 James Lowell could express this fundamental faith, telling an audience that "if there be one thing steadfast and of favorable omen, one thing to make optimism distrust its own obscure distrust, it is the rooted instinct in men to admire what is better and more beautiful than themselves." But it was ominous that Lowell was speaking to an audience in England, not America.[65]

Only gradually would it become apparent to Norton that the generous faith of Emerson and Mill might contain a fatal flaw. He was prepared by nature and training to expect that it might take more than a generation to clear away material constraints and false assumptions so that men and women could freely exercise and expand their higher capacities. But what the new ideas of New England had not prepared him for was the possibility that an open cultured elite, rather than strengthening the "virtue" of the republic in peacetime, might instead choose to align itself with forces that were deeply hostile to civic life. In the immediate postwar moment, a striving economic individualism seemed merely the powerful engine that was to provide the "best men" with the material basis for their "experiments of living." It was not yet conceivable that such an economic system might exert an ideological force so potent that even candidates for the open elite would become corrupted, lose any sense of a higher ideal of culture and choose themselves to plunge into the maelstrom of cut-throat economic competition, cultural philistinism and military aggression. It would be years before Norton would see this possibility. Through an accident of personal history, he would be absent from America as this darker configuration was taking shape. When he returned, it would be as a man changed by personal, spiritual loss confronting a nation changed by rapacious material gain. The rest of Norton's life would be a coming to terms with this double calamity.

CHAPTER FOUR

Eden and After

*H*is eye fixed on the bright horizon line of the future, Charles Norton was convinced that the abolition of slavery was simply the first of many emancipations to come. In the postwar moment, the scope of his expectations for America reached beyond outward political and social regeneration to embrace an inward change deeper still: a revolution in religious belief. Norton anticipated nothing less than a liberation from all theological "superstition," leading to the emergence of a genuinely religious life to be lived for the first time outside the church. "It is my firm conviction," he told a correspondent in 1865, "that we are just entering in this country on a new style of religious life, and a new manner of religious faith." Writing as the son of Andrews Norton, long known as the "Unitarian Pope," Charles did not hesitate to send to the same correspondent copies of some of his father's works. His gesture reveals the curiously intermixed loyalties—to unconventionality no less than to orthodoxy—that would thereafter mark both his private and public life.[1]

In fact, the deep change in religious disposition Norton looked for in 1865 had been underway elsewhere for some time. In England, such men as the poet Arthur Clough and the historian James Anthony Froude, rising to maturity in the tumultuous Oxford of the 1840s, had already fought their way clear of the Low Church, High Church and Broad Church orthodoxies within Anglicanism only to find themselves launched, as Froude would later say, upon an open spiritual ocean, with compasses awry, all intellectual lightships adrift and nothing left to steer by but the stars. Into the blackness of that desperate hour had come the rescuing voice of Thomas Carlyle. In the midnight of God's eclipse, declared Froude, "Carlyle was the first to make us see His actual and active presence *now* in this working world, not in rhetoric and fine sentiments, not in problematic miracles at Lourdes or La Salette, but in clear letters

98

of fire which all might read, written over the entire surface of human experience." Disenthralled from meaningless convention, seeking to live life honestly and in earnest service to their fellows, the generation of Froude and Clough found in Carlyle a sustaining creed and a path out of the pit of atheism.[2]

Norton's career in faith and doubt would take a different course from either Clough's or Froude's. For reasons of temperament, heritage, nationality and personal history, it was not surprising this should be so. But more unexpectedly, Norton would nevertheless end his religious transit with Carlyle. Writing in 1865 about his hopes for "a new manner of religious faith," Norton was still untouched by the bleak midnight of religious despair these other men had known. *Sturm und Drang* were foreign to his temperament. But within seven years of war's end Norton would discover on a personal level what the generation of Froude and Clough had already experienced. With the death of his wife Susan Sedgwick Norton in 1872, he would pass through the deep disorientation and utter at-sea-ness of one who found himself in a world gone void of meaning, without horizons. Overwhelmed, it would be then that he turned to Carlyle.[3]

⚡

Norton's private journey of faith and doubt would parallel at every turn his public career as editor, scholar and teacher. To understand his life in both its inward and outward aspects we must return to the place where both journeys began: Shady Hill, a spacious Federal-style house, set upon rising ground at the eastern border of Cambridge. Born there in 1827, Norton had spent his boyhood exploring its thirty-four acres of fields and woods and marshland, becoming an expert observer, collector and admirer of natural life. At the same time, Norton had absorbed himself in family life at Shady Hill with an emotional intensity that may now seem surprising, particularly in an old family of Puritan descent. But Catharine and Andrews Norton were unusually affectionate parents.[4]

When Charles was a child, his mother wrote on slips of paper "little phrases of affection for him, pinned at night to his jacket to meet the little boy's eye when he started early for school." Norton's earliest recollections of his father—the formidable Dexter Professor of Sacred Literature whose frown made grown men blanch—were of Andrews' keen "interest in all that concerned me, of his telling me stories, of his walking with me, of his waiting for me to come home from school to take me with him to drive." Later, Andrews encouraged nightly conversations with his son ("in them you let me talk to you of whatever for the moment most occupies my thoughts"). Charles's relations with his three sisters, Louisa, Jane and Grace, were no less devoted and affectionate. "It is quite unfortunate for me that I have such very charming sisters," he told Louisa in 1850 with a young man's *politesse,* "for I am sure it will prevent me from ever being married." He was more nearly right than he knew.[5]

Those permitted to glimpse family life at Shady Hill carried away an indelible impression of its prevailing sunniness and geniality. Henry Wadsworth Longfellow, visiting the Nortons at home sometime in the later 1830s after the death of his first wife, declared, "There I beheld what perfect happiness may exist on this earth, and felt how I stood alone in life, cut off for a while from those dearest sympathies for which I long." In September 1843, the young man who had just published *Two Years Before the Mast* made an afternoon call at Shady Hill. "The Nortons present the most charming family group that I know of," Richard Henry Dana, Jr., recorded in his journal. "An affectionate, intelligent mother, with many graces & faculties of mind & person, three daughters just coming into society, well educated, domestic, agreeable, good looking, well principled & with remarkably happy temperaments. Add to this a large house & beautiful estate in the country, with reading, writing, drawing, music & conversation."[6]

Into this serenely contented estate stepped the diffident yet resolute figure of Arthur Hugh Clough. Arriving in Massachusetts in 1852 seeking work as a tutor, Clough set in motion the first countercurrents of religious change that would eventually leave everything at Shady Hill changed for Charles Norton while seeming to keep everything untouched. Clough began by regarding the Nortons as "neither grand nor exclusive—very kind-hearted and good but perhaps a trifle too Unitarianish." Unlike many English people at this time, Clough felt no instinctive horror of Unitarians. But he found the Nortons in their Unitarianism "so awfully rococo in their religious notions that were I much in the way of hearing them expressed I should infallibly speak out and speak strongly."[7]

Clough's sincerity and integrity in matters of religious belief were not to be doubted. By the time he arrived in America, he had already resigned one of Oxford's most glittering prizes, an Oriel College fellowship, because of his conscientious inability to subscribe to the theological doctrines required by the Church of England in order to hold the post. For this self-denying act—which carried serious social and economic penalties in England—Clough's friends regarded him as a hero of intellectual principle. It is not clear Clough ever spoke his mind to the Nortons about their rococo Unitarianism, although he did decline to attend their church services. What is plain is that Charles Norton admired the nine-years-older Englishman enormously. As a boy, Norton had pored over pictures of the Spanish Inquisition and John Foxe's *Book of Martyrs*. Clough, at once reserved and funny, earnest and ironic, a poet and a social radical, was the first living martyr to conscience the younger man had ever met.[8]

Clough was the first in a succession of such witness figures to touch Norton's life—John Brown of Harper's Ferry would be another—men who pursued the truth despite the loss of external goods—friends, position, health, even life itself. Examples of such unswerving idealism embodied in living men and women would always move Norton strongly. But in the case of Clough there came into play another dynamic which would powerfully influence Norton's change in religious faith. Invited to America by Emerson, Clough had appeared in Cambridge at just the moment when Andrews Norton was slipping into the decline which would end in his death in September 1853. By this time, Andrews' violent and widely publicized denunciation of Emerson and the Transcendentalist movement in religious thought as "the latest form of infidelity" was already fifteen years in the past. But Andrews, as perhaps might be expected from a man notorious for the vehemence of his views and "his extreme dread and dislike of opposition to his own opinions," as the English traveler and Unitarian Harriet Martineau phrased it, had not changed his mind about Emerson. As Clough quickly discovered, Emerson was still "*very* wrong in the eyes of Ticknors and Nortons."[9]

Yet now as Andrews sank deeper into the heart disease which would end his life, Charles was pressing Clough about vexed questions of belief, and making his first personal contacts with the man his father regarded as an enemy—Emerson. Earlier, Charles had been repelled by the cool irony and detachment of Emerson's writings. Emerson's memoir of Margaret Fuller, as Norton told an older English friend named Arthur Helps, "seems to me cold & heartless,—with a too liberal display of the barrenness of religion in his heart." But when for different reasons both Helps and Clough asked Norton to write Emerson, and Emerson responded cordially to the overture, welcoming a closer acquaintance, there began a pattern of change in Norton's beliefs that would model the rest of his religious development. Representing his complex response to a father he deeply loved and respected, the change was slow but unmistakable: it was a revolution without a betrayal.[10]

For even as he was loyally editing Andrews' prose and poetry after his death, Charles was silently opening a path of resistance to his father's views. Andrews had been feared and disliked by the Transcendentalists—beyond all their larger religious quarrel with him—for his narrowness, his fierce intemperance of expression and an implacable hostility, approaching persecution, to all forms of dissent from his own highly idiosyncratic opinions. When George Ripley (attacked along with

Emerson in *The Latest Form of Infidelity*) responded in an essay of his own, he told Andrews, "You make no allowance for the immeasurable variety of mind which is found everywhere . . . but you advance your principle with the same want of reserve or qualification that a teacher of the Infallible Church would have exhibited before the Reformation." Given Andrews' hostility toward Catholicism, this was a punishing remark.[11]

Yet Charles Norton agreed with Ripley on precisely this point. In a biographical fragment written a few years after Andrews' death, Norton said of his father, "His imaginative faculties had never received much training,—and a consequent deficiency in the exercise[,] quickness and power of imagination sometimes led him to a somewhat narrow view of the variety in human nature, and the necessary diversity of men's opinions on the most important subjects." Rejecting Andrew's narrowness without at first rejecting his views, Charles would ever afterward seek out diversity of opinion and breadth of human nature among the men and women he met, just as he did with Clough. Reacting against Andrews, he would become more sympathetic, more curious, more of a man of the world. But Norton's pursuit of variety and openness in thought would at the same time become the inlet of unbelief which would overthrow the faith he had received from his father.[12]

By the 1860s Norton was eagerly seeking out works by men who had suffered for conscience' sake. In England, these were the "Seven Against Christ," seven Broad Church men whose fearless discussion of scriptural questions in a collection called *Essays and Reviews* had, as Norton anticipated, soon exposed them to persecution, and in the case of two of the writers, to prosecution in the Anglican ecclesiastical court. In France, such a figure was Ernest Renan, who had been evicted from his chair of Hebrew at the Collège de France for having boldly described Jesus Christ in his inaugural lecture as "an incomparable Man." Even more eagerly, however, Norton sought out personal acquaintance with men whose lives bore the livid marks of an earnest struggle with faith and doubt.[13]

When Leslie Stephen, visiting America as a pro-Union journalist, met Norton at Shady Hill in 1863, the two men discussed "certain points of religion." Stephen, like Clough, had just passed through a severe ordeal of doubt as a result of philosophical studies at his university. Ordained a clergyman in 1859 under relentless paternal pressure, Stephen had realized by 1862 that he could no longer in good conscience carry out the Church of England rites. Like Clough, Stephen would become an intimate friend, a man "whose affection," as Norton would say in another connection, "is better than fame." Clough had died prematurely, but the friendship that now opened with Stephen would become one of the bulwarks of Norton's emotional life. As with James Lowell and George

Curtis, theirs was a bond built on the communion of real talk—prolonged talk, at times made up as much of silence as of speech. William Dean Howells was to say after Norton's death that "[h]e could not sit down to talk with another, whether by the spoken or the written word, without wishing to talk seriously." Norton's social finesse was such that "he would not force the talk beyond smallness if that were the measure of his interlocutor." But in that case, Howells added, the talk would be small and brief. Serious talk could break through "the buried life," as Norton once said to Lowell, referring to a famous Matthew Arnold poem. In the midst of emotional constraint and empty social formulas ("How very hot it is!" "How very pretty Miss Podge looks!"), such talk could open the precious moment when "a bolt is shot back somewhere in our breast" and "what we mean, we say, and what we would, we know."[14]

Another witness figure who became intensely interesting to Norton during this time was Goldwin Smith, just four years older than Charles but already Regius Professor of Modern History at Oxford. Norton admired Smith because Smith had "fairly thought his way out of social and political feudalism, and out of that state Church which is its religious complement." During a visit to Shady Hill in 1864, Smith and Norton "talk[ed] as men talk when they really have something to say and something to learn from each other." Like Clough and Stephen, Smith would quickly become a model to Norton for the way "[a] liberal & independent thinker in these days, who has faith in God & in man must sooner or later think himself out of any orthodox creed."[15]

In his continuing effort to "think himself out of" the meaningless formulas of religious orthodoxy, Norton found no more rigorous guide than Chauncey Wright, an American utilitarian philosopher three years younger than himself but his master in analytic thought. From around 1864 until his early death in 1875, Wright became a permanent fixture at Shady Hill. Unlike the other visitors whose enacted witness to truth moved Norton, Wright did not strip himself of worldly goods or prizes to follow the path of intellectual conscience. This was because Wright, through a combination of circumstance and temperament, had entirely failed to amass any such goods. Handsome, sweet-tempered, and "radically modest," Wright lived at the edge of penury, wholly devoted to the life of mind. In his Cambridge rented room, as he told Norton with a sort of self-deprecating bravado, "I can attain, at will, the greatest beatitude,—that of complete abstraction from the external world, even in a day in June." Capable of immense concentration but wholly unself-absorbed, he was not so much a companion, Norton would later say, "as an agent for mental activity."[16]

Wright, whose heroes were Darwin and Mill, deepened Norton's already consistent distrust of "metaphysics" by insisting upon the philo-sophical emptiness and unearned claim to knowledge of most concepts commonly used in discussions of the most important subjects. Norton had regarded Roman Catholicism as a faith filled with "superstitions" ever since he first attended Unitarian services with his parents as a boy. But Wright's uncompromising nominalism pushed him to see that the scope of "superstition" extended more widely than just to doctrines of transubstantiation or immaculate conception. Understood as the ten-dency to presume upon grammatical convention in order to create en-tities wholly divorced from actual experience, superstition could be seen to characterize such terms as "the Infinite" and "immortality" and "God," invading Unitarianism itself. It would not be long before a Uni-tarian divine was heard complaining that Chauncey Wright was the one "who led Charles Norton astray."[17]

Yet behind the widened vista that Wright's analysis assisted in opening to Norton—the alternative moral horizon to belief in God that Norton would variously call "free religion" or the "religion of irreligion"—there hovered a shadow as yet invisible to him. William James would point to it when he came to write a memorial essay about Wright after the philoso-pher's death. James recalled that in an early essay about the debate sur-rounding the origins of the physical universe, Wright (who in working as a mathematician for the *U.S. Nautical Almanac* had become a skilled meteorologist) "used the happy phrase 'cosmical weather' to describe the irregular dissipation and aggregation of worlds." What James re-alized about his friend was that this fortunate metaphor captured for Wright not simply the operations of cosmological nature but the nature of being itself.[18]

For in contemplating the totality of being, Wright as James said, "preferred to think of phenomena as the result of a sort of ontologic weather, without inward rationality, an aimless drifting to and fro, from the midst of which relatively stable and so (for us) rational combina-tions may emerge." Wright explicitly advanced his view to combat what he considered the unearned optimism of Herbert Spencer's "Law of Evolution"—Spencer's widely popular notion that all change moved from simplicity to complexity and from homogeneity to heterogeneity. But in aiming at Spencer, Wright's underlying ontological assumption struck at the living heart of all Victorian progressivism. He argued that what might appear to careless or hopeful or tendentious observers to be "providence" or "progress" or "improvement," was to a properly scien-tific eye simply groupings of phenomena—arrays of existence that were neither orderly nor disorderly, just discontinuous movements and coun-ter-movements—resembling nothing so much as Democritus' whirl of infinite atoms in an infinite void. Behind these bare phenomenal facts,

Wright told his Cambridge friends, there was precisely *nothing*—a view the human consequences of which would not become completely plain until the twentieth century in Samuel Beckett's *Endgame*. With its nihilistic vision of endless, patternless, meaningless change, Wright's "happy phrase" possessed a power, as William James recognized in his own case, of making men quite miserable.[19]

If Norton remained as yet untouched by the icy currents of Wright's ontologic weather, it was because the drift in his own thinking towards such a conclusion was hidden from him precisely by the progressive element written into Andrews' Unitarianism. From his own childhood onwards, Norton had been taught to see that "childish" phases of human knowledge inevitably gave way to ever more advanced periods of enlightenment. Historically regarded, Protestantism had succeeded Catholicism, while the sequence of variant forms within Protestantism—from Lutheranism to Calvinism to Socinianism—pointed to a no less consistent pattern of ongoing "growth." Now, as Norton considered the last of these sects, he became convinced that in a new era when the right of private judgment and the utmost liberty of individual opinion were accepted as fundamental, a church would arise that would be freer still. "It will be the glory of Unitarianism," he told his co-religionist Meta Gaskell, "to have been the last step of the ascending series by which men reached at length the platform of the true Church Universal."[20]

Yet as Carlyle once demanded of an American Unitarian minister, "If so far, why not farther?" Why should a "free church" or "religious free-thinkers" hesitate to step beyond an orthodox belief in God? Some observers had long regarded Unitarianism as "a feather-bed for falling Christians," in Erasmus Darwin's famous phrase. But it now became apparent that the form of Unitarianism peculiar to Andrews Norton might hide the "progressive" seeds of its own decay. For Andrews' ironbound insistence that there could be but two sources of ideas—experience and testimony—reduced the sphere of religious belief to its narrowest base: empirical reason wreathed by a sort of humanitarian emotion, but rigidly denying any validity to the intuitions of religious truth. To his evangelical critics, Andrews seemed to have given his life to the barren proposition that the New Testament was not a revelation so much as the *history* of a revelation. To his Transcendentalist critics, he appeared to do something even worse: assert that religion consisted only in "knowledge" while denying the very kind of knowledge it genuinely consisted in.[21]

"To be true to your principles, you ought to be an infidel," the Benthamite historian Richard Hildreth told Andrews, "you ought to be an atheist." From Concord to Cambridge, serious people watched the Unitarian drama unfold in all its tragicomic irony: Andrews, a passionately sincere and deeply pious man making straight a highway for unbelief, a man who once taunted Calvinism for forcing its best minds into skepticism, now driving his own students with the hammer of "logic" into the deeps of Transcendentalism or the wilderness of agnosticism. Charles William Eliot, president of Harvard, would later say of his cousin Charles that "[t]he son came to see that the limits set up by the father did not exist—and cut adrift from all his father's beliefs." President Eliot had by then decided that Charles Norton's reaction from Andrews' theology "was a natural reaction," a revolution without a betrayal.[22]

⚜ ⚜

Natural and serene, Charles' successful effort to "think himself out of" orthodoxy took place at Shady Hill, where Norton discussed certain points of religion with visitors in the parlor and read Darwin and Mill in the library—once Andrews' sanctum and now his own. With its wide, columned porches and the green-shuttered white clapboard required by New England taste, Shady Hill has been for so long regarded as the domain upon which Charles Eliot Norton set his personal stamp that its shaping power over him, by contrast, can be difficult to see. Yet the house not only deeply formed him, as Norton's most recent biographer has well described, it also masked from him the extent of his own transformation. For with Shady Hill, the house of his birth, as a continuous background, enbosomed in its fields and marshlands and seeming to change only with the seasons, the ruptures of time and death were distanced and moderated, in effect disguised.[23]

Nowhere was this masking effect more remarkable than in connection with Norton's marriage in 1862. For in winning Susan Sedgwick as his wife, Norton found "an orphan," as he told his friends—a woman of distinguished family but possessing neither father nor mother—who saw no impediment to making her new home in the Nortons' old house. "Susan takes her place as happily and as peacefully amongst us," Norton told George Curtis, "as if she were the real daughter of my Mother, and the lifelong sister of Jane and Grace." Even Jane and Grace agreed that there had been an expansion, not a breach in the family circle, saying so with an enthusiasm a more cynical age may suspect but cannot entirely discount. "My highest hopes for my beloved Charles are fulfilled," Jane Norton told Curtis, "and that his engagement should bring me such unmingled joy is infinitely more than I ever dared imagine. I always knew his happiness would be my happiness after a sort, but not in this overflowing boundless measure."[24]

Yet the deceptive continuity in Norton's life at Shady Hill lay deeper than this, out of sight of the old rooms redecorated for new purposes and beyond the range of sisterly effusions or maternal pride. For Norton's marriage would gradually and silently assume the focus of transcendental aspiration he had earlier fixed on his religious belief. His marital love would prove to be the central moral source of his life, to adopt Charles Taylor's useful term—a good the love of which empowers a person to do and be good. At the same time, Norton's marriage would for a brief period shelter him from the colder consequences of his own unbelief. By the time he might otherwise have begun to feel the chill approach of something like Chauncey Wright's ontologic weather, Norton had married Susan Sedgwick. By the time he might have washed up on the bleaker shores of unbelief, he had diverted his impulses towards the search for ultimate meaning into his marriage.[25]

Even by the 1850s Shady Hill had become the center of what a later age would call Norton's "religion of the hearth"—the intensified celebration of family ties that compensated for a weakening of otherworldly beliefs by upholding values immanent in this world. In 1854, when Arthur Clough had sent over from England the first volume of a much-discussed poem, *The Angel in the House*, Norton seized on the book, quickly forgiving its occasionally cloying affectation. "[T]he sentiment is often true and tender," he told Clough, "and there is a quiet gentleness and purity of feeling running though it which is most pleasing." Norton was responding to the picture of the heroine's quiet home—"a tent pitch'd in a world not right"—where three sisters "On tranquil faces bore the light / Of duties beautifully done," keeping "their own laws, which seem'd to be / The fair sum of six thousand years' / Traditions of civility." Although a later day would treat "the Angel in the House" as a contemptuous by-word for nineteenth-century sentimentality and misogyny, in its original moment the poem expressed in compelling terms to Victorians on both sides of the Atlantic the new "religion of the hearth." A tent in a world not right, Shady Hill was the Nortons' temple to such a religion. "Do, when you write next to me," Norton begged Mrs. Gaskell in 1860, "send me a list of your birthdays. I like to keep the birthdays of those whom I love; they are my Saints Days."[26]

People who knew him well were thus not surprised when Charles Norton wrote back from Paris, "Dear Shady Hill! . . . I see every book in the library, I feel the handles of the doors, I see the patterns of the carpets." They were surprised when he got married. George Curtis confessed the news of the engagement "utterly surprises me." Dr. Holmes expressed delight mixed with amazement "to hear from yourself that you had found the counterpart whom those that knew you best might have doubted if you would ever find." For by 1862, Norton, now 35, verged on becoming a professional bachelor like Tom Appleton, witty and fastidious—perhaps too fastidious, as Holmes's letter delicately hints. A decade earlier, Charles had criticized American girls' placid uninterest in talking about anything beyond "the Opera, a sleighride, or the last novel." His female cousins tended to mistrust him, put off by a silken social manner that implied each one was his dearest woman friend. Occasionally, he would indulge his "natural gift for a peculiarly mordant sarcasm," or perhaps show "a certain amount of visible self-will, and a certain impatience with those who dissented from him"—all traits dangerously like Andrews' own.[27]

"Who is Charles' weakness this year? Or who are his half dozen weaknesses?" a Newport friend had asked Jane Norton in 1853. But as the appeal of flirtations and cotillions faded in the ten years following, so grew the attraction of Shady Hill, with its three extraordinary women: Catharine, "the loveliest of the post-meridian ladies," Jane, who "distilled civility and sympathy and charm," and Grace, the astringently intelligent confidante of Chauncey Wright and Henry James. "I suffer under the advantage," Norton once remarked in an attempt to explain his tepid response to a beautiful Irishwoman, "of having always known the most charming women in the world."[28]

Into this hospitable but self-sufficient circle of Shady Hill, Norton led Susan Sedgwick. Orphaned with her two younger sisters and brother upon the death of her father in 1859 (her mother died in 1856), Susan had grown up in Stockbridge, Massachusetts, where the Sedgwicks had been the leading family since 1785. Unitarian in religion, Federalist and then Free Soil in politics, the distinguished line of Theodore Sedgwicks—Susan's great-grandfather, grandfather and father all bore the same name—were notable public servants and vigorous anti-slavery men. As a child, Susan was gregarious and generous and, as one of her aunts observed, showed "a decided partiality for the other sex." As a girl, she adored dancing, telling her absent father with a suspicious breathlessness, "I have not polk[a]ed or waltzed but once since you asked me not to but really Bayendale and Willy polk[a]ed and waltzed in such a graceful and bewitching manner that I could not resist either of them but there is no danger of my doing it again as there is no one up here who dances in such a light and airy manner as Mr Bayendale and really his walking was inimitable[,] his feet hardly seemed to touch the ground. I hope he may remain some time to teach the young Americans how to walk à l'Anglaise."[29]

But when her mother's prolonged illness was followed by her father's painful cancer ("It is a Abscess [sic]," Theodore told his children, "filling the cavity of the Pelvis & extending three or four inches below the ligament known as Poupart's"), the burden of their care "for months & even years before their deaths" fell upon Susan, the oldest of the four surviving Sedgwick children. Her own health, complicated by a case of malaria contracted much earlier on Long Island, broke under the strain. In the "secession winter" of 1860–61, she was sent to England to recover, returning to Cambridge, where her brother Arthur had begun at Harvard, and her aunts had established a home for the three Sedgwick sisters "to give the girls a change of life after the trying & sad scenes they had lately passed through."[30]

With the onslaught of civil war, Jane Norton quickly enrolled Susan as an assistant in her project to secure employment for the poorer women in Cambridge by having them sew clothing for the Union army. Already disciplined by responsibility and sorrow, Susan proved exceptionally capable in the work, possessing besides "an intense remarkable power of sympathy." Soon, it appears, Jane began another project: marrying Susan to Charles. Amidst the heightened emotions, the sudden deaths and departures of wartime, the two became engaged in late March 1862, marrying two months later. The date chosen for the wedding was May 21st, Catharine Norton's own wedding day. Describing the ceremony with a novelist's eye for drama and detail, Susan's formidable great aunt was struck by the change in her. "She looked beautifully—queenly," Catharine Maria Sedgwick reported, "an expression of *perfect* contentment[,] of graciousness & dignity & of a certain assurance of power—not trenching on modesty either—impressed me." For at twenty-four, Susan had already passed through a hard and sorrowful life, watching by her parents' sickbeds when other young women were blithely waltzing the night away. Her assurance thus derived, not from a maiden's trust in hair-ribbons or a fetching dress, but from a woman's confidence in a proven friend. In Charles Norton she found a man who, remarkable in any age, prized firmness of character in a wife as much as fairness of face. In Susan Sedgwick, he found a woman, it appears, "free from self-consciousness, free from dogmatism and vanity, with feelings unformalized by creed or theory, with a deep and simple heart."[31]

In all, Catharine Maria Sedgwick decided, there was just one imperfection in the wedding ceremony: the bridegroom's extreme pallor. Perhaps, she declared sententiously, Norton's disquieting paleness would providentially remind onlookers "that even this beautiful vision is to be succeeded by a brighter that shall never pass away." Superstitious in its circumlocution, however, Sedgwick's indirection of speech reveals how darkly Charles's pallor seemed to cast upon the couple a shadow of early death.[32]

↯ ↯ ↯

A year after his wedding, Norton confessed to Meta Gaskell, "I had often wondered whether it were possible that a marriage should be what it seemed to me it ought to be." He was quite unprepared for how fully the answer could be "yes." After a single year of marriage, he had reached a remarkable conclusion: "It is the only experience of life in which the best ideal falls short of the actual." From the first, Norton regarded his marriage as "the great change & happiness of my life," the beginning of his own *Vita Nuova*. Precisely here, however, does direct testimony by either Charles or Susan Norton about their life together all but vanish. Norton fiercely guarded and sequestered all such personal testimony, regarding it as part of what he once in a letter to Mrs. Gaskell called "our united, sacred secret treasury of precious common memories & affections." After Susan's death, he would tell Ruskin of burning, one by one, "some of the sweetest love letters ever penned, because I would make sure that no eye but mine should ever see them," of watching "the sparks fly upwards to add to the brightness of the Ariadne's Crown that shines for me alone in the night." Even as his sacred rituals and religious silence have obscured Norton's marriage, however, they effectively reveal it.[33]

To grasp the significance of Norton's private life for his later public career, it is necessary to set his marriage against the background of a much larger social change: the evolution of a bourgeois ideal of companionate marriage that had been slowly developing in Protestant countries since the Reformation. The companionate ideal was ideologically positioned, on one hand, against the celibacy praised in Catholicism and, on the other, against the dynastic and landed property aims pursued by hereditary aristocracies. It centered in what Lawrence Stone and others have taught us to see as "affective individualism"—the pursuit of emotional and sexual intimacy within a zone of familial privacy. By the end of the eighteenth century, when it might be glimpsed in English epistolary poetry or the novels of Jane Austen or the marriage of John and Abigail Adams, companionate marriage had come to derive its own ideological prestige from an implicit appeal to the Aristotelian idea of ethical friendship, the friend—or spouse—as one's other self. This belief held that marital affection might extend beyond emotional and sexual gratification to reach "intelligent love," that Mr. Darcy (to take its most famous representation in fiction) might learn to curb his arrogant pride even as Elizabeth Bennet might recognize her own unjust prejudice. The notion that guidance in growth and conduct might be reciprocally given and accepted by each lover toward the other was new.[34]

In Unitarian New England, the companionate model quickly became the acknowledged ideal, to be vigorously invoked whenever either feverishly romantic or coldly mercenary versions of marital love threatened to displace it. In her 1857 novel *Married or Single?*, Catharine Maria Sedgwick depicted a wife insisting upon the vital importance in marriage of "a mutual dependence, and an individual freedom springing from reciprocal faith, love, and charity; each a life apart, and a life together."

As Catharine Maria's great-niece, the nineteen-year-old Susan Sedgwick, read the novel, she would have learned that anything less than this ideal, any "'next best' in marriage," as one of its characters says, must be regarded as unendurable. Norton in 1857 was reading and arranging to have published in the *Atlantic Monthly* a long narrative poem by Arthur Clough called *Amours de Voyage*. In it, Clough's witty and fastidious hero Claude explains to a friend that in seeking a woman's love, "I do not wish to be moved, but growing, where I was growing, / There more truly to grow, to live where as yet I had languished." Norton recognized that Clough's poem bore upon his own bachelor existence with an extraordinary urgency. As he was preparing to marry in 1862, Norton praised the work for the way it expressed "the emotions and thoughts which have more or less consciously been partaken of by every susceptible nature." Even more than when Clough portrayed the theme for which he was to be best known—the psychic plight of religious doubters—did the poet manage, as Norton insisted, to utter the hidden souls of his contemporaries in depicting their quest for companionate love.[35]

Yet what was perhaps less visible to Norton was how intimately related the two quests were, how dynamically the companionate ideal of marital love was expanding to fill the widening horizon left by the disappearance of God. In "Dover Beach" of 1867, the signature poem of their generation, Matthew Arnold would give lasting expression to the new existential landscape the Victorians found themselves in, as Arnold's poetic speaker turns in anguished hope to his wife in the darkness ("Ah, love, let us be true / To one another!") while the Sea of Faith shrinks back down the stony shore. Arnold saw so deeply into his contemporaries' situation—into the equivocal, sliding ratio they maintained between love and religious belief—largely because he himself was to retain a more nearly orthodox relation to the Anglican faith he had inherited from his father (while transvaluing its terms). This is why by contrast the most unequivocal expressions of the companionate ideal of marriage are most often to be found among the Victorian agnostic liberals.[36]

In George Eliot's novels, in particular *Middlemarch* of 1872, the companionate union shines forth with a luster that was to dazzle generations of readers, even as Eliot herself in her letters expressed her own devotion to the ideal—and to her de facto husband, G. H. Lewes—("I am very happy—happy in the highest blessing life can give us, the perfect love and sympathy of a nature that stimulates my own to healthful activity"). Leslie Stephen would later give expression to the same ideal in "Forgotten Benefactors," an essay eloquent in its silence about its real subject, Stephen's deceased second wife Julia. This kind of marital love, Stephen would then declare, meant absolute and reciprocal self-surrender. "To live in an atmosphere of the strongest and most un-qualified affection, to have the very substance of life woven out of the unreserved love of a worthy object, is its ideal." In sending Norton "For-gotten Benefactors," Stephen would say that the essay was "in the nature of a personal confession." In responding, Norton would tell his friend, "You have spoken for me in speaking for yourself."[37]

The most determined proclamation of the companionate ideal—J. S. Mill's *Subjection of Women*—appeared in 1869, just four years after the publication of the work Victorian agnostics regarded as their char-ter of religious freedom—Mill's *Examination of Sir William Hamilton's Philosophy*. The two works are sharply different, as an immensely pro-longed and plodding technical analysis of philosophical arguments will differ from a nimbly polemical tract. Yet within both works there played the jet of Mill's radical anger. The genuinely new idea put for-ward in Mill's *Subjection* was that the consecrated status and persistence of customary social arrangements made it impossible to say with any as-surance whether the apparently divergent characters of Victorian men and women arose from nature or culture. But it was another point en-tirely that struck William James as "revolutionary"—the ideal of mar-riage as ethical friendship. Reviewing the book for the *North American*, James cited a long series of disconnected passages from Mill's essay as evidence that this "new" idea of marriage "lurks as a hidden premise in all his reasoning." James rightly concluded his list with the following paragraph from Mill—rightly, because the passage he seized on con-tains, as if in a censer, the fragrantly burning heart of the liberal agnos-tics' companionate ideal:

> What marriage may be in the case of two persons of cultivated faculties, identical in opinions and purposes, between whom there exists that best kind of equality, similarity of powers and capacities with reciprocal su-periority in them—so that each can enjoy the luxury of looking up to the other, and can have alternately the pleasure of leading and of being led in the path of development—I will not attempt to describe. To those who can conceive it, there is no need; to those who cannot, it would ap-pear the dream of an enthusiast. *But I maintain, with the profoundest con-viction, that this, and this only, is the ideal of marriage*; and that all opinions, customs, and institutions which favour any other notion of it . . . are rel-ics of primitive barbarism.

In plain-colored but urgently peremptory prose, this was the romanti-cism of a rationalist.[38]

Not every Victorian liberal subscribed to Mill's account of marriage. But the Anglo-American liberals' sense of "regeneration" and imminent breakthrough, so characteristic of the later 1860s, are impossible to grasp unless one sees that part of the power they imputed to the moral and intellectual ferment of their moment derived from the innermost structures of their domestic life. Norton's own experience in watching Jane and Susan work for the army as well as in observing the labors of other women for the U.S. Sanitary Commission made him realize that "[t]here is at last not merely a promise, but a certainty, that society is to be perfected by the admission of woman to her full rights, and to essential equality with man."[39]

Surviving letters suggest the Norton family began discussing *The Subjection of Women* as soon as it appeared in 1869. The vital importance of Mill's essay, however, consists less in its direct influence upon either Charles or Susan than in the way it defined the furthest boundaries of a realm of social experiment on which they and their friends felt themselves to be embarking. Even before the Nortons left America for the long residence abroad that would so profoundly change their lives, Charles had taken up the cause of women's opportunities in education and political life. In 1865, Mill himself had reminded Norton that even should the Radical Republicans succeed in winning perfect civil equality between blacks and whites, "it will still remain to bring it into operation between men and women." In 1867, when George Curtis struggled to get a provision for female suffrage written into the revised New York State constitution, Norton lent a hand, publishing an article in the *Nation* bristling with the assumptions of Millite liberalism. With enhanced education, he declared, "women might—we see no reason to doubt that they would—vote as intelligently as men." With political equality, "they would, if we may trust to the lessons of past experience, grow more and more lovely and worthy of love, become more truly feminine, and be no longer the toy and the plaything, but the equal helpmate of man."[40]

It was, however, only when the Nortons reached Europe in 1868 that the full scope of the companionate ideal of marriage became genuinely available to them. Their quest was by no means exclusive, for both Charles and Susan went abroad for reasons of health, and traveled with a formidable entourage: Catharine, Jane, and Grace Norton, four children ranging in age from one to five years, two nursemaids and, from time to time, a Sedgwick sister. Yet it was in England and, above all, in art-filled Italy that the specifically Millite or developmental dimension of the companionate ideal would be most abundantly realized, where each spouse would continue "growing, where I was growing, / There more truly to grow, to live where as yet I had languished." In England, Charles, in repairing his breach with Ruskin, caught a desperate influenza and was compelled upon doctor's orders to remain through the winter. The fortunate consequence of this enforced stay was to allow both Nortons to become acquainted on more intimate terms than might otherwise have been possible not only with Ruskin, but with the younger leaders of the liberal revolution, swept into political power by W. E. Gladstone's electoral victory of autumn 1868.[41]

Such men as Dr. John Simon, Ruskin's friend and the physician who insisted that Norton remain in London, shared Norton's outrage and alarm at the degraded condition of English farm workers and of the urban working-class. Tirelessly active as the chief Medical Officer of the Privy Council, Simon was a pathologist acquainted with the London abyss, haunted by "[t]he certainty that every year in England there died 120,000, fourteen in every hour, who might have been and ought to have been kept alive." Fresh from the idealism and cooperation of postwar America, Norton was disheartened by the brutal cleavage between social classes he saw everywhere in London, and oppressed by the selfish indifference of the rich and the intense hostility of the poor. "I sit here," he said to a young woman at a sumptuous dinner given by Lord Coleridge, "I enjoy talking to you, I am not responsible for all the expense lavished on this dinner, I go home, the light of my carriage will fall on dark forms of misery and poverty in the streets—it must fall on them, it must strike as a terrible contrast." When the dismayed young woman asked what could be done, Norton said quietly, "I would have this thought, which must strike every one, not stifled but *enduring, abiding, living* with men, as a principle of action." Then he urged her to read Dante, and recommended Rossetti's translation of the *Vita Nuova*.[42]

Such a vignette may at first seem to say more about the difference between earnest Boston and worldly London than anything else. But Norton was not at odds with "advanced" London opinion in expressing such views. In fact, the winter of 1868–69 constituted a moment when imaginative art and social reform were not yet split apart into mutually incomprehensible and antagonistic camps. Walter Pater's review of William Morris' poems—part of which would later become the famous "Conclusion" to Pater's *Studies in the History of the Renaissance*—had just been published, declaring that both an aestheticist passion for "art and song" and a positivist "enthusiasm of humanity" could yield the "fruit of a quickened, multiplied consciousness." The utopian aim of the decorative arts firm of Morris, Marshall, Faulkner & Co.—to produce beautiful interiors under conditions of cooperative labor—had just been vindicated by a royal command to redecorate rooms in St. James's Palace. The *Fortnightly Review*, under the incisive editorship of John Morley, was deploying essays about art as camouflaged vehicles for the Millite message of "variety not uniformity" in order to attack the entrenched forces of orthodox religious and social belief. Now in its originating moment, Aestheticism was the "human face" assumed by Victorian rationalism and agnosticism.[43]

The Nortons achieved a remarkable social success in London during this year, but they preferred the company of "advanced" artists and writers who had managed to slip the heavy bridle of Victorian social convention. Norton made a point of getting know independent-minded women of sense and talent—among them, George Eliot, whose famous Sunday afternoon gatherings constituted the Radical party at tea, and Emilia Pattison, the intrepid young wife of the Rector of Lincoln College, Oxford. "Social discipline has not succeeded in crushing her," Norton told Curtis, using a phrase from Mill's *Subjection of Women*. Instead, Mrs. Pattison baffled it with wit, and "keeps up the most plucky & vigorous resistance against the social oppression to which most women meekly submit or even take part in supporting."[44]

The symbolic center of this attractively unconventional social resistance became for both Charles and Susan "the Grange," the quaint eighteenth-century home of Ned and Georgiana Burne-Jones, surrounded by what were then the open fields of South Kensington. "People who have done more for themselves than these two," he told Curtis, "in securing a due and desirable freedom of mind and soul, and in maintaining a genuine independence of life in the midst of the community which Mill complains of as that in which 'social discipline has most succeeded not so much in conquering, as in suppressing, whatever is liable to conflict with it,'—I have never seen." Picturesque in her Pre-Raphaelite dress, Mrs. Burne-Jones seemed to embody the new world of shared beauty and social amelioration the transatlantic liberals believed was coming. Norton glimpsed in her a "subtle quality in the faces of this generation of women which no painter has yet rendered; a look in many of them as if the perplexity of life bewildered them, but as if together with the bewilderment & finally to overmaster it were a fuller sense of life and a nobler self-reliance than women hitherto have felt,— a look as if moving in worlds not realized,—sure to be realized however in coming time."[45]

The Nortons dined frequently with the Burne-Joneses and William Morris during that year, Charles on one occasion talking with Morris about "the ideal [life] of the future." At other times they heard Georgie Burne-Jones read from a rare new translation of a long Persian poem, the *Rubáiyát* of Omar Khayyám. Borrowing her copy, Norton quickly decided to write a review of the startlingly contemporary *Rubáiyát*, declaring in the *North American Review*, "it reads like the latest and freshest expression of the perplexity and of the doubt of the generation to which we ourselves belong." For as rendered into plangent English by its as yet unidentified translator, Omar's quatrains put forward an audacious

doctrine: in a world apparently ended by death, the sacramental pleasures of life and love must suffice. The doctrine was neatly contained in
what would become the poem's most famous quatrain, "Here with a little bread beneath the bough, / A flask of wine, a book of verse,—and
thou / Beside me singing in the wilderness,— / O, wilderness were paradise enow." Later that year, after Norton bought his own copy of the
Rubáiyát, he inscribed it to Susan, writing on the title page, "—a book
of verse and Thou."[46]

As the Nortons looked forward in October 1869 to a winter residence
in Florence, John Simon, in his capacity as family friend and physician,
advised Susan "don't scamper about too frantically. You've a year before you. Move in a slow, expectant sort of way, as if Dante or Galileo
were round each corner." But there was little danger of any scampering.
Susan was six months pregnant with their fifth child. Only after she was
successfully delivered of a daughter in mid-January 1870, did Italy properly begin for her. After an unusually difficult and fatiguing pregnancy,
both husband and wife felt the joyous rebound from her prolonged weariness and his pressing fears ("a great weight is lifted from my heart,"
Norton told Lowell). As the spring advanced, Norton wrote Simon that
Susan "is delightfully well & strong, & young & blooming. She has not
looked so well for years as she does on fine days now. And she is as happy
in Italy as I could wish."[47]

Norton himself, encumbered by his stringent New England social
conscience, at first found it difficult "to learn to be content with the usefulness of doing nothing." Like other Bostonian men lingering abroad,
he heard more than the nightingale's song pulsing from the citron skies
of Italy. He heard what his friend Tom Appleton called "the whip of the
sky," a grating Yankee voice repeating and reproving, "Hurry up, jump
along, rest when you die!" Gradually, however, in the two years following
Susan's confinement, during long residences in Florence (twice), Siena
and Venice, Norton allowed himself "to accept & receive, instead of to
win & to conquer," and learned to live his Italian idyll. In Siena, where
from May to December 1870 the Nortons leased a large villa outside the
city, they found themselves in a humanely medieval world: "it is almost
pure old Italy of the days before the [Renaissance] tyrants were driven
out," as Norton told Meta Gaskell, ". . . free from the taint of this ten per
cent. stock broking age." Unlike England with its degraded rural peasantry, "there is no misery to wring one's heart; & one can give to beg-
gars without compunction." Charles carried out research in the Siena
archives, and took "lingering walks, never to be forgotten" with Susan
"through lovel[y] Italian *poderes*, with the bright Spring haze floating
over them, and the soft far blue horizon of the campanile-studded plain,
or of the hills crowned each with its shining town." With Ruskin in June,

he drank from the frowning medieval Fonte Branda where Dante himself had once paused, Ruskin later immortalizing the moment in one of the most famous passages of his autobiography: "We drank of it together, and walked together that evening on the hills above, where the fireflies among the scented thickets shone fitfully in the still undarkened air. How they shone! Moving like fine-broken starlight through the purple leaves."[48]

What the sojourn in Siena meant to Norton, he later that year sought to express to James Lowell. "To live in Italy in summer," he told his friend, "is to be made a poet for oneself." By this he meant that an ordinary man like himself, a sickly man who struggled against the cold, could feel the barrier between environing circumstance and inner consciousness drop away, and the friction between actuality and imaginative ideal melt. Such a man in Italy could live in imagination *directly*—without the mediation of poets or artists—just by living. After Susan's death, Norton would remember Siena as "the very heart of all that is most Italian," telling Henry James that "The poet, that is more or less consciously, in all of us is of no epoch or age,—but his native land is Italy." More than twenty years after Siena, Norton would speak of the intense delight one felt in Italy at "the calling forth and growth of faculties of the imagination . . . [,] in the enjoyment not of imagination through the poets, through literature, but of the very sources by which our imaginations are developed and relieved from their half unconscious, but always pressing thirst."[49]

What Italy meant to Susan Norton is only to be glimpsed indirectly, through Charles's eyes, after Italy was over for them both. "Life grew fuller & fuller of resource to her," Norton told Henry James. "All [her] powers of enjoyment, & of happiness increased from day to day." In Florence, Rome and Venice, she had spent hours in the presence of the greatest works of art, where to enter for the first time such a room as the Tribuna in the Uffizi or the San Lorenzo Chapel, as he said, "makes an epoch of one's life." Norton wrote Frank Child that "Every sympathy of her imagination & her heart seemed called into fresh and most delightful expression." Susan remained herself in Italy, while becoming more than she had ever been before, "her youthful freshness of spirit undiminished, but with a fulness & richness of maturity added to it such as few women have the character to attain." Struggling to say what he meant, Norton snatched a phrase from *Much Ado About Nothing*: "*Every lovely organ* and faculty *of her life* was at its full perfection."[50]

"To those who cannot conceive it," Mill had said, a marriage between two persons of cultivated powers with reciprocal superiority in them, each leading and being led in the path of development, might seem like a visionary's fantasy. Yet this is what Charles and Susan Norton seem to have achieved, most completely in Italy during the nineteen months from January 1870 to July 1871. Norton's transit from orthodox belief to the new secularizing idea of religion he expressed as "the striving to realize the ideal of our own nature" was now complete. In the *Vita Nuova* of a perfected marriage, there lay the power to be and do good, he realized—a moral source, shaping character, giving strength to right purpose, and helping others, a love therefore entirely distinct from "the selfishness of common love." As Charles would say much later, "the existence of that image of what we desire to be, and therefore really are, is the blessing of the one and only love."[51]

Beyond this, what the mysterious core of the Nortons' marriage may have been is now to be glimpsed only as it is contrasted with what it was not. At one extreme, the coolly external domestic affections among the English struck Charles as representing an emotional deficiency or lack, a matter "of mere juxtaposition, rather than of essential sympathy & comprehensive intelligence." At the other extreme, Leslie Stephen's uxoriousness towards his first wife impressed Susan, observing the couple at a London dinner party, as having injured Minny Stephen's perfect simplicity of manner. "[I]t is always a hard trial of simplicity," she wrote, probably to Chauncey Wright, "for a woman to have an adoring husband who lets his sun shine on the evil and the good equally, on the weaknesses and the strengths alike." In this incomplete letter, which even in its fragmentariness throws a clearer light than any other we have on the Nortons' own marriage, Susan continues, "At any rate, I know, it would have ruined me when I was young, and most women, I think, are better for a sense of their liability to be criticized, provided only the criticism comes from one who holds a high ideal of their possibilities." The Nortons' marriage began as a *Vita Nuova* of ethical friendship and "intelligent love," an earthen vessel for transcendental aspirations: their shared and reciprocal "striving to realize the ideal of our own nature." By Italy, the marriage had become, however briefly, "paradise enow."[52]

The Nortons' final four months in Italy, spent in Venice from April to July 1871, were if anything even more paradisal than Siena. A longtime resident of Venice, Ruskin's friend, Rawdon Brown, warned Charles about its disadvantages in summertime. "The mosquitoes begin to be troublesome at the end of July when the swallows take flight," Brown said, adding "the scavengers do their duty fairly in the streets." He meant the rats. But none of this mattered to Charles and Susan. Venice became for them "that city totally dedicated to Venus" (*Quella Città tutta dedicata a Venere*), in the Italian phrase about the old Venetian nobility Norton copied into his journal. In after years, he would note with a kind of religious fidelity the first day they entered the city and the last day they left it. By then, his retrospective view of Venice would be gilded by "some of the tenderest & most precious memories of my life," for Susan had been her happiest there. But even as he was living in it, Norton was depicting Venice with a saturated Shakespearean romanticism. "[T]he air [is] soft as in the old time," he wrote his mother in late June, "the moon at just the right height & sweetly dripping silver into the water & sleeping on the marble fronts of palaces as in the days of Jessica," the glimmering night silent except for "the occasional plash & ripple of a belated gondola." Then in a shift of tone, as if mocking his own sentiment, he added, "If Susan & I were younger & had not five children we should be romanticizing on the canal." In fact, though, the romance had already come to fruition: Susan became pregnant with their sixth child in Venice. Just before their departure in July, she would begin to experience morning sickness, bearing it, as Norton said, "patient as a Saint, & better than any Saint in the Calendar."[53]

❧ ❧ ❧ ❧

When Susan Norton died in Dresden on February 17, 1872, a week after giving birth to a healthy son, Charles Norton's life broke in two. As if silently marking the chasm it opened in his existence, his earliest biographers would end the first volume of Norton's life with her death and its immediate aftermath. In later years, Norton himself would say that no one truly knew him who did not know him before Susan's death. Quite simply, it was to prove the most decisive event of his private life, just as the Civil War would prove the most important public one. But the significance and consequences for Norton of his wife's death would be largely hidden. Some of these would be deliberately concealed by Norton himself as the price of his psychic survival. But others were to be unconsciously hidden, emerging only as the unintended side-effects of that same survival. Like Henry Adams after the death of his wife Clover in 1885, Norton would now begin his "posthumous life." Few people in later times, however, would ever realize that Norton had actually lived such a life, for he lacked both Adams' great talent for writing autobiographical prose and his equally great penchant for complaining in it.[54]

Yet Norton's friends did not fail to realize that in Susan's death he had suffered a "mortal wound." "You are plunged into this misery, from which you can never wholly be your old self again," one of them told him. Henceforth, said another, "you must be as one who is no longer himself[,] who has lost in some respect what was the best part of his own self." For those in America, the calamity seemed magnified by distance. The dreadful news was "overwhelming," Henry James, Sr., wrote Norton, "and even yet I can hardly get away from the shadow of your grief. It pursues me night and day." To W. J. Stillman in London, the terrible change was incomprehensible, for the Nortons' life together had seemed so proportioned and serene as to contain nothing perishable in it. "You had always something of the air of the immortals about you, & it seems as it might if one told me that Cambridge had slidden into the sea & was lost."[55]

Norton's first letters to his closest friends have disappeared. "I write now," he told Curtis on April 2, "less because I have anything but love to send you than that my last bitter note may no longer be the last." But the bitter note itself has vanished. As winter yielded to spring, and Norton with his mother, sisters and children left Dresden for Paris, Charles's outward calm and apparent physical strength reassured those closest to him. He sketched out an expanded edition of *Notes of Travel and Study in Italy*: a new second volume would be devoted to Siena and Orvieto, while a third volume would be given over entirely to Venice. He was looking forward with both dread and relief to returning to Shady Hill that autumn. But the tenant occupying the house, Alexander Agassiz, declined to vacate before the lease was up in the spring of 1873. Thus Norton, for whom it was a question of returning to his own home or none at all, was forced into an unwanted exile that became a ghastly counterpart to the emotional and spiritual exile he had suffered in Susan's death. Quartered in London from October 1872 until May 1873, he would live in limbo.[56]

Although Norton's surviving letters from this time resume their former commentary on people, places and events, there play beneath the surface of his sad composure, as those closest to him sensed, darker currents of depression and hopelessness. He wished to die. He would tell Ruskin he regretted living to see his own birthday that November, his forty-fifth. The London winter he lived through was to prove the rainiest ever seen until that time, as if in a hideous parody of its own randomness and meaninglessness, Chauncey Wright's ontological weather had reassumed its original meterological form. In his journal of these London days, Norton expresses a portion of his anguish, particularly in several lines he later deleted. Deciphered, these all but obliterated words reveal him struggling to find a foothold as he is buffeted by gusts of nihilism and despair. "The black and weariness of life oppress me," he writes, and "Life is little worth but I do try to make the best of it for the sake of the love I have had," and "I have my work, and I have every reason & motive to be the cheerfulest & best I can—but how full is 'my study of imagination' with one dearest, ever blessed, ever helpful image." In this last passage, Norton has returned to *Much Ado About Nothing*, to the scene where the Friar says of Hero, the heroine,

> Th'idea of her life shall sweetly creep
> Into his study of imagination,

Charles Eliot Norton

> And every lovely organ of her life
> Shall come apparelled in more precious habit,
> More moving, delicate, and full of life,
> Into the eye and prospect of his soul
> Than when she lived indeed.

In Shakespeare's play, Hero's death has been simulated. It is not real but instead the Friar's ruse to lure the alienated Claudio back into love with her. As the tender lines about the heroine's virtue and loveliness being heightened by death hovered in Norton's memory, they brought with them the dreary reminder that his own heroine would never return.[57]

As his friends were later to realize, this was the moment when Norton's tenuous, residually Christian faith gave way completely, leaving him to spurn as viciously false any notion of resurrection or immortality. Oppressed by the thought of Susan's corpse on its long journey back to buried in Mount Auburn cemetery in May and remembering the funerary customs he had seen in India, Norton, talking with Fitzjames Stephen and Thomas Carlyle, "expressed my wish that we could burn, instead of burying our dead." It pleased him when both men agreed. In this comfortless moment, Norton turned to Omar's quatrains, the volume he had inscribed to Susan seemingly so long ago. He learned the "book of verse" by heart, pressing it on such friends as Emerson and Carlyle, who both disliked it. But in the death-bounded horizon of the *Rubáiyát*, he found consolation. In its depiction of men as flickering shadows, he recognized himself: "For in and out, above, about, below, / 'Tis nothing but a Magic Shadow-show, / Play'd in a Box whose Candle is the Sun, / Round which we Phantom Figures come and go."[58]

Pulled taut between his meaningless daily responsibilities to his family and his intense need to maintain spiritual contact with his wife through memory and psychic communion, Norton felt himself change inwardly and become self-divided. He began to live a buried life. "The divorce between the inward & the outward man has rarely been wider in me than during the last month," he told Chauncey Wright in October 1872. "By degrees, I suppose with time & occupation the breach will grow narrower." But it did not. It grew wider. Five months later he would say to Henry James, "I am the nearest to a real ghost of any man you have ever seen, leading one real life, and another unreal but visible one." Four months after that, he would tell John Simon, "I am more solitary than I foresaw I should be; & the years to come will but close me more & more completely in a secret life of my own, while I lead a strange, unreal life in presence of my friends & the world." More than two decades later, Norton would be able to convey to Leslie Stephen, mourning for his second wife Julia in 1895, the bleak wisdom he had won from this dark London winter:

> [O]ne has to learn to live without joy, and without the hope of it. The hardest time is, perhaps, yet to come, when the excitement of immediate sorrow and the need of constant strenuous effort is past; when the dreary routine of the joyless days begins, and when the sense of solitude and of diminished personality weighs heavier and heavier. The death of her whom one has wholly loved is the end of the best of one's-self.

Amidst the black and weariness of this endless limbo winter, there was but a single gleam of light: Carlyle.[59]

Much later, twentieth-century critics would be disposed to regard Norton's friendship with Carlyle as proof of his reactionary temperament or his disdain for America. But Norton's affection for Carlyle, ripening from the acquaintance he had first opened with the sage in March 1869, was none of these, and had a different source. For in the winter of 1872–73, Carlyle was still mourning his own wife, even though Jane Welsh Carlyle had died almost seven years before. "She died at London, 21st April, 1866," read the inscription Carlyle had composed for her gravestone, "suddenly snatched away from him, and the light of his life as if gone out." Carlyle was in Scotland when the telegram came with the news of her death. "Not for above two days," as he would say in his *Reminiscences*, "could I estimate the immeasurable depth of it, or the infinite sorrow which had peeled my life all bare."[60]

In the years since Jane's death, Carlyle had come to realize, through reading her letters and a friend's recollections of her, how much his own actions had caused her pain and mortification—his exclusive focus on his writing, his failure to express his affection, his intimate friendship with Lady Harriet Ashburton, his inability to give Jane a child. Passing through an agony of remorse, he had been forced to confront his own life with the same unceasing honesty he had required of others since he first took up his pen. The effort had tempered him, imparting qualities of tenderness and nobility not usually associated with the literary figure many people still regarded as the cranky schoolmaster of Craiggenputtock. Visiting Carlyle in the summer of 1875, the American historian George Bancroft noted in his diary with surprise, "I never heard a man in conversation seem more sincerely moved by grief at the thought of having been bereaved of his wife."[61]

At first, Norton had himself regarded Carlyle in the usual way. Three years before Susan's death, in the meridian of his marital happiness, Norton had sought an introduction through mutual friends to the man Andrews Norton and George Ticknor had dismissed as an intolerable jester and stylistic coxcomb, Andrews seeming to Longfellow in 1838 "to take it as a *personal insult*, that anybody should write in such a style." But given the peculiar dynamic of psychological resistance to Andrews we have already noted in Charles, it was precisely his father's hatred of Carlyle ("Mr Norton . . . absolutely *hates* him," reported Longfellow), not less than his own curiosity to meet the notorious author of "Ilias Americana in Nuce," that prompted Charles's visit to Cheyne Walk in March 1869. There he found the brilliant literary lion he sought—extravagant in speech, reckless in opinion and wildly funny—but also a man whose fabled roughness of manner was underlaid by an unmistakable kindliness, visible only when one heard him in person and not from the printed page. In the course of several visits, Carlyle told Norton he wished to bequeath the books he had used to write his magisterial six-volume study of Frederick the Great "to some institution in New England, where they might be preserved, and where they would serve as a testimony of my appreciation o' the goodness o' your people toward me and o' the many acts o' kindness they have done me." Arranging that Harvard should receive the gift, both Norton and Emerson recognized that Carlyle's real desire was to repair the breach with Americans he had opened during the Civil War.[62]

When Norton renewed his acquaintance with the old man in the autumn of 1872, their common suffering and bereavement forged a deep bond between them. In their long walks together through the sodden London streets, Norton's earlier intuition of Carlyle's sorrow and solitariness grew, now strengthened by his own desperate need of a comprehending sympathy. "Each time I see him he seems better than before," he told Henry James, "more full of all sweet tenderness & all manly strength." Shunning the social whirl of the London season and "oppressed" even by the gaiety of his dearest friends, Norton found "[t]he chief and increasing pleasure and interest of my days here come from intercourse with Carlyle." For Carlyle spoke frankly of his own loss with a piercing force. Recalling his phantasmagoric stay on the French Riviera after Jane's death, living alone in a villa lent by a friend, he told Norton:

A beautiful coast, but very awful; the great mountains with bare heads and breasts, rugged an' scarred, an' wrinkled, an' horrible as the very Witch of Endor, but clothed on below with flowin' garments o' green stretchin' down to where they dip their feet in the water. Never in my life was I so solitary, and oppressed at heart as in my long walks through those chestnut woods with their brown carpet o' last year's leaves. I was bowed under heavy sorrow; & grief teaches one the measureless solitude o' life, when sympathy is of no sort of avail whatsoever; an' no comfort or counsel is good for aught except what a man can find in himself; and not much there, savin' as the conviction is borne in on him that in the mystery an' darkness everythin' is ruled by one Most Wise and Most Good, and he learns to say in his heart, 'Thy will be done.'

Just before Christmas, Carlyle gave the younger man a copy of *Sartor Resartus*. Published in Boston in 1836, this was the book that had marked an epoch in the intellectual development of an entire transatlantic generation. Yet it is possible that Norton had not read it before, since its electrifying message of existential courage in the face of a universe gone meaningless came deliberately clothed in an outlandish garb of wild metaphors and vehement Germanisms that would then have had little appeal to him. For Charles continued Andrews' emphatic preference for modest and transparent prose.[63]

Before Norton finished reading the book, however, he fell seriously ill. Amid the raw winds and dirty snow of February 1873, he faced the month beyond all others filled with painful memories and sacred associations—a month of "Saints Days," the birthdays of such intimate friends as Ruskin, Lowell, Longfellow, Child and Curtis, but much more poignantly, the anniversaries of Susan's death (on the 17th), her birth (on the 21st) and the birth of her now motherless son (on the 9th). Norton's last journal entry for February is dated the 7th. On the next page, he translates two poems from the Italian. One of them is "Discourteous Death" from *La Vita Nuova*, where Dante calls Death "by certain names proper to her": uncouth death, foe of pity, old mother of misery. Then Norton's journal breaks off for six weeks, as his lung congestion slipped into a case of full-blown pneumonia. Acutely aware of the physical peril posed to his friend by the mental stress of this time, Dr. Simon wrote Norton on February 21st to say, "I have thought of you very many times during the day: of what this anniversary used to be to you, and what, alas, it now is. . . . I have felt that, in this fortnight, sickness could hardly fail to be on you."[64]

When Carlyle was again able to visit Norton after the long siege of illness was over, he found that the invalid had finished *Sartor*. "An' how have ye got on thro' these days? dark enough days for ye, I daresay. Well, I'm glad if anythin' o' mine has afforded ye occupation. Poor old Sartor! It's a book in which I take very little satisfaction; really a book worth very little as a work of art, a fragmentary, disjointed, vehement production." All this was true enough. But what Carlyle could not see was that Norton had experienced the book, not as a work of literary art, but as the voice of a friend. "I fancy there is more of him in 'Sartor Resartus' than in his other books," Charles told Lowell, "at least his talk reminds me more frequently of that than the others." All the aphorisms poured out by the prophetico-satiric Professor Teufelsdröckh character in *Sartor Resartus*—"Do the Duty which lies nearest thee," "Renounce Happiness," "Work while it is called To-day," "Your America is here or nowhere"—became newly meaningful when they were expressed or silently enacted by Carlyle in his own person. Arthur Clough, John Brown, Leslie Stephen, Goldwin Smith—Carlyle's lived testimony now joined those given by the other witness figures in Norton's life. For despite his scholarly instincts and love of books, the knowledge that mattered most to Norton was always ethical knowledge in an embodied form, moral truth as it was witnessed to by an actual life. Amidst the ontological weather of the limbo winter of 1872–73, then, it was not neo-stoicism as an abstract system that rescued Norton. It was the religion of courage as he glimpsed it in a seventy-seven-year-old peasant's son from Ecclefechan.[65]

"I shall carry home few better possessions for myself," Norton wrote Henry James from London, "than my affectionate memories of [Carlyle]." Once returned to America, Norton, living his secret life of memory, resorted to Carlyle frequently in thought. "In all these months when I have not written," he told the old man a year after his return to Shady Hill, "I have not failed to hold you in constant memory. You have often been my honoured companion in my solitary walks, and I have gained much from the memory of our last year's talk." For out of their time together had come not merely courage, comprehending sympathy and "the really human sort of dialogues we used to have together last winter," as Carlyle put it with characteristic pungency, but for Charles the solution to an otherwise insoluble problem.[66]

Norton's memory of his life in Italy with Susan, where he felt his own imagination and hers had been "developed and relieved from their half unconscious, but always pressing thirst," was more real to him than his ordinary outward existence. Since her death, this memory had become "the secret treasure of my life," as he told Henry James in December 1873, "feeding all its springs with their sweetest & most healthful waters." Nor was this the merely temporary emotion of a widower still treading the empty round of his first year of bereavement. For five years later, Norton would tell a friend that at times he feared losing his memory, only to find "at some unexpected instant, in some sudden gleam, there comes a vision of the past so perfect that for a moment the heart stops beating with fulness of delight—and then throbs back to bare life again." In truth, Norton had survived but would never recover from the blow that fell upon him in February 1872—"the sorrow that changed and changes my life," as he described it to Lowell, "and that time makes old without making less." Less than a year before he was to die, Charles would tell another friend, "In a little more than three months I shall have lived thirty-five solitary sad years, and I would gladly live them over again could I live over again any two or three conscious days of the ten years which preceeded." Then he crossed out the word "days," and wrote above it "minutes."[67]

Norton was never able to speak of his ten years of marriage in detail or at length. That past belonged to a private realm of transcendence that he had regarded as sacred when his wife was alive—a "sacred secret treasury of precious common memories & affections," as we have heard him say—and now that she was dead, must be held utterly inviolate. Yet to say nothing at all was to fail in gratitude for what he had been given. Compelled to silence, he was no less obliged to speak. This was the problem Carlyle helped him to solve. For what Norton came to see was that under the guise of Carlylean work, he might take up in relation to the outward world the project that had formed the transcendental core of his relation to Susan—of "striving to realize the ideal of our own nature" through art and imagination. Publicly he would be doing "the Duty that lies nearest thee" and "working while it is called To-day," but privately he would be honoring the memory of their life together, and drawing its "sweetest & most healthful waters" to feed his parched and stricken roots.

Here lies the secret of the change in Norton's relation to art which so took Henry James aback when he encountered it at this time. Visiting the Louvre with Norton in September 1872, the novelist found that Charles "takes art altogether too hard for me to follow him,—if not in his likings, at least in his dislikes," as he told his brother William. Put off by an attitude he characterized as "a high moral *je ne sais quoi* which passes quite above my head," and disguising his uneasiness as airiness, Henry continued, "I daily pray *not* to grow in discrimination, and to be suffered to aim at superficial pleasure." In recent years, this episode has become a symbolic anecdote among critics writing about the two men, most often cited as evidence that while James sought an "inclusive" mode of aesthetic discrimination, Norton conceived of the aesthetic "as serene contemplation, a view that functions as part of a larger cultural strategy implemented by a Victorian, Protestant leisure class." Viewed against the actual background of Norton's tormented bereavement, such a reading seems ludicrously deficient. But James was not mistaken in sensing that a change was taking place in Norton. Another perceptive, if more ingenuous young man who had seen Norton in Paris a few months earlier told Charles, "Instead of depressing you sorrow if possible elevated, ripened and sobered your mind."[68]

A truer measure of the change in Norton's disposition toward art may be found in the long visit he made to the British Museum on the last day of January 1873. There, "amid the fragments of Greek work," as he wrote in his diary, "I felt the loveliness of love, and the joyfulness of life, and how beautiful is beauty,—& how love and beauty outlast knowledge, and are the expression of completed wisdom." When his first biographers published selections from this diary, they would omit the words "the loveliness of love, and the joyfulness of life, and how beautiful is beauty." But these tautological phrases are crucial for grasping the enormous emotional investment now shaping Norton's regard for art. For at the very moment he was contemplating the riders from the Parthenon frieze in their imperishable poised strength, what remained of Susan's body was lying in an unmarked grave in the frozen Massachusetts ground. During his morning in the British Museum, Norton perceived in a moment of transcendent intuition that love and beauty outlasted knowledge, and that thus the worthiest hope of human immortality lay with them.[69]

Nor was this all. During his ten years of marriage Norton, as he believed, had known the best life could offer, most of all in Italy with Susan where in being "brought into sympathy with the artistic emotions of Florence [and] of Siena," they had "experienced the fullness of resource of the world." Part of the burden of his bereavement had become, he told Lowell, looking "forward to the unending second best." The lengthening wake of the steamer carrying him back to America was but a measure of "the material distance between me and the best part of my life." Once reestablished in Shady Hill, Norton sensed that still vaster tides were carrying him away from the best he had known. "Day by day," he wrote Henry James, then in Rome, "America drifts farther & farther away from Europe. The great currents of cosmic life drive us— immense, floating, unattached continent that we are—farther away from all that is rooted in or anchored to the past." Then he added a sentence that contains all that his "posthumous life" in America would become. "It would be a wretched and unworthy patriotism, or mere love of paradox, or an unmanly timidity and self-distrust, that would hinder one, who has known the best, from saying distinctly, 'This is not the best & will not in our time be the best.'" In later years, Norton's relentless insistence on "the best" would be consistently misunderstood in America—as the captious complaints of a inveterate caviler or as the ideological plaint of a member of a dispossessed Victorian leisure class. At its core, however, his unceasing defense of "the best" would remain as what it began: a way of witnessing in America to the loveliness of love he had found elsewhere. For after 1872, Norton would never return to the heart of Italy. His "America" would be in America. Or it would be nowhere.[70]

CHAPTER FIVE

The Darker Day

The America Charles Norton returned to was not the America he had left. Before taking ship for England in July 1868, Norton had exclaimed to George Curtis, "How well the country is doing!" By then, the Radical Republicans had succeeded in wresting control of Reconstruction away from President Andrew Johnson, whose detestation of the Southern plantation system had always centered in rancor against the planter aristocracy rather than in any sympathy for its ex-slaves. When the Senate Republicans' attempt to convict Johnson of impeachment failed by a single vote in May 1868, Norton was relieved, feeling that the bad precedent of a wholly political prosecution had thereby been avoided. Although the battles for black suffrage and against high tariffs and repayment of the U.S. war debt in inflated greenbacks remained to be won, he was convinced that these great questions were well on their way to being solved. "I should not be willing to leave this country now," he had told Meta Gaskell, "did it not seem to me that its immediate future promised well." Meeting in Chicago in mid-May, the Republican party had just named as its presidential candidate the silent, granite-faced man who had saved the Union. "With Grant for the next President," declared Norton, "we may look for quieter times."[1]

During the next five years the raucous cacophony from the Grant "barbeque" had reached Norton but faintly. He was living with his family in a Swiss farmhouse with three cows grazing on the roof when the first great indictment of the spreading national corruption—Charles Francis Adams, Jr.'s "A Chapter of Erie"—appeared in the pages of the *North American Review*. In less than two years, Adams told his readers, Jim Fisk and the other rapacious directors of the Erie Railway had effortlessly reduced the New York stock market, judiciary and legislature to utter nullities. "A very few years more," he warned, "and we shall see corporations as much exceeding the Erie and the New York Central in both ability and will for corruption as they will exceed those roads in wealth and in length of iron track." Steal but enough, noted James Lowell acidly, and "the world is unsevere, / Tweed is a statesman, Fisk a financier." Was it for this a terrible civil war had been fought? "Office a fund for ballot-brokers made / To pay the drudges of their gainful trade," as Lowell raged in another poem, this one addressed to George Curtis. "Our cities taught what conquered cities feel / By aediles chosen that they may safely steal." Was it for this, Lowell demanded, that our young martyrs poured out their high-hearted blood?[2]

With E. L. Godkin brilliantly editing the *Nation* and Curtis at *Harper's Weekly* eloquently urging civil service reform, Norton's friends had sought to keep him abreast of American politics while he was abroad. "[W]hat a disappointment Grant has been to us!" Norton had admitted to Longfellow. "Your account of the Administration at Washington & of public affairs generally was depressing enough," he had told Curtis. "I sometimes long to be in the thick of the fight with you." But the urgency of the American civic struggle lost its edge in the Italian sunshine. "[W]ith every friend I have in the pell-mell of the fight with the devil & his allies," Norton had written Meta Gaskell from Siena in 1870, "I am now only waiting for the opportunity to rush in at a fair moment for dealing a good blow, and getting out of breath like the rest." But first there were medieval archives to explore and lingering walks to be taken with Susan through the bright spring haze. In another letter from Siena, Norton had assured Curtis, "You will not, I comfort myself, be in less need of such help as I can give two years hence."[3]

⚶

Now, returned to America at the end of May 1873, Norton found everything changed. Amidst his own grief and depression, he saw "a greater change in sentiment among the men whom I met, from confidence to want of confidence in our principles on which our social & political order rest, than I was prepared to expect, or than seemed to me altogether justified by the lamentable experience of late years." Even so passionate a believer in the American prospect as Walt Whitman was now finding the democratic vistas bleak—"The great cities reek with respectable as much as non-respectable robbery and scoundrelism," Whitman charged, adding "money-making is our magician's serpent, remaining to-day sole master of the field." Wearied by scandals and Southern political intransigence, strained by inflation and continuing high taxes, the expansive Northern energies of 1865 were in retreat, rolling back in upon themselves as every sector of the postwar American polity contracted into the racially conservative, localist and laissez-faire attitudes characteristic of the pre-war years. As if to punctuate the change, the country plunged into a great financial panic in September, when Jay Cooke & Co. failed, the bank that led in underwriting the Civil War. When the initial panic stretched out into a prolonged recession of trade, people grew anxious. "We think it may safely be said," ventured a writer for the *Nation* in May 1874, "that there is more doubt about the future than there was after the last panic [of 1857], and greater hesitation." In fact, the economic depression that appeared to begin with the failure of a single New York bank would reach world-wide and last until the mid-1890s, imperceptibly darkening the outlook of all those who lived under its iron dominion.[4]

Confronting a changed country, Norton at the same time was compelled to face his own personal territory on the changed terms decreed by his wife's death. At home, every room and outdoor walk had to be encountered for the first time without her, both at Shady Hill and at "The Locusts," the rambling eighteenth-century farmhouse in Ashfield, Massachusetts which Norton had secured in 1864, hoping to improve his family's ill-health with the cool upland air of the Hoosac hills. Susan had quietly presided at both places, casting about them a glamor of simple elegance and warmth. "[H]ow sorely I shall miss," a young professor told her just before the Nortons left for Europe, "those pleasant evenings by your work-basket, & the whole pleasant circle in which for the first time in my life I got a taste of what is meant by home." In Ashfield, to discover her "plain little mountain dwelling with all the books and elegancies[,] pictures and comforts amid the simplicity of the woods and rural ways," declared another visitor, was like walking down a dusty road and suddenly finding "a bracelet of gold set with rubies."[5]

As Norton struggled to re-establish his family life in Cambridge, he found the daily mass of domestic concerns—his mother's failing health, his sisters' flagging spirits, his children's need of nurses, tutors, music lessons—invading his consciousness and driving out the memories he cherished most. Even the sameness of Shady Hill—its grounds more beautiful now after five years of growth—seemed to mock his own changed life. Looking down the long avenue leading from the house to the unpaved road known as Kirkland Street, "[w]e seem to be far in the country, for not another house is in sight, and the woods apparently extend far away," as Norton described it to an English friend. In fact, he continued, "we are on the edge of a busy town and surrounded by all that is suburban and ugly."[6]

Not least of all, coming home meant returning to the soaring rates of inflation and taxation brought by the war. The Nortons were returning to "the dearest"—meaning the most expensive—"place in America, and therefore in the known world," as their friend Fanny Kemble called Boston at this time—Kemble herself deciding she could not afford to live there. The wartime tax on incomes had been repealed in 1872, but the rising property taxes on the Shady Hill estate became so onerous that Norton steeled himself to take a step he dreaded: selling off some of its thirty-four acres. Before leaving for England, he had asked his friend Frederick Olmsted to design a plan that would unify the estate with the surrounding neighborhood and, by opening a public pleasure-ground, provide a buffer between the old mansion and the new houses to come. Olmsted's design, an elegant serpentine of shaded walks and sweeping greensward, would have taken away over a third of the land available for the new building plots. But both men, aware they shared what Olmsted called "a personal bias in favor of the largest assumptions of taste in the community," believed in such a park, convinced that its sylvan beauty would offset any financial disadvantages. But not yet, decided Norton. His six young children—the oldest only eleven—were discovering Shady Hill, "growing familiar," as Norton said, "with the trees and the fields that I used to belong to." He wanted to postpone the subdivision project at least until Lowell returned from abroad. Cambridge, he told the poet, then absent in Italy, "is not home to me without you." Harvard Yard had changed out of all recognition. And upon the old triangle-shaped student athletic ground called the Delta was rising a "big building that covers it"—Ware and Brunt's gargantuan Memorial Hall.[7]

To shield himself from all these estranging changes, Norton sought absorbing work. From early boyhood on, he had obeyed the imperatives of the Protestant work ethic even to the point of physical collapse. He knew his father's inaugural lecture as Dexter Professor had ringingly praised every man "who feels that he is directing all his efforts, that he is devoting the whole energy of his mind, that he is pouring himself out like water, to swell the tide, which is to bear his country on to happiness and glory!" Thomas Carlyle's celebrated "gospel of work" was simply the most vigorous renewal of a motive that had ruled North Britain and Yankee America for generations. But Norton realized that his own relationship to work had now been permanently altered. As he told friends repeatedly during this time, "the spring of voluntary work is broken," and only compulsory labor could replace it. When his cousin, Charles William Eliot, the new president of Harvard, proposed that he teach a course on the history of art and architecture, Norton seized the opportunity. He knew that without proper textbooks and only scanty visual aids to assist him, the burden of giving weekly formal lectures and supervising thrice-weekly recitations would be heavy. But, as he told Ruskin, "I am not sorry to be forced to work,—the inner motive has lost its spring & must be replaced by external pressure." This reiterated stress on the externality of his motives reveals Norton still consciously living on the terms he had found in Omar's *Rubáiyát*: as a flickering, in-substantial shadow projected by the revolving mechanism of a magic lantern.[8]

At the same time, Norton in beginning to teach art history at Harvard was inwardly moved by an impulse that was unconscious or at most half-conscious. Arising from "the secret treasure of my life"—the soul-sustaining memory of his life with Susan—the motive is only to be distinctly traced at the outset of his long career as a teacher. Soon enough, it would become submerged beneath the polished surface of his role as professor and cultural authority, and the celebrated sequence of courses he taught at Harvard—Fine Arts III and Fine Arts IV—in quickly achieving classic status in the curriculum, would efface its deeper origins. But in the winter of 1873–74, as Norton prepared himself to begin his compulsory career of hard work, the professorial mask was not yet fitted to his face. "I have some ardours left," he insisted in a letter to Ruskin, "—and no whit of faith in the good as good, and to be aimed at whether attainable or not, has vanished from my soul." He had taken a Harvard teaching post to "be brought into close relations with youths whom I can try to inspire with love of things that make life beautiful, & generous." Such language reveals Norton readying himself to open the incomparable casket of "the best" to his students, to lead them to see what he himself had glimpsed in the figures of the Parthenon frieze: "the loveliness of love, and the joyfulness of life, and how beautiful is beauty." It is hardly surprising that William Dean Howells, reacting to Norton's austere new exaltation before art much as Henry James had done the year before, should tell James that Charles "comes home with a dreadfully high standard for us all. We may attain it as blessed spirits a thousand years hence."[9]

As he prepared his college course for the fall of 1874, Norton was si-multaneously working on a more immediate project that foregrounded the underlying ambition of his Harvard ministry: a public exhibition of and lectures on J. M. W. Turner's art. From his very first *Atlantic* essay in 1857, Norton had been attempting to convince Americans of Turner's wide-ranging genius and marvelous "truth to nature." During the intervening years, however, Turner's art had become identified with his own deepest personal experiences: his turbulent friendship with Ruskin, his life abroad with Susan, the initially perilous but ultimately trusting relationship that had arisen between his wife and his friend, and his own devastation at her death. Turner's pictures had served as the medium of exchange in all their transactions of love and friendship, Ruskin sending Turner drawings to adorn the Nortons' rental house in Kent, Susan sealing her welcome of Ruskin into her own marital life by expressing her intense delight in his "treasure house of Turners" at Denmark Hill.

Charles Eliot Norton

After her death, Ruskin sent Charles "a slight but interesting & beautiful sketch by Turner" for his birthday in 1872, "which pleases me," as Norton recorded in his journal, "because Sue saw it, four years ago, & liked it." A few weeks later, after spending the evening with Ruskin at Oxford looking over the teaching collection of Turner drawings the critic had given to the university, Norton again confided to his journal, "It is pleasant to admire them more and more, and I find them more wonderful and more unparalleled than ever." Then, in a passage he would later delete, he wrote: "Some of them were so tenderly associated in my memory with the delight they gave four years ago!"[10]

Delivering his two Turner lectures in April 1874, Norton may be assumed to have given discourses that were "the exact opposite of what our people are accustomed to hear from lecturers and public speakers of any sort." But popularity, if it had ever been, was no longer Norton's aim. Instead, he meant to deliver "a protest against the prevalent taste and the prevalent modes of artistic study & discipline." He told his audience that so long as such transcendent art as Turner's remained comprehensible to the advance-guard of humanity, "it matters not if it remains incomprehensible to the mass of beholders." The leading few would prize Turner because he had with sterling fidelity faced hard truths, depicting the earth as it really was—as "the home of man, the scene of his labours and his love, the theatre of all his hopes, & all his disappointments across whose stage generation after generation pass with beating hearts, sorrow and joy accompanying them hand in hand, and black fate constantly compelling, pass in endless succession from outer darkness into outer darkness again." Here the picture of the triumphant progress of humanity upwards from darkness to enlightenment that Norton had trusted to in the 1850s has given way to a somberer image: the celebrated comparison of human life to a sparrow's flight from darkness through a brilliant banqueting hall and out to darkness again, an image first put forward by the Venerable Bede in the unprogressive darkness of the eighth century.[11]

Norton considered his Turner lectures and exhibition very successful, with the two lectures producing, as he told Curtis, "the effect I hoped for." In defending Turner's darker vision of moral reality, Norton was at the same time defending the man he himself had now become. He outlined Turner's stoic creed with personal urgency: "If the fate of man be dark & sorrowful, it may be met with dignity; if it be dull & laborious, it may be endured with patience; if the best work of man be transient, this is no reason why he should cease to labour; if death destroy happiness and takes all joy from the passing days, not even death can take away the memory of love." Norton repeatedly championed the painter's flinty moral realism against Wordsworth's "dogmatic cheerfulness." But in fact his real target lay much closer to home. For when Norton insisted that such teaching as Turner's "is hardly likely to find ready or general acceptance in any community where prosperity had created a temper of shallow and fatalistic optimism," he was aiming at Emerson's America.[12]

Norton had returned from England on the steamer *Olympus* with Emerson himself, spending two hours every night in conversation with the older man. In the diary he kept during their ten-day voyage, he reflected that Emerson's "inveterate and persistent" and "dogmatic" optimism, though "a bigotry," did no harm in a person. By contrast, in a people it could become "dangerous doctrine," degenerating "into fatalistic indifference to moral considerations, and to personal responsibilities." It lay at the root, Norton now realized, "of much of the irrational sentimentalism in our American politics, of much of our national disregard of honour in our public men, of much of our unwillingness to accept hard truths, and of much of the common tendency to disregard the distinctions between right and wrong, and to excuse guilt on the plea of good intentions or good nature." At the Civil War's end, he had briskly dismissed Emerson as the friend of America's youth, the outgrown adviser of an earlier stage of national life. Now, cast into his own secret crucible of sorrow, he saw that the poet, who had turned seventy on the penultimate day of the voyage, was younger than he himself at forty-five could ever be again. He perceived as well that Emerson's fatalistic creed—his bigotry of optimism—might ultimately prevail as a national mentality over all hard truths whatsoever. Norton's "Emersonian June" had ended in February 1872. America's Emersonian season had scarcely begun.[13]

※ ※

The focus of his outward life—as an art professor, as "Charles Eliot Norton"—was ever afterwards to be Harvard. The stunning news in 1869 that his first cousin, hitherto a struggling young chemist at MIT, had been named president of Harvard College continued to cheer Norton upon his return from Europe in 1873. In Charles William Eliot, Lowell told him, "We have a real Captain at last." Norton was convinced that now the College could serve as "a real rallying-point for us all"— "our 'carroccio,'" as he called it, referring to the famous crimson battle cart of medieval Florence, "bearing the banner of the commonwealth against all the tides of plutocracy, and all the tempests of borderism." For Charles Eliot, like Charles Norton, was a Millite liberal. The provincial college Eliot was transforming into a world university was to become a vehicle for Millite ideas—the revolutionary elective system Eliot introduced being little other than Millite "liberty" expressed in curricular form. In this context, any tie of Eliot consanguinity meant little to the President compared to Norton's mastery of his field and his approach to it. That approach was Millite.[14]

Just seven years before, Mill's inaugural address as Rector of St. Andrews University in 1867 had marked a watershed in university studies by claiming for aesthetic culture a position as the third great branch of human training, "barely inferior," as Mill said, to that of intellectual and moral education. To regard the fine arts as they were regarded on the Continent "as great social powers" and the art of a country "as a feature in its character and condition," Mill acknowledged, went directly against the Anglo-Saxon grain. Yet no mode of education was better able to counterbalance the grinding influences that had so deformed Anglo-American life: commercial money-getting and religious Puritanism. Thoughtful contemplation of aesthetic works of a high order opened to students a vista of nobler aims and possible human perfection, prompting in turn "a feeling of the miserable smallness of mere self in the face of this great universe, of the collective mass of our fellow creatures, in the face of past history and of the indefinite future—the poorness and insignificance of human life if it is to be all spent in making things comfortable for ourselves and our kin, and raising ourselves and them a step or two on the social ladder." Education in the fine arts revealed "a higher conception of what constitutes success in life," breeding a valuable discontent with "what we ourselves do and are."[15]

Norton would take Mill's Inaugural as the charter for his own teaching of the fine arts, the battle standard he would continually flourish in explicit terms both in lectures and in examinations given to his Harvard students. Its assumptions are threaded through the 1874 letter Norton wrote to President Eliot, outlining his views of the proposed lectureship or professorship in the fine arts. In later years, he would repeatedly invoke Mill's Inaugural in lectures and essays directed to the public at large. At the same time, Norton's undisguised adherence to Mill must be seen in dynamic tension with the other great influence on his fine arts teaching—Ruskin. Norton's loyalty to Mill had long been a source of irritation to Ruskin, who at first reacted jokingly to the provocation, translating Hamlet's soliloquy into "Norton-&-Millesque" ("The question which under these circumstances must present itself to the intelligent mind, is whether to exist or not to exist") and sending an issue of *Fors Clavigera*, his monthly workingmen's letter, inscribed "Charles Eliot Norton (In memory of J. S. M.) From J. R., 1st January 1871"—Mill did not die until 1873. But as Ruskin slipped more and more into the fog of mental imbalance and irrational rages, Norton's insistence that his friend had wilfully misunderstood Mill became, at least in Ruskin's view, a bar between them. "[I]t is because you do not yet see the essential difference between divine work like Plato's—and such earthy gas vapour as Mill, that your sadness and darkness bear you down in heart," Ruskin told the still grieving Norton. He angrily dismissed all that Norton was attempting to accomplish in fine arts teaching in America as nothing other than "trying to leaven sand and scent the whirlwind" or "the dilution of the hot lava, and fructification of the hot ashes, of American character."[16]

Pained as he was by Ruskin's increasingly erratic vehemence and bitter vituperation of Mill ("loathsome cretin"), Norton would forsake neither teacher. For he needed both. Ruskin's divinatory imagination, his power of entering into every aspect of a painting or cathedral, must be made available to Harvard students as the great model of what sympathetic insight could achieve in grasping the inner meaning of the outer world. Ruskin's insistence that art lectures should always be accompanied by manual practice in art so that students might "understand the nature and difficulty of executive skill" would inform the Harvard fine arts curriculum, with Norton arranging for Charles Moore, his Pre-Raphaelite painter friend from the stirring days of SATA, to be hired to teach studio art classes. Ruskin's central doctrine that "the art, or general productive and formative energy, of any country is an exact exponent of its ethical life" would become the vertebral theme of Norton's fine arts courses, as he led his students along the path of human development from the languid mental twilight of Egypt through the shining noontide of Periclean Greece to the eloquent dusk of Venice. The arts, Norton would tell his audiences, both at Harvard and beyond, offered the "most unimpeachable evidence," served as the most "incorruptible witnesses" to the spiritual conditions of a people, to its soul.[17]

Norton's Harvard lectures quickly became an institution within an institution, attracting ever larger classes of students and soon such ardent outside auditors as Isabella Stewart Gardner, whose exquisitely Italianate Fenway Court would later embody an aspect of Norton's civic-minded aesthetics. Mixing acerbic remarks about undergraduate life and current events with earnest appeals to the young men's idealism, Norton presented himself less as an expert after the new mode of "Germanized" specialist scholarship than as a gentleman speaking to other, younger gentlemen about topics of urgent common concern: the human struggle for expression, the fate of republics, the mystery of supreme artistic genius. Norton spoke forcefully about the fine arts to hundreds of undergraduates at a time, "with great strokes of natural power," as one student remembered, "often with tears in his eyes, sometimes with sarcasm, sometimes dogmatically, but always successfully." In the years following 1875, however, art was no longer what art had been twenty years before. For the conditions that had roused in Norton's generation a keen new conviction of the need for art and imagination—industrial blight, social conflict, postwar barbarism, religious doubt, soulless materialism, plutocratic vulgarity—had in the course of their persistence provoked among younger artists and writers a response that represented at once a development of and a departure from the earlier reform of art carried out by Ruskin and the Pre-Raphaelites. This was Aestheticism.[18]

Liberal and utopian in its origins, English Aestheticism had begun in the later 1860s by seeking to treat life in the spirit of art, proposing that men and women enter into the superb intensity of artworks, and bear towards the world and their fellows the receptivity and imaginative sympathy of the great artists. In the famous words of the Aestheticist bible, Walter Pater's *Studies in the History of the Renaissance*, "To burn always with this hard, gem-like flame, to maintain this ecstasy, is success in life." Here, it seemed to many on both sides of the Atlantic, was a wholly unanticipated fulfillment of Mill's call for "a higher conception of what constitutes success in life." Accelerated by the rapid spread of education and disposable income among the middle classes seeking to express themselves "artistically," however, the Aestheticist gospel of art soon enough became vulgarized to the point of parody. George Du Maurier's drawings in *Punch*, Gilbert and Sullivan's comic opera *Patience*, F. C. Burnand's burlesque *The Colonel*, W. H. Mallock's *The New Republic*—all the incisive satires of Aestheticism date from the later 1870s and earlier 1880s.[19]

In response, certain leading partisans of the Aesthetic Movement mobilized doctrines from the parallel *l'art pour l'art* movement in France to thwart and harry their enemies. Whether expressed with crackling invective or negligent disdain, such men as Algernon Swinburne, James A. M. Whistler and Oscar Wilde insisted upon the unbridgeable enmity between art and nature, the complete divorce of art and morality and the absolute superiority of the artist over all other men. Whistler, for example, reduced to bankruptcy and seething resentment after his victorious but financially ruinous libel suit against Ruskin—(Ruskin had denounced the artist for the "Cockney impudence" of charging 100 guineas for "flinging a pot of paint in the public's face")—took out his revenge against all art critics, art professors and artistic middlemen in "The Ten O'Clock Lecture" of 1885. Art, the painter informed his audience, his monocle glittering in the gaslight, is "selfishly occupied with her own perfection only." Having no desire whatever to teach, "Art seeks the Artist alone," not the multitude or the million. Entirely false, Whistler declared, was Ruskin's asserted link between the state of art and the fate of the nation producing it, because "in no way do our virtues minister to its worth, in no way do our vices impede its triumph!"[20]

To understand the distinctive contours of Norton's Harvard career as Professor of Art is thus to see him teaching in a moment charged with cultural contradiction. He was a moral tutor who insisted on empirical evidence and scientific induction. He was a self-declared agnostic who believed in salvation by aesthetic grace. He was a republican aesthete. When Norton addressed his lecture room, students recognized in him "the American Ruskin," the defender of artistic "truth to nature" and the champion of art's incorruptible witness to a nation's ethical life. Yet they also saw the friend of Rossetti and Morris and Burne-Jones. Even more perplexingly, they heard Professor Norton express opinions that seemed very close to those of outright aesthetes like Whistler and Wilde. "Nature is imperfect," Norton told his students. "Hardly anywhere, not even in Italy, is there a scene which is thoroughly accommodating to the eye. The composition of the landscape is defective." ("Nature is very rarely right," Whistler had declared in his "Ten O'Clock," "to such an extent even, that it might almost be said that Nature is usually wrong." Nature, as one of Wilde's fictional spokesmen objects, is not merely "uncomfortable" and "indifferent," but "repetitive," "imitative" and hopelessly "behind the times.")[21]

Oscar Wilde's remarks are particularly salient because Norton felt himself to be inconveniently close at several points to the absurd young aesthete. When Wilde arrived in America in January 1882 for the lecture tour meant to advertise himself and a D'Oyly Carte production of *Patience*, he carried with him more than an "Aesthetic" regalia of plum-colored knee-breeches and low buckled shoes. He brought a letter of introduction from Ned Burne-Jones. "My very very dear Norton," the painter had written, "The gentleman who brings this little note to you is my friend Mr. Oscar Wilde . . . and any kindness shewn to him is shewn to me—and if some things in America should make him feel a bit that he has left home I know no antidote like your dear society—for he really loves the men & things you and I love." Such an appeal could not be disregarded, especially when Burne-Jones followed up with another letter two weeks later, promising Norton that beneath all Wilde's persiflage and pretension could be found "a quite genuine love & understanding of beauty." A earlier commitment to lecture at Princeton spared Norton from having to meet Wilde during his January visit to Boston. By June, however, the two men had dined together at Shady Hill, "among your beautiful trees," as Wilde said, adding characteristically, "How rich you are to have a Rossetti and a chestnut tree."[22]

By this time, the peripatetic aesthete's flamboyant progress through America had provoked reams of scurrilous newspaper abuse. But Norton's reluctance to meet him had less to do with the controversy swirling around him than with a queasy sense that Wilde was compromising the cause of beauty, imagination and culture he himself bore so closely at heart. The day before Wilde was to lecture in Boston, Norton wrote a former student, George Woodberry, then teaching at the University of Nebraska. A few days earlier, Woodberry had heard Wilde lecture in Lincoln, a windswept town of 15,000 that had added another horror to the American prairie by going "dry." "I do not want to see him," Norton told Woodberry, "for he cannot understand me, he can but receive a false impression of one whose moral nature is so different from his own, and yet has so many points of sympathy with the principles he professes and which he discredits." Then, struggling to distance himself still further from Wilde, Norton crossed out "points of sympathy with" and wrote "convictions similar to."[23]

Such distinctions were vital, if a generation of young men and women were not to be entranced and misled. Already, young Woodberry had been captivated by Wilde, spending hours with the aesthete before and after his lecture. Himself a rising poet thirsting amid the cultural desolation of Nebraska, Woodberry told Norton that Wilde "wants you to like him." "[A]nd I think you will," the young man went on hopefully, not least of all because "I have seen no one whose charm stole on me so secretly, so rapidly, and with such entire sweetness." Woodberry was similarly enchanted by Walter Pater's writings. He believed that in *Marius the Epicurean* of 1885—a stylized meditation on human consciousness disguised as an historical novel about Antonine Rome—what might at first glance seem like merely an "evangel of aestheticism" was in fact an evangelism of ideal—even religious—living.[24]

You overrate Pater, Norton told Woodberry. "[Y]ou have credited him with conceptions more deep & delicate than his own, and supplied by your imagination what is lacking in sincerity and definiteness in his work." But marooned on the Great Plains, Woodberry was scarcely alone in his response. Another Harvard student would remember Pater's cult of exquisite sensations as revealing the exaltation of an ideal world. For Pater's writings, as another reader stressed, ""have a special meaning to modern young men of an uncommercial turn." Even the sensibly socialist William Dean Howells found Pater's essays "written with so much toleration and decency that he might seem to be treating of anything but matters of art, which inflame controversy as nothing else but matters of religion can"—Pater's manner thus refreshingly "as unlike Ruskin's as possible." "No conception of art," a Dartmouth College student concluded triumphantly, "ever gained such a rapid and complete ascendancy over all classes as has 'Aestheticism.'"[25]

Faced with "art for art's sake," Norton declared that such a conception of art was not merely a travesty but an impossibility: "*Art cannot, if it would, divorce itself from morals.*" But neither, he insisted, was the ethical dimension of art to be located in invidious sermonizing or some tidy moral "message." Instead, it was a pervading disposition, an unconscious atmosphere. For "[i]nto every expression of man, into every work of art," he told his audiences, "whether the artist intend it or not, enters a moral element" because "[t]he beauty to which the artist strives to give form in his work takes her shape from his own spirit." It was a distinction many of his students would persist in misunderstanding, much as they misunderstood the man who made it. For Norton seemed to them, if not an aesthete, then as close to one as chilly Boston could produce. "The feelings I have had in hearing you speak," declared the aesthetic young man who would later be known as Bernard Berenson, "are like those that come to me when a dear friend speaks to me of the things that are nearest and dearest to both of us."[26]

What else but an Aestheticist "gospel of beauty," his students wondered, could have drawn forth Professor Norton's "power to make you feel by the contagion of example that beauty was the supreme value in life"? Why else would he say "We are corrupted by ugliness"? Barrett Wendell circulated a characteristic story about Norton's adamant insistence on the importance of taste:

> In a lecture about some aspects of the fine arts of Greece, he uttered devastating comments on the contrast between Greek articles of personal adornment and the machine-made scarf-pins, or watch-chains with dangling appendages, then observable in any company of American youth. A classmate of mine subsequently reproached him, in private, for lack of sentiment. The boy possessed some golden ornament, in the form of a horseshoe, affectionately given him by his mother; he was proud to wear it, he said, for her sake. Norton's reply, I believe, was gentle but final: an object of piety, he pointed out, is not consequently a thing of beauty. My friend's ardor of resentment took some time to cool.

So, what except an aesthete's fastidiousness could explain Norton's repeated complaints about Harvard architecture? From Ware and Brunt's Memorial Hall to Charles McKim's brick and iron fence around the Yard to Richard Morris Hunt's Fogg Art Museum, a true benefactor of Harvard, Norton declared, would pull down every building erected in the last fifty years. Who but an aesthetic mandarin or self-appointed *arbiter elegantiarum* would express such caustic disdain for American crudity and "semi-civilization"—what one of Norton's many mimics plaintively deplored as "the hor-ri-ble vul-gar-ity of EVERYTHING"? That old Norton—with his keen face and hooded eyes, swallowed up by his own overcoat as he walked bent but resolute through Harvard Yard—should himself look so obviously unaesthetic made the case even more puzzling.[27]

Read against a late-Victorian cultural background deeply colored by

Schopenhauer's philosophy, Swinburne's poetry and post-Darwinian theories of decadence, Norton's weary pessimism and frank professions of religious unbelief seemed to many of his listeners to express an identical fin de siècle attitude. "The dear old man looks so mildly happy and benignant while he regrets everything in the age and the country," a Radcliffe student recorded in her diary, "—so contented, while he gently tells us it were better for us had we never been born in this degenerate and unlovely age—that I remain fixed between wrath and unwilling affection." A Harvard student, after listening to Norton expound his religious views at Shady Hill one Christmas Eve, asked his host if Ruskin shared the same "pagan consciousness." It was a painful moment. "You think I am a *pagan?*" Norton demanded. Taken aback, the student apologized, explaining the positive connotation the word "pagan" possessed for his generation, reared as they were on Omar Khayyám. In fact, the plangent Epicureanism of the *Rubáiyát* had become one of the keynotes of the American 1890s—to be heard in the little poem written by another Harvard student beginning "Brother, Time is a thing how slight! / Day lifts and falls, and it is night" and ending, "Seize, then, what mellow sun we may, / To light us in the darker day." But of course it was Norton himself who had opened the words of the *Rubáiyát* to Americans some thirty years before.[28]

Disdaining to explain himself, too weary to unbend, Norton frequently seemed to audiences and observers alike to be haughty or contemptuous. With the brutal candor of his mania, Ruskin told Norton that it was all the fault of "your stuck-upness and too fineness." Unpleasant stories about Norton began to circulate—people whispering that his demands for sympathy and service had drained his sister Grace and his two Sedgwick sisters-in-law of all their vitality, that he maintained a cruelly open and outspoken preference for Sally, the beauty among his three daughters. Even those younger friends who admired and were grateful to Norton grew at times impatient under the weight of his dogmatism and disillusionment. Edith Wharton would recall with exasperation Norton's alarmed response to news she was writing another society novel like *The House of Mirth*—Norton "imploring me to remember that 'no great work of the imagination has ever been based on illicit passion'!" But Wharton prized Jean Racine's tragedy of sexual obsession and incest, *Phèdre*, as a milestone in her own artistic experience. A Harvard undergraduate from the Midwest, invited to a small musical party at Shady Hill, was asked by his host, "Do you enjoy Bach?" "I know nothing of music," the young man replied, "but I am glad to listen to it." "That is right," Norton responded. "That is the way culture comes." Thirty years afterward, the remark still rankled—"I was infuriated," the grown man declared.[29]

Here, then, lie the origins of the now-standard version of Norton as a priggish, embittered aesthete, a notion that has served as one of the received ideas about the American Gilded Age to the present day. It is a view given classic expression in Van Wyck Brooks's hostile portrayal of Norton reading Dante aloud to students at Shady Hill "like a learned, elegant and venerable priest dispensing sacred mysteries to a circle of heretics, perhaps, who were unworthy of them." Even those keener-eyed observers of Norton at this time, who perceived he was in no common sense an aesthete, concluded that he must instead represent some species of aesthetic pretender or evolutionary hybrid, thrown up during the transition between a paleolithic pre-aesthetic era and the new age of artistic modernity in which art was freed to become entirely self-referential. "A man born blind," as his former student John Jay Chapman was to describe Norton in June 1898, "[preaching] the religion of pictures, a deaf man worshipping music, a man devoid of sensuous experience erecting altars to the Aesthetic." Henry James decided that Norton's life offered a case study of "how race and implanted quality and association always in the end come by their own." Writing just after the older man's death in 1908, James then proceeded to seize with a feline grace upon the contradiction which seemingly lay at Norton's heart, professing to wonder how:

> a son of the Puritans the most intellectually transmuted, the most liberally emancipated and initiated possible, could still plead most for substance, when proposing to plead for style, could still try to lose himself in the labyrinth of delight while keeping tight hold of the clue of duty, tangled even a little in his feet; could still address himself all consistently to the moral conscience while speaking as by his office for our imagination and our free curiosity."

As soon as the Norton essay appeared, William James wrote to congratulate his brother on his "tiptoe malices." The "way in which you subtly killed him was inimitable," William crowed. "But only the few will understand the neatness."[30]

At the outset of his teaching career, Norton had imagined that Harvard might serve as "our carroccio," the communal vehicle around which defenders of the republic would rally against the menacing forces of plutocracy. The learnedness of his reference to the Florentine battle cart obscures its militant character—and his own. For Norton, even with his quick sympathies and graceful manner—"such graces of mind and heart as I have known in no other," as Howells would later say—possessed a bulldog tenacity within his stooped and sickly frame. Despite his private sorrow, he entered the public sphere with a civic commitment surpassing anything most modern "public intellectuals" can show. For all his cautious invalidism, the Harvard Professor of Fine Arts poured himself out like water, to swell a slack tide that was about to turn against him. As one of his younger friends recognized, Norton was teaching art to the general public through the unlikely medium of college boys. Unfolding the grandeur and pathos of human achievement, pointing to the fate of past republics as revealed through their visual arts, urging a "noble discontent" with every ignoble aspect of the present, insisting upon a democracy "liberal enough to include genius," Norton was a militant but clear-eyed idealist of a type that would become all but incomprehensible after 1914. That most of the American public and many of the college boys of his own day mistook him for a caviling aesthete was simply the first of the bitterly ironic reversals to come.[31]

⚜ ⚜ ⚜

The modern reputation of Charles Eliot Norton as a carping, hypocritical, neurasthenic elitist would be determined largely by what he wrote and said as an old man. From 1895 to 1902, from the age of 68 to 75, Norton expressed himself in such a way as to suggest both to his contemporary critics and their twentieth- and twenty-first-century inheritors that none of the earlier Nortons we have seen—not the earnest young reformer of the 1850s or the skillful publicist for American democracy of the 1860s or the tender husband and father of the earlier 1870s—had ever existed. Again and again, Norton's critics would seize upon such discourses as "Some Aspects of Civilization in America" of 1896 or "True Patriotism" of 1898 or his 1896 commencement address at Bryn Mawr or (after their publication in 1913) his letters from these years, for evidentiary proof of his dislike or contempt or betrayal of America. It is not accidental that John Jay Chapman gave his sneering description of what he considered Norton's hypocritical incapacity—"a man born blind with the religion of pictures," as we have heard Chapman say, "a man devoid of sensuous experience erecting altars to the Aesthetic"—in June 1898. For the year 1898, like the years of 1895–96, would become a crystallizing moment in Norton's civic career. It would be at these two junctures that he emerged as the seemingly self-deluded Don Quixote of the genteel tradition, the impotently patrician "man without a country" that has since passed as his posthumous reputation.

1898 marked the outbreak of the Spanish-American War. 1895–96 saw the eruption of a less well-known emergency: the Venezuelan crisis which for a few precarious months in President Grover Cleveland's second administration threatened war between the United States and Great Britain. The volcanic impact of these two moments upon Norton's civic consciousness marked the end of his long journey as a reformer and

The Darker Day   143

liberal. In the 1880s, Norton's trust in the shaping influence of a certain quantum of highly cultivated people, J. S. Mill's "best men," to guide national life wisely in America remained unshaken. But his supreme confidence in the steady approach of an ideal community—a "moral commonwealth" as he called it—the faith he shared with so many others in 1865, had dimmed and diminished. The Franco-Prussian War of 1870–71 had suggested to him that "England & America, no less than the rest of Europe" might first have to "pass through a fiery furnace, to come out purified into the likeness of a true commonwealth." Later, the fierce opposition mounted by New York tavern-owners and proprietors of souvenir shacks to the campaign to preserve Niagara Falls from commercial spoilation had given him pause. "The growth of wealth and of the selfish individualism which accompanies it (and corrupts many who are not rich)," Norton told one of the organizers of the Niagara campaign, "seems to weaken all properly social motives and efforts." Instead, he continued, "Men in cities and towns feel much less relation with their neighbours than of old; there is less civic patriotism; less sense of a spiritual and moral community."[32]

By the 1880s, Norton seems quite consciously to have sought the moral commonwealth "elsewhere." His greatest effort to preserve his postwar faith in America as "the first nation which deserves the name of commonwealth" involved displacing it onto smaller structures than the existing republic. Here lies the real significance of his 1880 book *Church-Building in the Middle Ages*, where he repeatedly focuses upon those moments in medieval and early Renaissance history when the European peoples first felt themselves coalescing within "a vast and real, however vague, moral commonwealth" or later, when artist and audience found themselves united in mutual bonds of expressivity and sympathy in a reciprocity of intelligent criticism. This is why, for example, Norton so prized Giorgio Vasari's story of the sculptor Donatello in Florence. Flattered and prosperous while working in Padua, Donatello had nonetheless decided to return to his native city. Only in Florence, amidst its spirited and opinionated citizens, the sculptor declared, could he be "sure of blame, which would make him work and acquire glory." In 1859, the little republics of medieval Italy had seemed to Norton to exist upon the same plane of historical actuality as Rhode Island and Delaware, offering Americans a not-impossible model of how their own states might conduct their sociocultural life for the future. By 1880, this dynamic relation of the medieval past to the American present had lost meaning for him. He had now come to regard that past as a detached repository of accomplished facts, passively conserving republican possibilities against a brighter day.[33]

This displacement of Norton's hopes for true commonwealth in

Charles Eliot Norton

America onto a smaller domain is to be glimpsed as well in his relation to the little hill town of Ashfield, the site of his summer home. He had invested himself deeply in Ashfield, in a material sense, by buying more land and encouraging his friends Curtis, Lowell and John W. Field to acquire properties near his own. More significant, however, was Norton's psychic investment in the little town. For like the Siena of sacred memory, he found that to live in Ashfield was to live "where nobody is suffering want, where everyone has selfrespect, where there are no great differences of condition." Norton poured himself out in civic and charitable activities for the village—raising money for a library, reviving the common school, known as Sanderson Academy, with the economic resources provided by annual fund-raising dinners held every August. Begun in 1879, with the genial and charismatic Curtis presiding in the chair, these "Academy Dinners" quickly became famous both for the hearty abundance of their farmhouse cooking and the distinction of their invited speakers—notable men and women discussing significant national issues without resort to buncombe or blarney.[34]

Today, one suspects, there would be a tendency to view Norton's Ashfield projects as "Federalist nostalgia" or the civic slumming of a summer tourist. The townspeople themselves, however, were ready enough to regard Norton as a friend and fellow citizen. If a town meeting was to be held, they remarked that he and Curtis "were pretty sure to be there, not for the purpose of influencing or criticising the proceedings, but to observe the ways of doing business, to see the citizens in a mass, and also probably to get a little recreation from it." At the same time, the Ashfielders got a little recreation from their professor. When Norton expressed his strong disapproval at a farmers' club meeting of the new barbed wire fences, declaring he had much more respect for the beautiful vine-covered stone walls left over from colonial times, one grizzled farmer observed, that might well be so, but the cows had much more respect for the barbed wire. In the end, Norton and Curtis, first drawn to Ashfield by its salubrious air and deep quiet, came to care most for the opportunity the town offered them, as one woman put it, "to win the good will of their friends and neighbors, and to work with them as fellow-citizens and fellow-residents." But the rancorous tumult of the larger polity would penetrate even here.[35]

When Curtis died in August 1892—exactly a year after Lowell—no Academy Dinner was held that August. By the time Norton came to speak of Curtis at the dedication of a commemorative plaque to his friend in the Ashfield town hall, it was August 1896, and the world looked very different. For by then the country had passed through the Venezuela crisis. A minor quarrel between Venezuela and Great Britain over a disputed border (British Guiana's) and unpaid debts (Venezuela's) had, incredibly, escalated to the brink of war between the United States and Britain. Pressed by Democratic politicians impatient to overcome the Republican electoral advantage with "a little Jingo" and by newspaper editors eager for exciting conflicts, President Cleveland had sent an aggressively anti-British message to Congress in December 1895. "[It] fell like a thunderbolt out of a clear sky," Norton told Leslie Stephen, "shatter[ing] with its stroke his reputation with all serious and right-thinking men." For Cleveland, though a Democrat, had been a hero to Mugwump and independent voters in 1884 when he first gained the Presidency, his firmness and integrity prompting them to shift their electoral support away from the regular Republican candidate, the sonorously corrupt James G. Blaine. No one had thought then, as Norton said, "that Cleveland himself would fail, so long as he was in office, to resist the popular disposition toward war."[36]

Now, despite his own desire for peace, Cleveland had yielded to the Anglophobic fury of Irish immigrants and "patriotic American" demands for war ("I don't care whether our sea coast cities are bombarded or not," stormed Theodore Roosevelt, "we would take Canada"). Shocked by their onrushing peril, a large portion of the British public as well as influential segments of American public opinion—especially in New York and Boston—demanded a peaceful solution to the dispute. After secret negotiations, this was eventually achieved through international arbitration—the second such resolution of its kind. But the episode left a bitter aftertaste. "I am more indignant than I can say at the action of the Harvard people," Roosevelt told Henry Cabot Lodge. "Our peace at any price men," as Roosevelt said, meaning such figures as President Eliot, William James and Moorfield Storey, have "convinced me that this country needs a war."[37]

Norton was one of the men Roosevelt meant. The Venezuela crisis left him feeling him as if Cleveland and his assertive secretary of state, Richard Olney, had deliberately roused belligerent passions and delusions among the mass of Americans that could not easily be quelled again. He became convinced that "[t]he best gains of a hundred years have been flung away at a single cast," a belief William James shared with him. Once truly awakened, the war-lust could not be escaped from, James told an English friend. "This your European governments know; but we in our bottomless innocence and ignorance over here know nothing, and Cleveland, in my opinion, by his explicit allusion to war has committed the biggest political crime I have ever seen here." This signal failure in the moral imagination of the nation's leading men—not least of all in Lodge, Roosevelt, and William Randolph Hearst, Harvard '71, '80, and '86 respectively—outraged and alarmed Norton. If such men failed—privileged "political swaggerers" striking at civilization itself by disparaging peace and good will between nations—how could anyone expect that less advantaged voters in the seething cities or the unbridled West would resist the intoxifications of war and conquest? In the West, he knew, they lynched suspected horse thieves within a half hour of bringing them into town, and "they did it laughingly." In a few years more, Norton would hear President Roosevelt declare in his hearty, boyish way that the only trouble with the war against Spain was "there was not enough of it to go around."[38]

This was no unreal peril, no figment of a desponding pessimism, Norton told readers of *The Forum* in February 1896. It was instead "a peril indefinitely enhanced by the optimistic indifference of the people at large, and their childish conceptions concerning the greatness and power of the United States as compared with other nations." Thirty years had passed since the end of the Civil War. A new generation had grown up, with no memory of its horrors, much less any direct experience of organized bloodshed. A large portion of the nation now lived geographically and intellectually remote from any real knowledge of other countries or cultures, dozing in an Emersonian optimism. In just two years more, the satiric sage of Chicago, Mr. Dooley, would have occasion to say that the American people did not know whether the Philippines were islands or canned goods. "Vaguely and uneasily," one of Cleveland's own friends noted soberly, "that part of the beast in man appears to be rousing in our country." "Some chance spark," warned Norton, "may fire the prairie."[39]

The full depth of Norton's civic alarm may be measured by his remarks to the Bryn Mawr graduating class that June. For the man who in 1867 had joined George Curtis in the campaign for women's suffrage in New York State now told the young women seated before him that he could no longer support such a measure. The evils of universal male suffrage had been unmasked by the howling popular demand for war during the Venezuelan crisis. America had become a nation of venal, unprincipled and trivial-minded voters, insistent upon aggressive action in the Caribbean even when they were unclear as to where exactly the Caribbean might be, blind to the expense of blood in attacking the world's greatest naval power, indifferent to the cost in honor in assaulting the nation above all others bound to America through its language, literature, history, politics and law. Such evils would only "be increased by extending the suffrage to women, and no compensating good be acquired." For as Norton had taught his Harvard students, wars were "the result of lack of imagination." In this time of national disgrace, women, endowed with sympathetic powers far beyond the other sex, must—especially now—hold fast to their more important role as active custodians and exemplars of the moral imagination.[40]

Their effort, joined with that of honest men, would continue what Norton, Curtis and the other transatlantic liberals had called "the good fight"—the ongoing battle of civilization against barbarism. In waging such a struggle, the truest partisans, as Norton said at the end of his *Forum* essay, "are enlisted for the war." He was using a phrase from thirty years before, from the Civil War, when young men enacted their full-hearted commitment to the Union cause by enlisting in its army, not for three months or a year, but for the duration of the conflict as long as it might take—"for the war." Slight as it is, the allusion signals the high civic stakes involved for Norton in the Venezuelan crisis. "A light across the sea, / Which haunts the soul and will not let it be, / Still beaconing from the height of undegenerate years," the memory of their great war—its fearful sacrifices, its final victory, its triumphant vindication of democracy—was ever present to him after 1895, as the last years of the nineteenth century in America slid with headlong rapidity from mere threatenings of war to war itself. For even as the Venezuela crisis was roiling the American homefront, resistance to Spain's colonial rule by Cuban revolutionaries was reviving hopes among partisans of American expansion that their cherished "large policy" might finally be fulfilled. "Free Cuba," Henry Cabot Lodge promised his Senate colleagues in December 1896, "would mean a great market to the United States; it would mean an opportunity for American capital."[41]

⚜ ⚜ ⚜ ⚜

The Spanish-American War that was to gain for Teddy Roosevelt national renown would gain Norton national infamy. In June 1898, as Roosevelt and 200,000 other volunteers desperately schemed to embark for Cuba (only a third of them would ever actually leave the States), an avalanche of abuse—including threats of physical violence—fell upon the seventy-year-old professor's head for urging his Harvard students to reject President William McKinley's call to arms. Sixty years earlier, Emerson had warned that "Whatever outrages have happened to men, may befall a man again, and very easily in a republic." Emerson made the remark in his lecture on "Heroism." He was speaking of Elijah Lovejoy, the abolitionist printer who had been killed by an Illinois mob intent on smashing his printing press. Tar and feathers, slander, fire, the noose—the specific means of rectifying a man's opinion in America might change but the popular impulse to do it would always remain, returning, said Emerson, "whenever it may please the next newspaper, and sufficient a number of his neighbors to pronounce his opinions incendiary." So it proved in Norton's case. "We of America believe that our country loves freedom of thought and of speech," he told a younger friend as the avalanche of abuse still rattled around him, "yet is it not

148   *Charles Eliot Norton*

true that no force was ever more pitiless to either than the public opinion of our democracy?"[42]

A contemporary journalist has left a description of the scene that became the occasion for Norton's national pillorying. "Imagine, if you can," he wrote,

> a great, bare lecture-room, filled, every inch of it, with eager undergraduates, all looking in one direction. On the slightly raised platform sits Professor Norton, stooping badly over the desk, his spare figure clothed in elegant black, and an atmosphere of scrupulous care pervading his person. His sonorous tones, unaccompanied by any gesture, would seem hardly to carry beyond the platform; yet that student in the far corner by the door catches every word.

Addressing the four hundred students in his fine arts class immediately after their return from spring vacation on April 26, 1898, Norton told the young men that their genuine patriotic duty lay—not in waging the "criminal" war against Spain declared by Congress just the day before—but in improving the lives of the less fortunate people around them. He called upon the young men to disregard the President's appeal for volunteers, explicitly urging them not to enlist. He termed the war "criminal" because he was aware that on the eve of his message to Congress McKinley had brushed aside a final Spanish offer which might have secured the peace. "Who is Professor Charles Eliot Norton," a newspaper demanded the day after he spoke, "that he should declare, from his seat in the lecture room of his 'fine arts' class, that those Harvard men who enlist in the service of their country are not to be credited with patriotism? Is this the kind of 'fine arts' that he is engaged to teach the students at Harvard?"[43]

In our own day of narrowly focused professorial expertise, undergraduate vocationalism and "customer-oriented" universities, such questions perhaps seem reasonable enough. But Norton was speaking from quite another tradition—the republican humanism of J. S. Mill's Inaugural Address, which held that arts education, by revealing the ideal perfection that artists eternally aimed at without ever wholly attaining, could develop in its students a healthy dissatisfaction with every work they did, and most of all, with their own characters and lives. In its widest scope, this was civic education. Such study, as Norton had told his students in his very first year of teaching, "leads to refinement without selfishness, to sensitiveness not sensuality, to delicacy but not effeminacy, to sound & active critical judgment, but not to petulant & feeble fastidiousness." He was modeling his remarks on one of the sacred texts of nineteenth-century civic liberalism—the Funeral Oration of Pericles.

Now, measured against the ideal standards of art to be found in Fine Arts III and IV—against Phidias, Polygnotus and the Parthenon—an ignoble war for coaling stations and expanded commerce in the Caribbean hastily glossed with an hysterical humanitarianism could only appear as a profound betrayal of the American ideals that had been rebaptized with blood in the Civil War. And Norton said so.[44]

In ordinary times, Norton's remarks might have reverberated in the lecture hall and then died away without an echo. But these were not ordinary times. A student correspondent, a "stringer," was present in the crowded hall. The next day, the *Philadelphia Public Ledger* was on the story, printing an editorial that damned Norton's "Fine Arts Toryism." How incredible, the paper fumed, that "this great republic having entered upon an absolutely unselfish war in the cause of humanity and human freedom, the distinguished professor of fine arts at Harvard College fails to grasp the high moral spirit of the struggle." The story of Harvard's traitorously "Tory" professor then rocketed around the country, sped by an off-the-record conversation with a newspaperman in early May that Norton unwisely believed the reporter would not quote. When he attempted to clarify his position in a public lecture on "True Patriotism" in early June, the national outcry against him redoubled. When the Polonius of the Republican party, Senator George Frisbie Hoar of Massachusetts, denounced Norton by name from the podium of Clark University in mid-July, the piquant scandal of two septuagenarians, Harvard classmates and old friends, furiously battling each other in the press assured that the tidal wave of anti-Norton invective would continue to swell. Swept up in the passions of the moment, Edward Everett Hale, another old acquaintance, reissued his celebrated Civil War story, prefacing it with a stern warning: "The man who, by his sneers, or by looking backward, or by revealing his country's secrets to her enemy, delays for one hour peace between Spain and this nation is to all intents and purposes 'A Man Without a Country.'" Everyone agreed that Hale was referring to Norton.[45]

"The bitterest disappointment in regard to America," Norton told a correspondent that August, "which I have had to bear in a life of more than seventy years is to find the conscience of the people so dead to the crime of war, and their imagination so dull to its brutalizing horrors." He had been prepared for the rabid newspaper sensationalism at the sinking of the *Maine* in February. He had been unsurprised by the conscienceless advocacy of war put forward by Lodge and Roosevelt—for Lodge's icy and ill-founded assertion (after Commodore Dewey's victory over the Spanish fleet in Manila Bay on May 1) that "all Europe is seizing on China, and if we do not establish ourselves in the East that vast trade, from which we must draw our future prosperity, and that great

Charles Eliot Norton

region in which alone we can hope to find the new markets so essential to us, will be practically closed to us forever." He had suspected McKinley's potential cravenness in the face of ferocious political and party pressures—McKinley in the end abandoning all efforts at peace when Republican Congressional leaders told him they would cross the aisle and vote with the Democrats unless he did so. What Norton could not anticipate—nor did anyone else in the American leadership class—was that an enthusiasm for war would rise to the pitch of hysteria precisely because the people's imagination had been so powerfully stirred.[46]

For through a perverse irony, the very forces Norton had earlier trusted to build America as moral commonwealth—the power of human sympathy, the power of a free press—had combined to "fire the prairie" of popular reaction. Neither the imperialists nor the *Maine* disaster had succeeded in infecting the populace with war fever as did a single 30-minute speech made on the floor of the U.S. Senate by one man, the flinty, unemotional Redfield Proctor of Vermont. "Torn from their homes, with foul earth, foul air, foul water, and foul food or none," declared Proctor, reporting on Cuban peasant suffering under the *reconcentrado* or concentration camp policy of the Spanish, "what wonder that one-half have died and that one-quarter of the living are so diseased that they can not be saved?" Proctor's speech galvanized the nation, its impact vastly heightened by the silent revolution in journalism taking place during the 1890s: the consolidation of news-gathering and dissemination services among a handful of New York City newspapers including Hearst's *Journal* and Joseph Pulitzer's *World*. "Little children are still walking about with arms and chest terribly emaciated," Proctor told the Senate, "eyes swollen, and abdomen bloated to three times the natural size." Re-transmitted to countless small-town papers across the nation, Proctor's words provoked what was only later recognized as an hysteria of humanitarian sentimentality. Even religious and business leaders who had adamantly opposed the war changed their position seemingly overnight. "If we were asked where was the most direct agency in bringing on the war, at last," the *Boston Herald* observed in August 1898 after the scene of military operations had shifted to the Philippines, "we should find it in Redfield Proctor of Vermont." Proctor's tale of horrors had fired the shallow imagination of a volatile public whose explosive reaction in turn frightened its ostensible leaders into war. "It is not easy," the *Herald* writer conceded, "to stop to reflect and reason when tales of starvation are being told."[47]

"Mr. Norton appears to look upon American patriotism as mere hysteria," the *Springfield Republican* noted reprovingly later that August, after McKinley had signed a preliminary peace accord with Spain. Instead, "[a]s a poet and a friend of poets and a student of poetry,

Mr. Norton ought to have been able to appreciate the uplifting of the national imagination." In fact, the national imagination was already sagging, deflated by press stories about the lethal inefficiency and interservice rivalry on Cuba, soon to be confirmed by the soldiers themselves, returning home diseased and disillusioned. By mid-September, the *Boston Herald* observed that "[f]rom an eagerness for war, the pendulum of public opinion has apparently swung back to a horror of war. . . . We doubt whether in the history of this or any other civilized country there has been, in so short a space of time, such a complete reversal of opinion." Despite a concentrated campaign by Norton, Carl Schurz, William James and other members of the Anti-Imperialist League, a formal peace treaty with Spain providing for U.S. annexation of the Philippines was to be ratified by the Senate in February 1899. Nonetheless, the fighting would continue.[48]

For now American forces found themselves struggling to put down the Filipino insurgents bitterly resisting U.S. annexation. "It is all a miserable affair," Norton told his daughter Sally that February, "a kind of world's comi-tragedy,—with a beginning of fine humanitarian pretensions under which could even then be seen grinning the sardonic features of the old enemy who brought death into the world." Justifying the annexation with the same high-toned appeals to "civilization" and "humanity" and "Christian religion" he had invoked when declaring war on Spain, McKinley had begun to substitute "keen effective slaughter," said E. L. Godkin in the *Nation*, "for Spanish old-fashioned, clumsy slaughter." Soon, American soldiers would find themselves burning whole villages, torturing their Tagalog prisoners for information, and later, firing their rifles into the bowl of an extinct volcano where cowered 600 Muslim men, women and children, killing them all. Meanwhile, Lodge's vaunted "new markets" and "vast trade" of the Far East did not materialize. A poem of 1901, "On a Soldier Fallen in the Philippines," expressed the shame and bitterness of this unexpected outcome by ending, "Let him never dream that his bullet's scream went wide of its island mark, / Home to the heart of his darling land where she stumbled and sinned in the dark." Writing the poet to thank him, Norton said, "you fulfil[l] one of the highest functions of the poet, in giving true expression to sentiment latent in the heart of a great body of the people."[49]

"Latent in," "a great body of"—the qualifications Norton is forced to use here reveal his struggle to keep alive his hope in America as moral commonwealth. Before the outbreak of the Venezuelan and Spanish crises, he could persuade himself that taken as a whole, the American people meant, in their own phrase, "'to do about right.'" The vast majority of them had risen within the space or two or three generations from the ranks of the world's oppressed—from the servile class or the peasantry,

Charles Eliot Norton

lacking not merely traditions of intellectual life and habits of sustained reasoning but often literacy itself. Thrown into the struggle for life in a new land, it was not surprising they should prove shallow-minded or materialistic or even occasionally brutal. Given such circumstances, the wonder was, as Norton said, "they are not worse." After the outbreak of the criminally unnecessary war of 1898, however, this position became untenable. In the face of Western newspapers urging war as a boost to trade, of religious congregations demanding imperialism as an aid to Christian proselytizing, of the "best men" abdicating their posts of moral leadership out of fear, and of the great and self-governing majority's indecent haste to deny any self-governance to non-American peoples, the fundamental conditions of possibility for any ideal of America as moral commonwealth seemed to melt and disappear.[50]

In the midst of the outcry over his "un-American" words, Norton had written to W. J. Stillman, his old Pre-Raphaelite friend from the 1850s. Together in Newport, the two men had once dreamed of "a new art & a new American life." Now it seemed, he told Stillman, "as though I were witnessing the end of the America which we have loved, and for which, in spite of all doubts, we have hoped." The new America both men had lived to see was not Lincoln's "new birth of freedom" but an aborted monster, begotten on American ignorance and selfishness by Old World aggression, corruption and lust for imperial spoils, and now entering, as Norton said, "on the ways of ancient wrong." Despite all the earlier portents of evil, he continued, "it has been possible to believe that in the long run the better elements of the national life would prevail over the worse," that the nation's moral progress would follow in the footsteps of its astonishing material advance. Until now. But the disastrous, shameful, needless war of 1898 unmasked the fallacious ground of these liberal hopes, "the mistake," as Norton called it, "of believing that happier conditions than man had experienced elsewhere would work a change in human nature itself." Instead, "the same old Adam has turned up in our Fool's Paradise."[51]

From a viewpoint well beyond that of 1898, it has proved easy to deride the bitter disappointment at the loss of "the old America" of men like Norton, Godkin, Moorfield Storey and William James. After Auschwitz and the Somme, after My Lai and Montgomery and Little Big Horn, their repeatedly expressed anguish over the tarnishing of American ideals may seem wholly disproportionate or wilfully sentimental, the "nostalgic" fetishizing of an impossibly pure nation that in fact never was. But in sorrowing over the loss of the old America, Norton was at the same time mourning a larger belief about the world that had animated his young manhood and middle age: the idea of progress, of an infinitely slow but ceaseless growth towards the light in the mass of men and women that would recapitulate and crown the individual acts of self-development in those he had once so much trusted to lead: the "best men." This is what Norton meant when he told Stillman that "our New England teachers all led us wrong." He was referring to Emerson, Longfellow and Lowell, to be sure, but also at no very great remove, to such teachers as Arthur Clough, George Curtis and J. S. Mill—to the whole midcentury generation of transatlantic liberals whose idealism had once seemed about to remake the world. Only Ruskin had dissented from this reasonable and "scientific" faith in human progress. But silent in his maddened senility and "absolutely childish or worse than that," Ruskin had died in 1900.[52]

Before 1898, Norton's hopes for an American moral commonwealth could plausibly be displaced upon smaller domains in art and life. Now, even these more circumscribed areas were being breached by forces indifferent or hostile to the needs of genuine community. Invaded by loafers and tramps, the Shady Hill estate had to be fenced against trespassers and patrolled by a policeman. At Harvard, the architect Charles McKim, commissioned to design a structure to encircle the College Yard, disdained all appeals to integrate the new fence with existing buildings or even to consult with those who were to live and work within its perimeter. Built slowly, thoughtfully and lavishly, the Harvard Fence, like Pisa's famous Campo Santo, might have expressed through its form the character and history of the institution it enclosed. But instead of acknowledging Harvard's human past with a series of memorial tablets as Norton proposed, the new wall—that "crude globiferous fence" as one student called it, parodying Norton—was deliberately designed to be "abstract and impersonal." For McKim, unlike Donatello, did not relish discussion and intelligent criticism from his fellow citizens: "I decided that, if I was to build a fence," the architect declared imperiously, "I would build a fence; if I was to build a graveyard, I would build a graveyard. But I would not build the two in one." Norton was reduced to presenting his views as a minority opinion in a Harvard Overseers' committee report.[53]

Here, in turn, lies the larger significance of the final Ashfield Academy Dinners. After Curtis' death, Norton had necessarily assumed an expanded role at the annual banquets, introducing the speakers, but also giving speeches himself in the place of the golden-throated Curtis. In 1898, the crowd was unusually large, drawn in anticipation of hearing what the embattled Norton would say about the war. "This remote little hall," the *Springfield Republican* reporter reminded his readers, "is a sort of whispering gallery where the lowest tones can be heard all over the country, and both Prof. Norton and President Hall preach most effective sermons there every year." It had become the custom for G. Stanley Hall, an Ashfield native and now president of Clark University in Worcester, to report on news from the world of science. This year, the reporter noted, Professor Norton's "kindly pessimism and ill-concealed distrust of present tendencies" contrasted forcibly with Hall's "glowing prophecies for the future." He noticed that the audience, though cordial to Norton, showed its marked preference for "the more aggressive patriotism" of another speaker, a clergyman who, perhaps hoping to appear "vital," declared of the war in Cuba, "When I read of the charge at El Caney I wept that I was not with them."[54]

During the next three years, Ashfield audiences heard a series of incisive attacks upon the presidential policy in Cuba, Puerto Rico and the Philippines. In 1899, five of the six speakers condemned it. Leading them off, Norton demanded to know, "by what right are we murdering the people of the Philippines and devastating their homes?" The following year, Norton told his listeners that the question "you, men and women of Ashfield, have each of you to answer" was this: "Shall materialism, in its various disguises of jingoism, commercialism and imperialism, continue to drag the flag in the blood of the innocent till all the stars are blotted out from it?" That August, none of the six Academy Dinner speakers rose in defense of McKinley's "large policy." Thus by August 1901, many audience members were growing impatient under the continuing anti-imperialist critique. That year, Norton arrived in Ashfield after having fiercely opposed the honorary degree Harvard bestowed on President McKinley, and having refused to attend its graduation ceremonies. When the main Dinner speaker, Daniel Chamberlain who deplored the actions of "an unscrupulous and deceitful president," was reproached for his remarks by Stanley Hall, the banqueting room burst into a storm of clapping. This "noise of applause," the *Springfield Republican* reporter noticed, "differed in character from that given to Prof Norton's utterances."[55]

All this lay in the background of the tumultuous Ashfield Academy Dinner of 1902, contributing, along with lowering skies and spattering rain, to the charged atmosphere inside the hall that August day. As diners seated themselves at the long tables, it became clear that a local campaign to boycott the banquet had achieved a small but visible success. Welcoming the audience, Norton pointedly thanked "those who have come in spite of the threatening weather without and the prospective weather within." During the preceding twelve months, local criticism of Norton's management of the Dinners had become severe, prompting him to offer to resign his post—provided his chief critic would assume the role. When his critic declined this proposal, Norton made it clear he would continue to speak his mind plainly and invite other speakers who did so. Several people muttered that the professor and his anti-imperialist friends were lucky they did not live where men with offensive opinions were treated to a coat of tar and feathers.[56]

In his Academy speech, Norton directly confronted Ashfield's unhappiness with "controversial" opinions about matters "foreign" to the town. "No man can be more sorry than I," he told his listeners, "that some of my friends here find the dinner[s] no longer as pleasant as they used to be." But two points must be considered. Were these matters of war and aggression truly "foreign" to Ashfield? Where should they be of interest, if not here? "Who should be concerned about them, if not we?" Was not a true republic precisely "that in which every individual feels and acts on the conviction that the affairs of the nation are his personal concern?" But there was something else to consider: "Wisdom is the product of the working of many minds," he said, invoking one of J. S. Mill's great teachings. "It is the result of free discussion." Except for a small band of anti-imperialists, Americans had clamored for war with a single brazen throat. Looking out at the audience from his place at the head table, Norton saw his neighbors assembled in a town hall that had originally been a Congregational church. "We understand little of the need of a nation," he reminded them, "if we do not regard freedom of speech as sacred."[57]

If by such words Norton hoped to stake out a protected space for the free expression of hard truths, he was quickly disappointed. The towering indignation of the next speaker, Edwin Burritt Smith of Chicago, at the horrifying carnage, destruction, censorship and duplicity attendant upon the official U.S. policy of "benevolent assimilation" in the Philippines soon roused the simmering hostility of the audience. As Smith denounced "a policy of oppression and suppression," castigating by name—Lodge, Taft, Root—the men who were its civil instruments, people began hissing. As soon as Smith concluded, Stanley Hall, interrupting his own prepared speech, angrily denounced all "epithets" and "aspersions of motives of public men whom this community respects" and "methods of antagonism and partisanship and propaganda." Asserting the right of the majority "to hear the expression of their own sentiments here," Hall went on to deliver his bitter and elaborate rebuke to Norton for having changed the Academy Dinners into occasions for propaganda and proselytism. There was "much applause" when Hall finished. Although three speakers remained to be heard from, the proceedings were summarily ended after the first of them, a courageous "sound money" man from Colorado, delivered an unusually eloquent address. "There will be no more speaking," Norton announced abruptly. "The dinner is ended."[58]

At this moment, Norton's ideal of Ashfield and the Ashfield Dinners can only seem to have been utterly vanquished. He and Curtis had once

Charles Eliot Norton

glimpsed in such small New England towns the vital republican qualities needed for the true commonwealth: integrity, self-reliance, intelligence, neighborliness, civic participation. At first greeted by "acquiescent indifference," then struggling against implacable socio-economic pressures sucking the life out of such dwindling agricultural hamlets, Curtis and Norton had sought to stabilize and reconstruct Ashfield by investing its homely republican virtues with the atmosphere of the best thought from the larger world. Distinguished visitors—James Lowell, Booker T. Washington, Charles Dudley Warner—seeming to dazzled onlookers like "magazine pictures who were made flesh and dwelt among us"—arrived to speak at the Academy Dinners. A stream of summer residents and tourists followed. Soon a new hotel was put up. Yet in their train had come all the homogenizing and materializing forces of scientific and metropolitan sophistication that posed the greatest danger to Norton's vigorous civic ideal.[59]

In August 1902, these forces were incarnated in Stanley Hall, the Ashfield farmer's son, who had gone to Germany to study physiological psychology, and returned to become a professor. Now, asserting his authority as an expert in anthropology, Hall defended his fellow Ashfielders as an endangered tribe or race whose primitive beliefs must be cherished and left undisturbed. Flexing his authority as a university president, Hall treated the assembly as if it were a scientific conference or academic senate rather than a civic occasion, feeling free to reject strong opinions as "propaganda" and spurn coherent arguments as "proselytizing." Speaking a little confusedly, under the pressure of his own anger, Hall declared, "Academies like ours, to thrive, must be of, for and by the people." But beneath his emptily Lincolnesque phrase was to be glimpsed the shrunken idea of democracy and the inert conception of civic life that had already begun to shape the American future. For even now Hall was working on the vast treatise that would introduce "adolescence" as the "apical" phase of human development, superior in its openness and intensity to maturity itself. "This golden stage," as Hall would call it, urging that it be privileged and prolonged, would prove "the only point of departure for the super anthropoid that man is to become." In 1909, the year after Norton's death, Hall would invite Sigmund Freud and Carl Jung to lecture at Clark University, opening the door to a therapeutic world-view that would eventually reduce civic conceptions into mere preferences of the personal psyche.[60]

It remained only for Norton to say farewell to the Ashfield Dinners. This he did the next year—in August 1903, on the twenty-fifth anniversary of their founding—disengaging himself from Ashfield with such a consummate grace that the defeat and humiliation of the year before were transmuted into a sort of victory. With a heroism of reticence,

Norton would simply vanish from the public sphere. He would become the Ghost of Shady Hill. With a quiet confidence in their kindly regard, he told his neighbors, "I have not a word to retract of what I have said here in former years. . . . I do not regret having maintained opinions which were for the time unpopular." Then he recalled to them, as if in a grand procession, the noble men who had spoken in this plain town hall. "As I name them the illustrious figures reappear, glorifying this humble room, and for a brief moment, as they pass before our inward vision, it is peopled by the famous dead and by their worthy compeers among the living who in past years have been seen and heard here."[61]

In summoning the Ashfield civic heroes to inward vision, Norton was displacing the last vestige of his moral commonwealth idea to the "elsewhere" of imagination. It was the last, best resort left to the kind of patriot he had become. In earlier years, it had become the fashion among young Harvard aesthetes to say they were willing to do anything for their country—"except live in it." But Norton's patriotism was of another kind. Imagination allowed him to live in the actual America while glimpsing a better one beyond the limits of his own brief life, a brighter day when—surely—the sun would shine "on fairer prospects, and on generations of men more brotherly to him than his own."[62]

Abbreviations

ADV	Aubrey de Vere
AHC	Arthur Hugh Clough
AN	Andrews Norton
AtMo	*Atlantic Monthly*
CEN	Charles Eliot Norton
CN	Catharine Eliot Norton
CW	Chauncey Wright
DGR	Dante Gabriel Rossetti
EBJ	Edward Burne-Jones
ECG	Elizabeth Cleghorn Gaskell
ELG	Edwin L. Godkin
FJC	Francis James Child
GEW	George E. Woodberry
GN	Grace Norton
GPM	George Perkins Marsh
GS	Goldwin Smith
GSH	G. Stanley Hall
GWC	George William Curtis
HCL	Henry Cabot Lodge
HJ	Henry James, Jr.
HL	Houghton Library—all materials quoted by permission of the Houghton Library, Harvard University
HWL	Henry Wadsworth Longfellow
JBH	Jonathan Baxter Harrison
JN	Jane Norton
JR	John Ruskin
JRL	James Russell Lowell
JS	John Simon

JSM	John Stuart Mill
LS	Leslie Stephen
MG	Meta Gaskell
NAR	*North American Review*
NELPS	New England Loyal Publication Society—all materials quoted permission of the Rare Book Room, Boston Public Library
NP	Norton Papers, quoted by permission of the Houghton Library, Harvard University
NY	New York
RWE	Ralph Waldo Emerson
SATA	Society for the Advancement of Truth in Art
SGW	Samuel Gray Ward
SSN	Susan Sedgwick Norton
TC	Thomas Carlyle
TR	Theodore Roosevelt
WJ	William James
WJS	William J. Stillman

Notes

Preface: The Ghost of Shady Hill

1. Norton, quoted in "August Breeze at Ashfield," *Springfield Republican*, 22 August 1902, p. 4.

2. Hall, quoted in "August Breeze at Ashfield," *Springfield Republican*, 22 August 1902, p. 4; the *Republican* reporter, noting that Hall delivered his "pedagogic scolding" of Norton "with all of a schoolmaster's magisterial emphasis," observed that "This must have made Prof. Norton feel quite like a schoolboy."

3. Cf. Norton, as quoted in a *New York Sun* editorial of 27 April 1898: "The duty you have to perform, gentlemen, is one for the improvement of the lower classes, to whom such issues as the present war appeal strongly. Your academic training does not impose on you the necessity of encouraging barbarous warfare" (clipping preserved in Records of the Hour, Vol. 1, a scrapbook about the Spanish-War controversy kept by Sally Norton, NP [bMS Am 1088.3]); *Los Angeles Times* of 19 May 1898, clipping in Records of the Hour, Vol. 1; *Chicago Tribune* of 10 May 1898, clipping in Records of the Hour, Vol. 1.

4. Cf. B. T. Washington: "The further we go as a nation in the direction of engrafting the ignorant and irresponsible of foreign islands into our government, the more will we be tempted to depart from the old landmark—'that the right to govern rests upon the consent of the governed.' In the South for years I fear we have disregarded this principle," quoted in "Annual Ashfield Dinner," *Springfield Republican*, 26 August 1898, p. 4.

5. Norton, quoted in "Philippine War Arraigned at Ashfield," *Springfield Republican*, 18 August 1899, p. 5; Smith, quoted in "August Breeze at Ashfield," *Springfield Republican*, 22 August 1902, p. 5.

6. Santayana's various remarks on this topic have been collected in *The Genteel Tradition: Nine Essays*; see Shklar, "Emerson and the Inhibitions"; cf. also Santayana on the American "diffidence as to quality": "The democratic conscience recoils before anything that savours of privilege; and lest it should concede an unmerited privilege to any pursuit or person, it reduces all things as far as possible to the common denominator of quantity" (in "Materialism and Idealism," p. 187).

7. Brooks, *Flowering*, 458, 459; see Hofstadter, *Age of Reform*, 135–43; Hofstadter's heirs include Hoogenboom, Persons and Sproat; Tucker and Butler represent recent, valuably revisionist accounts of the Mugwumps.

8. The most influential historians in the progressivist portrayal of Norton

have been Fredrickson, Solomon and Beisner, with Trachtenberg, Brodhead, Freedman, Posnock, Duffy and Menand offering recent versions of the same hostile portrayal in literary history. Lears and Gurstein represent recent distinguished exceptions to the stereotypical view of Norton; C. Chauncey Stillman to CEN of 1 August 1898, NP (bMS Am 1088 [7056]); Hoar to CEN of 18 July 1898, *Worcester Evening Gazette*, 18 July 1898, reprinted in Hoar, *Quality of Our Honor,* unpaginated.

9. Norton, "Partridge's," 249.

10. CEN to JRL of 16 Nov 1884 in *CEN Letters,* 2:166.

11. Berkowitz, *Virtue and the Making,* xiii.

12. CEN to WJ of 1 June 1901, James Family Papers, HL, [bMS Am 1092 (628)]; CEN to SGW of 26 Apr 1896 in *CEN Letters,* 2:244.

13. CEN to JR of 28 Sept 1888 in *JR/CEN Correspondence,* 502; cf. CEN to M. Laird Simons [editor of Duykinck's *Cyclopaedia of American Literature*] of 30 Jan 1873: "I do not regard it as suitable for a writer to prepare a notice of himself and his works, or even to supply the material for such a notice, for a work that pretends to be an independent and critical review of contemporary literature," Duykinck Collection, Rare Book and MSS Dept., NY Public Library and CEN to Edward Lee-Childe of 18 May 1874: "I know no worse calamity that can overtake a man than to have a thirst for publicity, and yet it is the common vice of able men in this epoch of the newspaper reporter" in *CEN Letters,* 2:47 and CEN to Nathan Haskell Dole of 26 Aug 1897: "It would be so greatly against my taste to have my portrait inserted in the new edition of the Rubaiyat, and it would seem to me so much out of place, that I trust that you and Messrs. L. C. Page & Co will pardon me for withholding my consent," NP [bMS Am 1088.8].

14. Brown, "A Self-Indulgent," 174; CEN to HJ of 5 Dec 1873, James Family Papers, HL [bMS Am 1094 (379)]; CEN to HJ of 23 Mar 1873, James Family Papers, HL [bMS Am 1094 (378)].

15. WJ to Alice James of 23 Aug 1891 in *WJ Selected Letters,* 137; Norton had just been named Lowell's literary executor; earlier he had published prose translations of Dante's *Divine Comedy* and *The New Life,* edited the correspondence of Carlyle and Goethe, and had been the intimate friend of Ruskin, the American utilitarian philosopher Chauncey Wright and Edward FitzGerald, the translator of the *Rubáiyát of Omar Khayyám* (which Norton had introduced to an American audience in 1869); if William James's responses to Norton seem unusually heated here as elsewhere, it is well to remember what James once said of himself: "I write this with . . . an appearance of vehemence which in me is inseparable from the writing act" (WJ to W. M. Salter of 18 Nov 1898 in Perry, *Life and Character,* 2:310).

16. Norton, Address given at the dedication of the Slater Memorial Museum, 22 Nov 1888, NP [Nor 5257.25f*].

17. Cecil Spring Rice to Stephen Spring Rice of 24 Jan 1890 in Spring Rice, *Letters and Friendships,* 1:102; Bryce, *American Commonwealth,* 2:21; Curtis, "Public Duty," 269, 267, 265; Lucius Annaeus Seneca, *De Tranquillitate animi,* ch. 2: *Nunquam inutilis est opera civis boni: auditu enim, visu, vultu, nutu, obstinatione tacita, incessuque ipso prodest,* quoted in Latin in CEN to Mountstuart Grant-Duff of 19 Apr 1896 in *CEN Letters,* 2:241.

18. Josiah Royce to Sally Norton of 1 Nov 1908 in Royce, *Letters*, 532; cf. CEN to JS of 8 July 1885, NP [bMS Am 1088.2 (Box 6)]: "Of all mortal poisons flattery is worst,—worse far than calumny. Calumny sometimes kills outright, which flattery never does; but instead of that creates a morbid appetite for itself like opium, and then the victim will take any means, no matter how unworthy to secure his portion, and the dose will benumb all the finer faculties"; Burke's "Flattery corrupts both the receiver and the giver, and adulation is not of more service to the people than to kings" forms the epigraph to Chapter 1 of Norton's *Considerations on Some Recent Social Theories*; Norton, "Notices of Gillett's *Huss*," 270.

19. Wendell, "Charles Eliot Norton," 84; Ruskin, *Praeterita*, 522; EBJ to CEN of "Saturday" [21 June 1884] in NP [bMS Am 1088 (781)]; Bertram Grosvenor Goodhue to CEN of 18 Feb 1908, NP [bMS Am 1088 (2750)]; cf. William Dean Howells on Norton's criticism of a draft essay Howells had written about Lowell: "I have always felt myself indebted for his censure which made me save the day" ("Charles Eliot Norton," p. 842).

20. Emerson, "New England Reformers," 162 (my emphasis).

Chapter 1: The Art of Reform

1. Brooks, *Dream*, 247, 245.

2. M. A. DeWolfe Howe, C. E. Norton Notes, HL [bMS Am 1826 (417)]: "His uncle Mr Ticknor strongly disapproved of C. E. N.'s opinions after his first return from Europe [in 1851]. There was little sympathy between them"; thereafter, though the overt breach between uncle and nephew was healed, relations were never again easy, Norton telling James Lowell in 1860 "[a]s long as he and I keep off from approaching certain dangerous topics [i.e. slavery], we have a pleasant time" (CEN to JRL of 29 June 1860 in *CEN Letters*, 1:209); Norton, "Dwellings," 470; Morison, "Reminiscences," 364; Russell Sturgis to CEN of 1 Jan 1900, NP [bMS Am 1088 (7255)]; in 1854 Norton charged the boys 25 cents apiece, Expense Book for Evening School, NP [bMS Am 1088.5 (Box 5)]; Norton, "Dwellings," 473.

3. McCarthy Family gravestone, Pawtucket, RI; Norton, autobiographical recollections of 1908, quoted in *CEN Letters*, 1:27; the detail about the milk-cart is from E. W. Emerson, "Charles Eliot Norton," 9; inscription by Patrick McCarthy, dated 1913, in author's copy of CEN's *Notes of Travel and Study*.

4. Fanny Longfellow to Emmeline A. Wadsworth of 16 Apr 1852 in Longfellow, *Mrs. Longfellow*, 187; Curtis, *Potiphar*, 18.

5. Kossuth, Mazzini and Blanc, quoted in Norton, *Considerations*, 5–17.

6. Norton, *Considerations*, 36; Philippe Vigier, "Les victimes du coup d'État" <http://napoleontrois.free.fr/victimes.htm>; Norton, *Considerations*, 47.

7. Norton, *Considerations*, 35, 36.

8. Curtis, *Potiphar*, 163 (my emphasis).

9. For Leroux, see Norton, *Considerations*, 55, 67–68; follower of Cabet, quoted in *Considerations*, 74.

10. Sumner to Samuel Gridley Howe of 30 Dec 1851 in Sumner, *Selected*

*Letters,*1:343; CEN to Arthur Helps of 1 Dec 1851, NP [bMS Am 1088.8]: "I sincerely regret his coming,—not so much because it is most difficult to form an estimate of his real deserts, although it is very certain that they are less than the enthusiastic popular voice has claimed for him,—as because at this time the question of intervention in foreign politics is becoming a very prominent one with us [a third attempt by largely U.S. "filibusterers" to annex Cuba had failed in August], & is likely to receive an unfavorable determination from his arrival & influence. The tendency of the democracy in this country is to desert the sound principle established by Washington in the affairs of foreign states."

11. CEN, "Manchester," 33; Dickens, *Hard Times,* Chap. 5; Green usefully sets Norton in the British "culture and society" tradition defined by Raymond Williams (see *Problem of Boston,* pp. 15–16, 25–26).

12. Howells, "Charles Eliot Norton," 843; personal expenses notebook of 1846, NP [bMS Am 1088.5 (Box 2)]; Morison, "Reminiscences," 365.

13. Smith, *Theory,* 9.

14. Smith, *Theory,* 22, 317.

15. Smith, *Theory,* 18, 9, 21.

16. James Woodrow in 1808, quoted in Introduction to Smith, *Theory,* 3; Mill, "Bentham," 91; Eliot, "Natural," 13; Eliot to Charles Bray of 5 July 1859, in *Letters,* 3:111.

17. Miller, *American Thought,* ix; Rand notes that Stewart's *Elements* was a required text for Harvard juniors during 1841–1848 ("Philosophical Instruction," p. 190); Turner has said the Scottish doctrine of imagination "reworked, would provide the core of Norton's own pedagogy" (p. 49); Stewart, *Elements,* 378 (my emphasis).

18. Dickens, *Nicholas Nickleby,* Chap. 8; Gaskell, *Mary Barton,* Chap. 6; reviewing anonymously in the *North American Review* for 1847, James Russell Lowell complained about reform-minded agendas evident in too much recent literature: "Adam Smith gets us inexorably by the button in the corner of some shilling novel, and Malthus entraps us from behind the unsuspected ambush of the last new poem. Even the tragic Muse drops her mask, and behold, Mr. Ricardo!" ("D'Israeli's *Tancred,*" p. 215).

19. Eliot, "Natural," 14, 13.

20. Olmsted, *Cotton,* 32; E. P. Parker in 1868, quoted in Camfield, "Moral," 322.

21. Gaskell, *Mary Barton,* Chap. 35.

22. Stowe, "Introduction," iii; Stowe's introduction is dated May 22, 1844; Dickens, *American Notes,* Chap. 6; AN to Nathan Appleton of 11 Nov 1844 (copy), AN Papers, HL [bMS Am 9029 (1305)]; AN to CN of 15 Mar 1845, NP [bMS Am 1088.2 (Box 13)]; Andrews was keenly aware of the effect of English factory work on children: "the distortion of their bones, the twisting of their joints, constant disease, death by slow torture, and, worse, far worse than all, the annihilation of every thing intellectual and moral in the human being" (A. Norton, "Hamilton's *Men,*" p. 99).

23. Norton, "Dwellings," 468; CEN to Sarah P. Cleveland of 12 Sept 1849, NP [bMS Am 1088.2 (Box 1)]; Norton, "Dwellings," 469n, 489 (my emphasis).

24. Gaskell, *Mary Barton*, Chap. 35; Norton, "Dwellings," 468; Norton, "St. Nicholas," 511.

25. Norton, "Manchester," 33.

26. Longfellow, *Mrs. Longfellow*, 211; CEN to CN of 2 July 1857 in *CEN Letters*, 1:173–74; A. Sedgwick, "Words," 430.

27. Ruskin, "Cambridge School," 171; Ruskin, *Notes*, 6; Ruskin, "Study of Art," 460.

28. Ruskin, "Essay," 370; Ruskin, *Modern Painters— Vol.* 2, 287, 257.

29. Ruskin, *Modern Painters— Vol.* 2, 60.

30. Ruskin, "Academy Notes/1858," 152; Ruskin, *Praeterita*, 311; Ruskin, *Stones of Venice— Vol.* 2, 173.

31. Ruskin, *Modern Painters— Vol. 1*, 624.

32. Louy Leavitt [?] to Frank Sanborn of 7 Feb 1855, F. B. Sanborn Papers, Special Collections, Georgetown Univ. Library, Washington, D.C.; Stillman, "*Modern*," 239; Young, *Pre-Raffaelitism*, 301, 257.

33. Hawthorne, *English*, 550.

34. Longfellow, *Mrs. Longfellow*, 211; Hawthorne, *English*, 550.

35. Norton, "*Common Objects of the Seashore*": "[The aquarium] becomes like a secret cave in the ocean where the processes of Nature go on in wonderful and silent progression, and the coy sea [word missing] displays its rarer beauties of life, of color, and of form before the watching eyes" (p. 253); Sturgis, "Pre-Raphaelites," 182; Barringer, *Reading*, 117; Wood, *Pre-Raphaelites*, 62; Hawthorne, *English*, 550; Norton, "Manchester," 46.

36. CEN to CN of 16 Oct 1856 (typescript copy), NP [bMS Am 1088.2 (Box 11)]; Ruskin, *Praeterita*, 486; Carr, "Edward Burne-Jones," 72; Burne-Jones, *Memorials*, 1:144.

37. CEN to CN of 16 Oct 1856 (typescript copy), NP [bMS Am 1088.2 (Box 11); this characterization of the proposed portrait is Ruskin's (JR to CEN of 10 Dec [1859] in *JR/CEN Correspondence*, p. 55).

38. For the loan, see Turner, *Liberal*, 129; CEN to William S. Bullard of 18 Sept 1856, NP [bMS Am 1088.5 (Box 1)]; Norton, MS lectures delivered to the School of Drawing and Painting, Museum of Fine Arts, Boston, Apr–May 1892, NP [bMS Am 1088.5 (Box 6)]; cf. also Harris, "Charles Eliot Norton": "He met every situation with a sane radicalism; the dominant note was ever:— 'We want nothing but the best.' The best always costs a great deal of money, but where the treasury [of the American Institute of Archaeology] was empty, he still insisted, with far-seeing courage, on the best" (pp. 51–52).

39. CEN to CN of 15 July 1857, NP [bMS Am 1088.2 (Box 10)]; Norton, "Manchester," 45.

40. Norton, "Manchester," 44.

41. Cf. Fraser, *Victorians*: "the glorious early Renaissance culture which the name of the movement conjured up was connected in people's minds with an idealized conception of political conditions which prevailed under the Italian republics, and thence with the modern struggle for emancipation" (p. 95).

42. Burrow, *Whigs*, 108.

43. Turner notes that CEN met Lyell in 1841 during the geologist's Amer-

ican lecture tour (p. 61); Darwin to Leonard Horner of 1844, quoted in Max, "Two Cheers," 74.

44. Curtis, "Emerson," 27; Carlyle, "History Again," 256.

45. Carlyle, "On History," 232; Carlyle, "History Again," 245; Emerson, "History," 16; TC to RWE of 19 July 1842 in *TC/RWE Correspondence*, 2:6.

46. CEN spent 75 cents for *Past and Present* in May 1847; he had previously bought Carlyle's *Heroes and Hero-Worship* in Oct 1846, 1846–48 account book, NP [bMS Am 1088.5 (Box 2)]; Carlyle, *Past*, 170; excerpt from RWE's Diary, ca. late April 1843 printed by Norton in *TC/RWE Correspondence*, 2:34n.

47. Carlyle, *Past*, 54, 55; Burne-Jones, *Memorials*, 1:143.

48. CEN's review, published in the Sept 1855 number of *Putnam's Magazine*, is reprinted in Murdock, *A Leaf.*

49. Ruskin, letter of 1887, quoted in Rosenberg, *Darkening*, 126; Ruskin, *Seven Lamps*, 82.

50. CEN, "Introduction" to *Seven Lamps*, ix.

51. Ruskin, *Stones of Venice— Vol.* 2, 192, 190.

52. In Ruskin's *Modern Painters— Vol.* 5, Chapter 1 of Part 8 is entitled and devoted to "The Law of Help" (pp. 203–16).

53. During 1853–54 William Morris (who inherited a fortune in 1854) and Edward Jones made plans to found a monastic brotherhood; the New York lawyer is George Templeton Strong; see his *Diary* 2:128.

54. Ruskin quoted in Hollis, *Oxford*, 97; Woodward, quoted in Blau, *Ruskinian*, 68; Norton, "Oxford," 768.

55. Ruskin, letter to H. G. Liddell of 12 Oct 1844 in *Modern Painters— Vol. 1*, 668; Norton, *Notes of Travel*, 103.

56. Ruskin, *Praeterita*, 521; Norton, 1856 travel diary, entry for 26 July 1856, NP (bMS Am 1088.5 [Box 15]); in *Stones of Venice— Vol.* 2, Ruskin had written, "I never yet met with a Christian whose heart was thoroughly set upon the world to come, and, so far as human judgment could pronounce, perfect and right before God, who cared about art at all. . . . I have never known a man who seemed altogether right and calm in faith, who seriously cared about art." (pp. 124–25).

57. AHC to Blanche Smith of 8 Feb 1853 in Clough, *Correspondence*, 2:378; CEN to E. G. Squier of 29 Apr 1849, Ephraim George Squier Papers, Library of Congress; Norton was still sending out Andrews' books to religious seekers as late as 1865, saying to one man, "It is natural that to me there should be few books on theological subjects so satisfactory in the main as his" (CEN to JBH of 19 Mar 1865, NP [bMS Am 1088.2 (Box 4)]; Norton, "Manchester," 46.

58. Norton, 1856 travel diary, NP (bMS Am 1088.5 [Box 15]).

59. Norton, "Introduction" to *A Joy For Ever*, viii; when Ruskin reprinted the Manchester lectures in 1880, he retitled them *A Joy For Ever (And Its Price in the Market).*

60. Ruskin, *A Joy*, 51.

61. Norton, "Manchester," 36.

62. *Boston Daily Evening Transcript*, quoted in Casteras, "1857–58 Exhibition," 116; *New York Times*, quoted in Casteras, 122; *Philadelphia Sun Dispatch*, quoted in Casteras, 130; after Siddal's death, DGR requested the return of *Clerk Saun-*

ders, offering either to repay the original purchase price or to make another drawing (DGR to CEN of 19 April 1869). Norton complied, accepting Rossetti's offer (made in DGR to CEN of 23 April 1869) of a replacement drawing of Jane Morris. Although Rossetti duly received *Clerk Saunders* (DGR to CEN of 22 Jan 1870), Norton had not received the Jane Morris drawing by 26 March 1873, the last letter of the Rossetti-Norton correspondence preserved in NP [bMS Am 1088 (5852, 5853, 5855, 5857)]; in 1886, Ruskin, at that time subject to erratic moods, demanded the return of *A Block of Gneiss*: "America, as long as she worships Mr. [William Merritt] Chase, and pirates the teaching of the living, and taxes the teaching of the dead,—can get no good work or word of mine, and no friend of mine should disgrace my work by keeping it there" (*JR/CEN Correspondence*, p. 491). Again Norton complied.

63. Strong, *Diary*, II:460; Strong is reacting to a later Pre-Raphaelite exhibition of 1859; Augustus Ruxton to William Michael Rossetti of 10 Oct 1857, quoted in Rossetti, *Ruskin, Rossetti*, 182; the young artist is William Trost Richards, cited in Ferber and Gerdts, *New Path*, 214; "The British Gallery in New York," 501–507.

64. CEN to AHC of 8 June 1858, NP [bMS Am 1088.2 (Box 11)].

65. James, "Sense of Newport," 529, 533; for Newport and CEN's artist friends there, see Turner, *Liberal*, 105, 147, 157, 435 n25.

66. Critic's remark quoted in Ferber, "Clearest Lens," 100; WJS to CEN of 28 June 1894, NP [bMS Am 1088 (7148)].

67. A note by Norton in NP indicates the Rowse portrait was done in June 1858 [bMS Am 1088.5 (Box 5)]; Wendell, "Charles Eliot Norton," 85.

68. Norton, *Notes of Travel*, 101, 103, 105, 106, 104 (I have expanded Norton's original phrasing: "that of the imagination").

69. Norton, "'The New Life,'" 65; these quoted passages were preserved in the earlier editions of the book version of *The New Life of Dante* (1859 and 1867) but—except for the phrase "at once the fruit and the seed of glorious energy"—all of them were dropped, as Mark Stirling kindly informs me, from the later editions of 1892 and 1895, their disappearance effectively marking the contraction of Norton's hopes for "a new American life."

70. Acton, *Acton in America*, 63; Norton carried out his extensive researches into the history of medieval church-building in the spirit of a scientific induction from "facts." His pre-existing emotional loyalties, however, largely determined what phenomena would count as "facts." Cf. for example, his translation in "'The New Life' of Dante" of a medieval decree concerning a new cathedral for Florence: "'no work of the commune should be undertaken unless the design be *to make it correspondent with a heart which is of the greatest nature, because composed of the spirit of many citizens united together in one single will'*" (p. 65, my emphasis).

71. Norton, *Notes of Travel*, 108, 109, 303; cf. also *Notes of Travel*, 107–108: "The periods distinguished in [post-classical] history by a condition of intellectual excitement and fervor have been usually, perhaps always, followed at a short interval by epochs of more or less moral energy, which has borne a near relation to the nature of the moral elements in the previous intellectual movement." Thus the Renaissance, "an intellectual period of pure immorality,

was followed close by the Reformation, whose first characteristic was that of protest."

72. Norton, *Notes of Travel*, 292, 320, 298; cf. CEN to AHC of 24 Sept 1860: "The new birth of Italy is already the grandest event of the modern period" (in *CEN Letters*, 1:210) and after Abraham Lincoln's election, CEN to MG of 25 Nov 1860: "not even in Italy is a struggle going on of more importance to men, involving more lasting consequences, or in which justice, truth, & all good are more deeply involved than that which is now taking place here," NP [bMS Am 1088.2 (Box 4)].

Chapter 2: War and Democracy

1. "Harvard University has, we believe, a larger percentage of graduates in the Federal army than any other northern college" ("Patriotic Young," p. 1). Lowell mentions the heat and the locusts in a letter to JN of 25 July 1865 in *JRL Letters*, 1:386–88; Emerson's address is quoted in E. W. Emerson, *Early Years*, 402.

2. James, *Notes*, 477; Norton, "Partridge's," 249, 250.

3. Norton, "Paradise," 44; CEN to SGW of 9 March 1903 in *CEN Letters*, 2:334.

4. Moorhead, *American*, 189; Lowell, "Ode," 399; Norton, "Life of Curtis" (1896), in *Memorials*, 82 (I have adjusted Norton's original word order to fit my sentence).

5. Under the provisions of conscription act which became national law on 3 March 1863, Norton was categorized as a Class 2 enrolled man (i.e. a married man over 35). Such men were virtually never drafted (see McPherson, *Battle Cry*, pp. 600–601). When Norton contributed $575 on 16 July 1864 for John Riley to serve, he did so in the words of the official Certificate of Substitute as "an enrolled man, not drafted" (NP, bMS Am 1088 [Box 14]). Norton thus paid for a substitute when he was not legally obliged to. His entirely voluntary contribution meant not only that John Riley's family would be taken care of during his prospective three-year absence but also that another man, perhaps one much less able to go, would not be drafted in Riley's place—for Cambridge was required by law to fill its quota of men by 5 September 1864. Although alien or even repellent to modern ethical sensibilities, the system of military substitution and commutation by purchase was a traditional practice in America and, in the absence of public welfare or social services, a humane one (see McPherson, pp. 602–603). Earlier, in September 1862, Norton had contributed $100 to the Cambridge Volunteers (NP, bMS Am 1088.5 [Box 12]).

6. See Turner, *Liberal*, 136; CEN to William S. Bullard of 18 Sept 1856, NP [bMS Am 1088.5 (Box 1)]; Henry Yates Thompson saw Norton in July 1863: "Called on Mr Charles Eliot Norton at Cambridge. Little man with moustache and tendency to baldness" (*Englishman*, p. 42); according to his passport, Norton's height was 5'9", about average for men at the time; that Thompson considered him "little" suggests that the osteoporosis or whatever condition it was which would later so severely bend Norton's frame had already begun; Bundy's

description of CEN as "owl-eyed" is exact (*Nature of Sacrifice*, p. 4); the observer was Edward Emerson who was 18 in 1863 (*Early Years*, p. 238).

7. CEN to GWC, quoted in Turner, *Liberal*, 175; Norton describes his work for NELPS in an 1871 letter in *CEN Letters*, I:221–23; see also Turner, *Liberal*, 179.

8. Mary Pringle Mitchell to W. A. Pringle of 6 Nov 1862, quoted in Lee, *South Carolina*, 119; married to the writer Donald Grant Mitchell ("Ik Marvel"), Mary Pringle Mitchell was at this time living outside of New Haven, CT; her brother Edward Pringle, Harvard '45, was one of CEN's closest Southern friends; Gov. Oliver P. Morton to Abraham Lincoln of 27 October 1862, quoted in Wood, *Hidden*, 116; *Columbus (OH) Crisis* of 21 January 1863, quoted in Wood, *Hidden*, 125.

9. Wood, *Hidden*, 131; Vallandigham, quoted in Wood, *Hidden*, 119.

10. McPherson, *Battle*, 584; Grant, quoted in Wood, *Hidden*, 132; Col. Lucius Fairchild to "Sarah" of 30 Jan 1863, quoted in Wood, *Hidden*, 133; GWC to J.J. Pinkerton of 17 Feb 1863, quoted in Cary, *George William*, 163.

11. N[orton], "Slavery at the North or Freedom at the South," NELPS editorial of 19 March 1863, NELPS Papers; see Norton's essay "The St. Nicholas [Hotel] and the Five Points."

12. N[orton], "Slavery at the North or Freedom at the South," NELPS editorial of 19 March 1863, NELPS Papers; Carlyle's "*Ilias Americana in Nuce* [The American Iliad in a Nutshell], a short dialogue between Northern Peter and Southern Paul," was published in *Macmillan's Magazine* for August 1863; N[orton], "Mr. Carlyle and the American Iliad," NELPS editorial of 27 Aug 1863, NELPS Papers.

13. For Norton's reading of Carlyle's *Cromwell*, see CEN to GWC of 7 Sept 1862, NP [bMS Am 1088.2 (Box 2)]; N[orton], "Mr. Carlyle and the American Iliad" NELPS editorial of 27 Aug 1863, NELPS Papers.

14. See Norton, "Advantages of Defeat"; Chesnut, *Diary*, 92; CEN to GWC of 7 Sept 1862, NP [bMS Am 1088.2 (Box 2)].

15. CEN to GWC of 11 May 1862, NP [bMS Am 1088.2 (Box 2)]; in Louis Menand's *The Metaphysical Club*, a Norton demanded by Menand's own "progressive" preconceptions is created through selective quotation. Thus, for instance, Menand is able to take this remark by Norton to Aubrey de Vere—"pray we may have suffering enough"—as being about wounds and death suffered by Union soldiers in combat. This then becomes the basis of Menand's sneering comment about Norton's "high-minded satisfaction in agonies actually being sustained by other people" (*Metaphysical*, p. 52). In fact, however, the full context shows that Norton was speaking to de Vere about the national suffering brought about by the war as "the great expiation" of the "great national sin" of slavery, his point being that tolerance of chattel slavery has eroded the foundations of civic morality since the beginnings of the American republic: "I trust," says Norton of the struggle to eradicate slavery, "we shall come purified out of its fires. But we have many weaknesses, many faults, many ignorances, to be purged from, and the process must be long & painful to be effectual. *I pray that we may have suffering enough to make us as a nation nobler & worthier of our unexampled opportunities and our unbounded hopes*; that we learn the true art

of self-government, and acquire that liberty which is the fulfilling of the law," CEN to ADV of 2 Oct 1861, NP [bMS Am 1088.2 (Box 3)] (my emphasis). In the same way, a too-hasty turning over the Norton Papers leaves Menand with the impression that Norton's "take on the war was Spartan," and that "he regarded it as an opportunity to toughen up an elite class of young men who had been made effete by too much prosperity" (*Metaphysical*, p. 51). This is of course precisely the attitude later expressed by Theodore Roosevelt, against whom Norton would wage the last bitter struggle of his long career. As regards the Civil War, however, Norton specifically said about the young Harvard men who enlisted on the Union side that "*There was no need of long military or Spartan training to make these boys good soldiers*; such principles as those in which they had been bred made them good men alike in war or in peace" ("Harvard Memorial," p. 508 [my emphasis]). In 1899, when Quinet's widow sent Norton her two-volume memoir of her husband, he responded, "It is now more than forty years since I first became acquainted with the work of Edgar Quinet, and learned to hold his name in honor as that of a man devoted to the service of the noblest Ideals." CEN to Mme Edgar Quinet of 23 Mar 1899, Bibliothèque Nationale de France [BNF-Richelieu NAF #15517, ff. 31–32]; Norton, *Notes of Travel*, 300.

16. James Jackson Lowell and William Lowell Putnam were first and second lieutenants, respectively, of Company E, 20th Massachussetts Volunteers (Bruce, *Twentieth*, p. 11); a third Lowell nephew, Charles Russell Lowell, was Colonel of the 2nd Massachusetts Cavalry; Lieut-Col. Frank Palfrey was the son of the Free-Soil Congressman, abolitionist and historian of New England, John Gorham Palfrey.

17. Holmes, "Bread," 346–47, 348.

18. Lt. F. A. Stearns to his father of 9 March 1862, quoted in Norton "Our Soldiers," 188; Holmes, "Bread," 346; cf. Palfrey, "Ambulance": "By correspondence, through the press, by personal communication with officers and men, we are in closer relations with our armies than ever people was before" (p. 86).

19. Bruce, *Twentieth*, 414; the newspaper was the *New York Examiner*, Ridley Watts to CEN of 5 Aug 1864, NP [bMS Am 1088 (7885)]; John Murray Forbes to CEN of 15 Aug 1864, NP [bMS Am 1088 (2260)]: "In order to try everything[,] I have sent to Will [Forbes's son] Greenbacks[,] checks on Boston Bank, £2 Bills drawn by a Banker to his Order, Ward's credit a[t] Lenox to his order. Clothes & tinned meats, &c &c"; for Forbes's aid to the Ball's Bluff captives, see Miller, *Harvard's Civil War*, 94–95.

20. CEN to GWC of 8 June 1862, NP [bMS Am 1088.2 (Box 2)]; Robert Gould Shaw was the brother of Anna Shaw Curtis; Joseph Bridgham Curtis, Lt.-Col. of the 4th Rhode Island, was the son of George Curtis's father's second wife; CEN to James Parton of 30 Oct 1864, James Parton Papers, HL [bMS Am 1248.1 (209)].

21. JRL to CEN of [25 Oct 1861], JRL Papers, HL [bMS Am 765 (91)]; JRL to CEN of July 1862, JRL Papers, HL [bMS Am 765 (91)]; the exception is CEN to JRL of 22 Oct 1864 on the occasion of Charles Russell Lowell's death at Cedar Creek: "My dearest James, Your sorrow is ours also. . . . I can scarcely write for tears in thinking of poor Effie [C. R. Lowell's wife Josephine Shaw Lowell, sister to the deceased Robert Gould Shaw and to George Curtis' wife

Anna],—of her mother & his. May God sustain them!" in JRL Papers, HL [bMS Am 765 (583)]; CEN to JRL of 19 Dec 1861 in *CEN Letters*, 1:249; CEN to JRL of 20 Jan 1878, JRL Papers, HL [bMS Am 765 (598)]; CEN to JRL of 11 May 1884, JRL Papers, HL [bMS Am 765 (604)].

22. Norton, "Francis James Child," 168; Norton, Address to 20th Mass. Volunteers, NP [bMS Am 1088 (Box 14)]; because Norton fell sick during the journey down to Washington, D.C., to deliver the address, his speech had to be given in absentia by Palfrey's father on Dec 25, 1861; the red silk flag, inscribed with "Ball's Bluff 21st Oct 1861" and the motto "Having Done All, To Stand" (from Ephesians 6:13: "Wherefore take unto you the whole armour of God, that ye may be able to withstand in the evil day, and having done all, to stand"), was the gift of the sisters of Willie Putnam and James Jackson Lowell; of the flag Lieut. Col. Palfrey told Norton "we, with one accord, regard it as the most sumptuous & beautiful flag we have ever seen," NP [bMS Am 1088 (5204)]; cf. Dr. Henry Bryant: "Poor Lieutenant Putnam was lying near the fireplace with his intestines projecting from a wound in his abdomen," quoted in Miller, *Harvard's Civil*, 81; Col. Lee at 53, was accounted second-oldest field officer in the Army of the Potomac (Miller, "Trouble," p. 41). Lee was one of the prisoners chosen by lot to be hanged by the Confederates in retaliation if Lincoln's announced policy of hanging captured Confederate privateer crews as pirates were carried out; in the end, Lincoln backed away from the policy.

23. Sumner to Richard Henry Dana, Jr., of 14 Dec 1861, quoted in Donald, *Sumner*, 48.

24. CEN to CN of 14 Feb 1846, NP [bMS Am 1088.2 (Box 9)]; CEN to FJC of 15 March 1855 in *CEN Letters*, 1:122; CEN to MG of 25 Nov 1860, NP [bMS Am 1088.2 (Box 4)]; cf. CEN to ADV of 24 Feb 1861: "[There are] many persons amongst us, many good people too, who would do anything, make every concession to Slavery, for the sake of preserving the Union. The Union is to them the chief object of desire,—and in their eyes I & the men who feel like me are little better than traitors. But for my part I have no wish to preserve the Union if it can be preserved only at the expense of the Freedom and the Justice which it was formed originally to promote" [bMS Am 1088.5 (Box 3)]. Norton's earlier doubts about abolitionists were so far erased by 1864 that he asked Wendell Phillips to write an essay about William Lloyd Garrison for the *NAR* that "might by its judicial fairness do something to remove the prejudice which still in many quarters prevents the career & the character of Mr. Garrison from being appreciated as they deserve" [CEN to Wendell Phillips of 9 Feb 1864, HL [bMS Am 1953 (936)].

25. The observation that Norton "did not believe in racial equality" (Menand, *Metaphysical*, p. 51), frequently and uncritically handed about in recent scholarship, seems to have had its origin in George Fredrickson's claim in *The Inner Civil War* that "Just before the outbreak of the war, Norton adopted what amounted to an anti-Negro, antiegalitarian 'free-soil' doctrine" (*Inner Civil*, p. 47). This is a notion Fredrickson apparently deduced from a single essay, Norton's *Atlantic Monthly* review (February 1861) of Sidney George Fisher's *The Laws of Race as Connected with Slavery*. The problem is, that in the portions of the review that make such a deduction even remotely possible, Norton

is paraphrasing Fisher's opinions, not giving his own. When Norton does express his own views, it is to disagree with Fisher. In *The Union Party*, Mark E. Neely has recently drawn attention to Fredrickson's distortions of evidence in *The Inner Civil War*. As an example of the sort of selective quotation that is then used to support judgments like Menand's (who cites this very page of Fredrickson's book), the following may be taken as representative. First, a sentence as it stands in its entirety in Norton's *Atlantic Monthly* review of Fisher's book on race and slavery:

The black is in many of his endowments inferior to the white; but until he and his children and his children's children have shown an incapacity to be raised by a suitable training, honestly given, to an intellectual and moral condition that shall fit them for self-dependence, we have no right to assert that slavery is necessary condition, if in the meaning of necessary we include the idea of permanence. (Norton, "*Laws of Race*," p. 253)

Now the portion of the same sentence quoted by Fredrickson as evidence of "an anti-Negro, antiegalitarian" doctrine:

The black is in many of his endowments inferior to the white. (*Inner Civil*, p. 47)

Neely's analysis supports the notion that Fredrickson's anti-establishment bias always had more to do with the 1960s—when the word "endowments" was identified with gifts of nature—than with the 1860s—when "endowments" still referred to advantages bestowed *either* by nature or by fortune. In Norton's case, at any rate, serious work with the primary materials immediately suggests as much.

26. CEN to GPM of 27 Apr 1862, GPM Papers, Special Collections, Bailey/Howe Library, Univ. of Vermont; CEN to GWC of 23 Sept 1862 in *CEN Letters*, 1:256–57; CEN to GWC of 30 Sept 1862 in *CEN Letters*, 1:257.

27. CEN to GWC of 16 Apr 1863, NP [bMS Am 1088.2 (Box 2)]; Sumner to Edward L. Pierce, quoted in Donald, *Sumner*, 118; cf. the letter of Willie Putnam to his mother written a week before his death at Ball's Bluff: "God grant that every river in this land of ours may run with blood, and every city be laid in ashes rather than this war should come to an end without the utter destruction of every vestige of this curse so monstrous," quoted in Bundy, *Nature of Sacrifice*, 197.

28. CEN to GPM of 9 May 1863, GPM Papers, Special Collections, Bailey/Howe Library, Univ. of Vermont.

29. CEN to John Murray Forbes of 27 Dec 1863, NP [bMS Am 1088.5 (Box 3)]; CEN to GWC of 24 July 1864 in *CEN Letters*, 1:274; W. T. Sherman to U.S. Grant of 29 Jan 1865 in Sherman, *Memoirs*, 740.

30. See McPherson, *What They Fought For, passim*; James H. Bradd Diary, entry for 18 Apr 1864, quoted in Hess, *Union Soldier*, 141.

31. CEN to GPM of 19 April 1864, GPM Papers, Special Collections, Bailey/Howe Library, Univ. of Vermont; Lowell, "Causes," 267.

32. Lowell, "Causes," 267.

33. Mill, "Contest," 142; John Lothrop Motley to Oliver Wendell Holmes of 26 Feb 1862 in Motley, *Correspondence*, 2:64; Holmes to Motley of 8 Mar 1862 in Motley, *Correspondence*, 2:69.

34. Mill, "Contest," 135.

35. See Woodworth, *While God, passim*; cf. Mill, "Contest," 141: "But war, in a good cause, is not the greatest evil which a nation can suffer. War is an ugly thing, but not the ugliest of things: the decayed and degraded state of moral and patriotic feeling which thinks nothing *worth* a war, is worse" (Mill's emphasis).

36. Terry, "New Sangréal," 344.

37. Norton, "Advantages," 364–65; Norton, "Our Soldiers," 177–78.

38. Oliver Wendell Holmes, Jr., to CEN of 17 Apr 1864, NP [bMS Am 1088 (3532)]; Maj. James A. Connolly, quoted in Hess, *Union Soldier*, 130.

39. Norton, "Harvard Memorial," 507–508, 498; Norton, "Our Soldiers," 185; Norton, "Harvard Memorial," 507, 509.

40. Norton, "Harvard Memorial," 506.

41. Norton, "Advantages," 362; Norton, "Our Soldiers," 198; cf. the hidden tribute Norton offered to his brother-in-law Arthur Sedgwick in a passage praising General John Sedgwick, killed at Spotsylvania: "As we call the roll, each name answers for others beside him who bore it. Sedgwick, the self-poised, modest, thorough soldier" ("Our Soldiers," 175).

42. Bellows, "Sanitary," 158.

43. Norton, "Work," 145n, 150; Bellows, "Sanitary," 183.

44. Norton, "Emancipation in the Middle Ages," MS lecture given at the Lowell Institution on 1 Jan 1863, NP [*46M–66F]; Norton, "Work," 154.

45. Norton, "Work," 145n; Norton, "Goldwin Smith," 524.

46. Norton, *Notes of Travel*, 110; CEN to MG of 2 Oct 1865, NP [bMS Am 1088.2 (Box 4)]; Norton, "Draper's *Civil*," 408.

47. Norton, "International," 608; Emerson, "American Civilization," 511; Norton, "Wilson's *Anti-Slavery*," 239; CEN to GWC of 2 Oct 1861, NP [bMS Am 1088.2 (Box 2)]; CEN to MG of 2 Oct 1865, NP [bMS Am 1088.2 (Box 4)].

48. CEN to GPM of 29 Dec 1864, GPM Papers, Special Collections, Bailey/Howe Library, Univ. of Vermont.

49. CEN to ADV of 25 March 1867, NP [bMS Am 1088.2 (Box 3)]; cf. Norton's reaction to the panic rout of the first battle of Bull Run: "From the first Grace [Norton's younger sister] took the news bravely, and as for me I was optimist as usual. I could not regard the defeat, even at the worst, as a serious disaster" (CEN to JN of 20 July 1861, NP [bMS Am 1088.2 (Box 10)]).

50. CEN to GPM of 29 Dec 1864, GPM Papers, Special Collections, Bailey/Howe Library, Univ. of Vermont; Whittredge, *Autobiography*, 43; Clarence Cook, quoted in Ferber, "Determined," 36, n43; Smith and Judah, *Life in North*, 296; cf. also Norton, "Beadle's Dime Books": "And it is a striking fact, to be learned from Messrs. Beadle & Co.'s account of sales, that the best books on their list are those for which there is the greatest demand" (p. 308).

51. "The 40th Exhibition," 26; Werner, *It Happened*, 209, 190; Bellows, NY Sanitary Fair memorandum of 18 Nov 1863, quoted in Werner, *It Happened*, 191; *Boston Transcript*, Sanitary Fair supplement of 18 Dec 1863, n. p.

52. *Boston Transcript*, 3 Dec 1863, n. p.; *Boston Transcript*, Sanitary Fair supplement of 18 Dec 1863, n. p.; Norton became a proprietor of the Athenaeum in 1849, taking over the share of William S. Bullard; in 1856 he acquired an

additional share, which upon leaving for Europe in 1868 he transferred to Arthur Sedgwick; Norton was a trustee of the Athenaeum from 1852 to 1864 (*Catalog of the Athenaeum*, pp. 5, 12, 24).

53. See Ruskin's *The Two Paths*, 310; Russell Sturgis to CEN of 2 June 1863, NP [bMS Am 1088 (7280)]; Norton sent his Rossetti watercolor, "Before the Battle" to Charles Herbert Moore on extended loan (Charles Herbert Moore to CEN of 11 Mar 1867, quoted in Mather, *Charles Herbert*, p. 24).

54. JR to CEN of 28 July 1863 in *JR/CEN Correspondence*, 79; JR to CEN of 6 Aug 1864 in *JR/CEN Correspondence*, 80.

55. *New Path* 1, i (May 1863): 4; *New Path* 1, xiii (Dec 1863): 94; *New Path* 2, i (May 1864): 4.

56. Norton, "*The New Path*," 303; Stein, "A Flower's Saving," 90.

57. Emerson, "Fortune," 396; *New Path* 1, ii (June 1863): 17; *New Path* 1, iv (Aug 1863): 41–42.

58. *New Path*, 2, iii (July 1864): 35; Sturgis, "Condition of Art," 18 (Norton commissioned the article from Sturgis for the *NAR*, revising it so heavily that he may be considered its co-author—see Vanderbilt, *Charles Eliot Norton*, pp. 89–90); James, *William Wetmore*, 1:297.

59. "Peter Bonnet Wight," *DAB*, 20:196; Wight, "Reminiscences of the Building," 25; Wight, quoted in Norton, "Wight's National," 587: " 'I believe,' Mr. Wight continues, and we heartily adopt his belief, 'that there is great hope for art in the future, and that the day when modern architecture shall attain its greatest glory from the association of all other arts with it will surely come, even though not in this generation . . . . [ellipsis in original] The art of the future will grow out of the wants of the future. I believe it will be one of the results of unseen regenerative influences which have been felt through the world to a greater or less extent during this generation, and of which modern war, and especially our civil war, have been no small part.' "

60. Fry, quoted in Jenkyns, *Legacy of Rome*, 9; Norton, Art in America MS lecture, NP [bMS Am 1088.5 (Box 6)]; Kemble, letter of 27 May 1835, in *Records*, 14; Olmsted, *Cotton Kingdom*, 425.

61. "Art and Art-Life," 599; Dicey, *Spectator*, 61; *New Path* 1, vii (Nov 1863): 80; Norton, "Wight's National," 586.

62. Norton, American Culture MS lecture, NP [Nor 5752.25f*]; *New Path* 2, ii (June 1864): 25.

63. "Yale College Art," 115; Norton, "Wight's National," 586; *New Path* 2, vi (June 1865): 85; Wight, quoted in Norton, "Wight's National," 588.

64. *New Path* 1, xi (Mar 1864): 142; Hersey, *High Victorian*, 197; Norton, "Oxford Museum," 769.

65. Wight, quoted in Norton, "Wight's National," 588; *New Path* 2, ii (June 1864): 29; cf. Orlowski, "Frank Furness": "The National Academy of Design became an important example [of Ruskinian principles] for architects of Furness' generation. Furness based his design for the Pennsylvania Academy of Fine Art (1871–76) on Wight's model" (p. 152).

66. Norton, "Paradise," 44.

67. Norton, "Harvard and Yale," 35; Shaffer, "Ruskin, Norton," 223.

68. CEN to Charles Loring of 28 July 1865, A. A. Lawrence Papers [Box 19],

Massachusetts Historical Society, Boston, MA; A. Sedgwick, "Words," 437; GEN to Charles Loring of 28 July 1865.

69. Norton, "Harvard and Yale," 34; perhaps seeking to repair the breach, Norton in 1878 sought information from Van Brunt about the constructional principles of Brunelleschi's dome for the Florentine cathedral; he received a brusque reply (Henry Van Brunt to CEN of 20 Nov 1878, NP [bMS Am 1088 (7542)]); when Frederick Withers' 1866 design for Yale's Battell Chapel failed to secure adequate funding, a new plan by Russell Sturgis was accepted for construction in 1874.

70. Ephraim W. Gurney to JN of probably late July 1867, quoted in E. W. Emerson, *Early Years*, 432; Norton, "Harvard and Yale," 35; the medieval Florentine decree is quoted in Norton, "New Life," 65, 66: "The records of few other cities contain a decree so magnificent as this."

71. Norton, "Harvard and Yale," 35; R. W. Emerson, "The Problem," 496.

72. CEN to GPM of 29 Dec 1864, GPM Papers, Special Collections, Bailey/ Howe Library, Univ. of Vermont.

73. Sturgis, "The 45th Exhibition," 341: "Landscape art disappears year by year from our exhibitions . . . [and] the public take no interest whatever in landscape. It is a languid enough pleasure that they take in pictures of any kind"; Fite, *Social and Industrial*, 256: "With prices soaring publishers brought out only standard books of permanent value, for which there was an immediate and sure sale, and nothing was taken on speculation. This accounts for the surprisingly high tone of the new books"; the facade of the National Academy of Design building was saved and, in 1904, re-integrated into Our Lady of Lourdes Roman Catholic Church on 142nd Street in New York City; Shaffer, "Ruskin, Norton," 277n.

Chapter 3: Culture as Virtue

1. GWC to CEN of 4 Apr 1865 in GWC Papers, HL [bMS Am 1124 (263)]; Strong, *Diary*, 3:574–75.

2. CEN to GPM of 9 May 1863, GPM Papers, Special Collections, Bailey/ Howe Library, Univ. of Vermont; CEN to MG of 12 and 25 May 1863, NP [bMS Am 1088.2 (Box 4)]; Chesnut, *Diary*, 379.

3. Norton, "American Political," 564; McPherson, *Struggle*, 335; Richardson, *Death*, 16–17; cf. Norton on Johnson: "As a 'mean white' he has learned to hate [the slave-holding class]; but as a man he has not learned to hate slavery or to recognize the right of the black to political equality with the white" (CEN to GPM of 21 Aug 1865, GPM Papers, Special Collections, Bailey/Howe Library, Univ. of Vermont).

4. Riddleberger, *1866*, 12–13; Norton, "American Political," 564.

5. Norton, "American Political," 554–55, 564–66.

6. Norton, "Advantages," 361; Boswell, *Life of Johnson*, 2:155: "He would not admit *civilization*, but only *civility*. With great deference to him, I thought *civilization* from *to civilize*, better in the sense opposed to *barbarity*, than *civility*; as it is better to have a distinct word for each sense, than one word with two senses,

which *civility* is, in his way of using it." Boswell, as a Scot, was familiar with the newer four-stage terminology.

7. Bagehot, "Adam Smith," 255.

8. Pocock, "Tucker," 188.

9. Ferguson, *Essay*, 81.

10. Bushnell, *Barbarism*, 20, 18, 19.

11. Olmsted, *Cotton Kingdom*, 553, 534.

12. Cairnes, quoted in Mill, "Slave Power," 146; Mill, "Contest," 141.

13. Sumner, "Barbarism," 127.

14. Strong, *Diary*, 2:299; De Forest, *Miss Ravenel's*, 55.

15. Harper, *Memoir on Slavery*, 35.

16. Dew, "Review of the Debate," 338–39; Simms, *Morals*, 185, 271.

17. Bushnell, *Barbarism*, 18.

18. The photograph of the Pringle-Norton group is reproduced in Middleton, *Life in Carolina*, opposite p. 61; for Edward Pringle's pamphlet *Slavery at the South*, see Turner, *Liberal*, 110–11; William Porcher Miles to CEN of 11 May 1853, NP [bMS Am 1088 (4709)].

19. *Lotus-Eating: A Summer Book*, Curtis's collection of travel sketches illustrated by John Kensett, was published in 1852; GWC letter of 10 Aug 1854, quoted in Cary, *George William*, 89–90.

20. CEN to Thomas Gold Appleton of 9 Aug 1854, NP [bMS Am 1088.5 (Box 1)]; "Clytie," ca. 40–50 CE, forms part of the Townley collection in the British Museum; Mary Hering Middleton to Eliza Middleton Fisher of 16 Jan 1840, quoted in Harrison, *Best Companions*, 100: "He considers her the most clever of his family which I have always thought the case"; Chesnut, *Diary*, 353; Richard Baird Smith to JN of 17 June 1853, NP [bMS Am 1088.1 (89)]: "Is he 'kinder partial' to that pleasant Miss Middleton still?" (that Smith was referring to Matilda and not Ella is clear because Victorian social convention prescribed that the oldest unmarried daughter was referred to as "Miss [Family name]," while her younger sisters were known as "Miss [Given name] [Family name]"; in 1854 Matilda Middleton was 24, Ella, 23 and Norton, 27.

21. The Middletons' visit to Shady Hill is mentioned in CN to Mrs. Oliver Hering Middleton of 25 Nov 1854, Middleton-Blake Papers, South Carolina Historical Society; CEN to AHC of 5 Apr 1855 in *CEN Letters*, 1:122; CEN to FJC of 15 Mar 1855, NP [bMS Am 1088.5 (Box 1)]; CEN to JRL of 6 Apr 1855 in *CEN Letters*, 1:125; CEN to CN of 15 Apr 1855, NP [bMS Am 1088.2 (Box 10)]; the two clauses following "saved" and ending with "improvement" were deleted sometime later by Norton, presumably after he lost his belief in immortality.

22. From Chesnut's autobiographical fragment "Two Years—Or the Way We Lived Then," quoted in Woodward, "Introduction," xxxii; Holmes, "Inevitable Trial," 88: "Slavery gratifies at once the love of power, the love of money, and the love of ease; it finds a victim for anger who cannot smite back his oppressor; and it offers to all, without measure, the seductive privileges which the Mormon gospel reserves for the true believers on earth, and the Bible of Mahamet only dares promise to the saints in heaven"; Chesnut, *Diary*, 253 (entry of 28 Nov 1863); Chesnut, *Private Mary*, 117 (entry of 31 Aug 1861); CEN to CN of

21 Mar 1855, NP (bMS Am 1088.2 (Box 10)]; William Porcher Miles to CEN of 26 Apr 1853, NP [bMS Am 1088 (4708)]; CEN to FJC of 15 March 1855 in *CEN Letters,* 1:122.

23. CEN to AHC of 7 May 1855, NP [bMS Am 1088.2 (Box 11)]; CEN to CN of 21 Mar 1855, NP [bMS Am 1088.2 (Box 10)].

24. JN to Mrs. Oliver Hering Middleton of 6 Sept [1855], Middleton-Blake Papers, South Carolina Historical Society; CEN to GWC of 9 Feb 1862, NP [bMS Am 1088.2 (Box 2)]; Chesnut, *Private Mary* (entry of 20 Nov 1861), 205; Matilda Middleton to Mary Chesnut of April 1865 in *Mary Chesnut's Civil War,* 778; in autobiographical notes dictated in 1908 (NP, bMS Am 1088.5 [Box 15]), CEN recalled "the severing of all relation with [the Middletons] when the war broke out—severed by them in profound & perhaps natural bitterness of heart"; various references in NP, however, indicate that Matilda Middleton continued to write affectionately at least into 1863, perhaps breaking off the correspondence only after young Oliver's death (on 30 May 1864); CEN to ELG of 20 July 1865 mentions "a very remarkable letter from Miss Middleton" to Jane and Grace in which "[t]he old spirit is intensified to an incredible degree of bitterness" (ELG Papers [bMS Am 1083 [613]]); there are no Matilda Middleton letters preserved in NP.

25. *Mary Chesnut's Civil War,* 782; Wells, *Sketch,* 48–52; W. Eric Emerson, *Sons of Privilege,* 81; more than three weeks after Noll's death, Oliver Middleton, Sr., wrote William Porcher Miles for help in retrieving his son's body (see W. Eric Emerson, p. 91); in a long letter of 27 Aug 1874 (marked by Norton's daughter Sally, "About Southern friends. *Burn*"), CEN tells JN what he has learned about the postwar fate of the Middletons from their cousin, John Middleton: "The Oliver Middletons have very scanty means, but yet enough to live on without actual suffering from want. . . . [Mr. Oliver Middleton]'s feelings toward the North are of deep hatred, & John Middleton says he thinks he would not cross the Potomac even, if by so doing, he could recover his property. He retains the plantation at Edisto, & goes there once a fortnight; it is worked under a negro foreman, but it is very little worked, & produces scarcely anything. Matilda is not much changed in appearance, but is very much altered, so her cousin thinks, in character. She seems to him to have grown hard & generally embittered. She insults him, he said, whenever he sees her. She told him since the war, that she still loves Jane & Grace Norton, but she wished never to see them again," NP [bMS Am 1088.2 (Box 10)].

26. Wimsatt, *Major Fiction,* 173–7; Strong, *Diary,* 4:362.

27. CEN, "Advantages," 361; Theodore Tilton in 1875, quoted in Fox, *Trials of Intimacy,* 115; *Othello,* III:iii.

28. Timrod, "The Cotton Boll," 316; CEN to JRL of 21 July 1861 in *CEN Letters,* 1:237.

29. Sherman quoted in Davis, *Sherman's March,* 16; Massachusetts soldier quoted in Rable, "Hearth, Home," 100; Robert Gould Shaw to Annie Haggerty Shaw of 12 June 1863 in Shaw, *Blue-Eyed Child,* 343; just two weeks earlier, the Confederate Congress had affirmed a policy of punishing captured Union officers of black troops as "criminals engaged in inciting servile insurrection," with the death penalty to be inflicted upon conviction (McPherson, *Battle Cry,*

p. 566); Charles Russell Lowell to Josephine Shaw Lowell of 5 Oct 1864, quoted in E. W. Emerson, *Life and Letters*, 353.

30. Sherman to Halleck quoted in Liddell Hart, *Sherman*, 358; cf. Harriott Middleton to Susan Matilda Middleton of 21 Mar [1865]: "Weehaw is gone—lying in ashes. . . . I mourn over Frank's garden as I would over a dear friend, and the Yankees cut down the oak trees everywhere. Susan—I know now what it is to hate! I believe that the destruction of Frank's garden has taught it to me. My dear do you know (Do not tell) that I would like to *see* the Yankees lying in their blood" (*South Carolina Historical Magazine*, 65, ii (Apr 1964): 105; Harriott's brother, Francis Kinloch Middleton, of the Charleston Light Dragoons, had been severely wounded on 28 May 1864, dying two days later—on the same day as Matilda's young brother, Oliver Middleton, Jr.

31. Trent, *William Gilmore*, 281; Simms, *Sack and Destruction*, 44; Harriott Middleton to Matilda Middleton of 28 Feb 1865 in *South Carolina Historical Magazine* 65, ii (Apr 1964): 102–103 (ellipsis by *SCHM*).

32. Norton, "Waste," 302; Holmes, "Inevitable," 113; for price of fruit in 1863, see Chesnut, *Diary*, 263 and Holmes, "Inevitable," 113.

33. *Ladies' Repository*, quoted in Moorhead, *American Apocalypse*, 225; John Sherman, quoted in Morison, *Concise History*, 325; Howells, *Hazard of New*, 1:230.

34. Strong, *Diary*, 4:488.

35. Ferguson, *Essay*, 206.

36. See McLachlan, "American Colleges," 202; see also Turner, *Liberal*, 48, 117, 183–84.

37. CEN to John Bright of 8 May 1863: "slave owners must be exterminated or suppressed or driven away," British Library [Add. MSS. 43391, f. 148–151]; CEN to GPM of 9 May 1863, GPM Papers, Special Collections, Bailey/Howe Library, Univ. of Vermont: "We must thoroughly subjugate, & if necessary exterminate the slave holding class, leaving them no power politically or socially, & this is not a quick process"; unnamed Englishman quoted in Trollope, *Domestic Manners*, 242; Trollope's view of Americans in 1832 may be compared to J. S. Mill's opinion, expressed in his *Principles of Political Economy*, that in America "the life of the whole of one sex is devoted to dollar-hunting, and of the other to breeding dollar-hunters" (*Principles*, 754); Norton read Mill's *Principles* on his long voyage out to India in 1849; Mill dropped the remark from later editions.

38. De Forest, "High-Toned," 206, 208.

39. CEN to ADV of 25 Mar 1867, NP [bMS Am 1088.2 (Box 3)]; CEN to ELG of 20 July 1865, ELG Papers, HL [bMS Am 1083 (613)]; Norton, "Good Manners," 571.

40. Whittier, "In War-Time," 236.

41. Andrews' "On the Duty of Continual Improvement (Philippians iii:13,14)" was published in 1825; Ware's "Duty of Improvement" was preached on 31 Dec 1826, quoted in Ware, *Memoir of Henry Ware*, 180; Motley, letter to his mother of 9 June 1862 in *JLM Correspondence*, 2:76; see also Turner, *Liberal*, 183–84.

42. CEN, Reminiscences of 1908, NP [bMS Am 1088.5 (Box 15)]; Morley, "Death of Mr. Mill," 671; cf. George Curtis on Mill: "the truest American will

find upon his heroic pages the gleams of a fairer and ampler America than ever in vision even Samuel Adams saw" ("Eulogy of Sumner," p. 123).

43. CEN to Chauncey Wright of 13 Sept 1870 in *CEN Letters* 1:399; Charles Francis Adams, Jr., *Autobiography*, 179; CEN, Reminiscences of 1908, NP [bMS Am 1088.5 (Box 15)].

44. See Hall's "Victorian Connection"; Bagehot, *English Constitution*, quoted in Kent, *Brains*, 46.

45. Strong, *Diary*, 4:187; Gladstone quoted in Collini, *Public Moralists*, 112.

46. R. W. Emerson, *English Traits*, 54–55; Thompson, *Englishman*, 61.

47. Dicey, *Spectator*, 266; Smith, "Experience," 218; John Lothrop Motley to his mother of 16 Mar 1862 in *JLM Correspondence*, 2:71.

48. Stephen, *Some Early*, 102; Buchan, *Spare Chancellor*, 179.

49. Mill, *On Liberty*, 267.

50. Tocqueville, *Voyages*, 206–207; Arnold, "Function of Criticism," 261; cf. Norton, echoing Arnold, in an address given at the dedication of the Slater Memorial Museum in Norwich, CT (22 Nov 1888): "For its happy & productive exercise the creative imagination requires a certain spiritual & intellectual atmosphere, and this America does not yet supply," NP [Nor 5257.25f*]; when Norton described the chill and airless environment of Cambridgeport, Massachusetts as having stunted the genius of the American painter George Washington Allston, he used the same word, declaring Allston's story "is pathetic, for it is that of an exquisitely-endowed nature struggling to exist in atmosphere that was wholly uncongenial. He was like a plant needing a rich soil that had struck its roots in the sand. He never succeeded in expressing himself. The fire that burnt within him needed more oxygen than the air about him supplied" ("Definition," p. 37).

51. JSM letter to James M. Barnard of 28 Oct 1869 in *JSM Collected Works*, 17:1662 (my emphasis).

52. My account of Mill and self-development in this and the next 3 paragraphs depends upon Wendy Donner's analysis in *The Liberal Self.*

53. Mill, *Utilitarianism*, 211.

54. Mill, *On Liberty*, 269, 270.

55. Norton, "Goldwin Smith," 526; HWL to Charles Sumner of 20 Apr 1862 in *HWL Letters*, 4:277.

56. Mill, *On Liberty*, 266.

57. Norton, "Sir Alexander," 107; CW to GN of 13 Jan 1870 in Wright, *Letters*, 162.

58. Norton, "American Political," 565; Norton, "*History of New*," 640; Curtis, "The Good Fight," 176.

59. Harper, *Memoir on Slavery*, 35; CEN to JBH of 20 Mar 1864, NP [bMS Am 1088.2 (Box 4)]; Curtis, "The Good Fight," 170.

60. JSM to ELG of 24 May 1865, quoted in Ogden, *Life of ELG*, 1:43; Norton, "*History of New*, 639, 640; cf. the *Home Missionary* for Nov 1869: "New England has declined—into America. Plymouth Rock is only the doorstep of a house that reaches to the Golden Gate" (quoted in Power, "A Crusade," p. 653); cf. also CEN to JRL of 19 Dec 1861: "A few years hence and Boston will be a place of the past, with a good history no doubt, but New York will be alive. It seems to

be getting what Paris has so much of—a confidence in the immortality of the present moment" (*CEN Letters*, 1:247–48).

61. JSM to James M. Barnard of 26 Jan 1870 in *JSM Works* 17:1691; in CEN to JSM of 10 Apr 1868, Johns Hopkins Univ. Library, Norton urged Mill to "speak of the delusiveness of the seeming prosperity based on unlimited issues of irredeemable currency"; JSM to CEN of 24 Nov 1865 in *JSM Works*, 16:1119 (my emphasis).

62. CEN to FLO of 24 Jan 1864 in *CEN Letters* 1:268; Norton, "Paradise," 44.

63. CEN to Carolyn H. Dall of 8 Feb 1868, Carolyn H. Dall Papers, Massachusetts Historical Society; CEN to CW of 13 Sept 1870 in *CEN Letters* 1:399.

64. R. W. Emerson, *English Traits*, 178; Mrs. Jameson on Allston, quoted in Brooks, *Flowering*, 165; Greenough, *Travels*, 129; R. W. Emerson, "Progress of Culture" (1867), 215.

65. JSM to ELG of 24 May 1865, quoted in Ogden, *Life of ELG*, 1:43; Trollope, *Domestic Manners*, 253; Parker, quoted in Lowell, "Democracy," 16; Lowell, "Democracy," 27.

Chapter 4: Eden and After

1. CEN to JBH of 19 Mar 1865, NP [bMS Am 1088.2 (Box 4)].

2. Froude, *Life of Carlyle*, 419–20.

3. Cf. *CEN Letters*, 1:181: "*Sturm und Drang* were foreign to his temper of mind."

4. For Norton's Puritan heritage, see Vanderbilt, *Charles Eliot Norton*, 7–12; as Vanderbilt has encouraged the impression that Norton "appears never to have been a child at all" (p. 22), it may be worth giving this report by the seven-year-old Charles of an overnight visit to his Aunt Guild's house in Brookline: "[A]fter I got there I played with Charley Guild up in a tree to play ship, played about an hour then it was time to go to dinner. [A]fter dinner went into the garden & climbed another tree. [W]ent to see the pigs, & played in the asparagus. [W]ent into the garden & played with the four wheels of a little waggon. Mr. & Mrs [Henry R.] Cleveland came, & we had supper. [W]ent into the East parlour & dressed up like a Siberian & said a little poetry." The next day the two boys "went to our ship in the tree," then "played with the four wheels & rode on sticks for horses, played by the Pigs sty"; Norton's dictated report is preserved on a slip dated [24 &] 25 July 1835 in the so-called "Child Papers" notebook, NP [bMS Am 1088.5 (Box 2)].

5. Catharine Norton's notes to CEN are mentioned in *CEN Letters*, 2:91; CEN to AHC of 17 Sept 1853 in *CEN Letters*, 1:94; CEN to AN of 25 Feb 1849, NP [bMS Am 1088.2 (Box 9)]; CEN to his family of 9 July 1850, NP [bMS Am 1088.2 (Box 9)]; Louisa Norton, four years older than Charles, married William S. Bullard in 1851; Jane Norton was three years older than Charles, while Grace was seven years younger.

6. Longfellow quoted in Fields, *Authors and Friends*, 23; Dana, *Journal*, 1:218.

7. AHC to Blanche Smith of 4 Jan 1853 in Clough, *Correspondence*, 2:360; cf. J. C. Shairp to AHC of 20 Jan 1853: "It may be strange, but I had always an instinctive horror of this (Unitarianism) — and even when at any time driven that way in thought I felt like a man would, who was being immersed in polar ice" (Clough, *Correspondence*, 2:367).

8. For Norton's looking at pictures of the Inquisition at age 8, see "Child Papers' notebook, NP [bMS Am 1088.5 (Box 2)]; Norton's commonplace book with long quotations from Foxe's *Book of Martyrs* is in NP [bMS Am 1088.5 (Box 3)]; as a boy of six, Charles had met the Italian patriot and political refugee, Piero Maroncelli, see Turner, *Liberal*, 33.

9. First published as "The New School in Literature and Religion" in a Boston newspaper, Andrews' attack on Emerson's July 1838 Divinity School Address was later expanded to book length and issued as *A Discourse on the Latest Form of Infidelity* in 1839; Martineau, *Retrospect*, 2:99; AHC to Blanche Smith of 4 Jan 1854 in Clough, *Correspondence*, 2:360.

10. Cf. CEN to AHC of 20 Dec 1853: "Seriously, I wish you were here again for I think I may have grown brighter since [AHC's departure]. I should not have to force you to intelligibility as I used to, at any rate" (quoted in Biswas, *Arthur Hugh Clough*, p. 457); Turner has suggested that Andrews's symptoms were consistent with heart disease (see *Liberal*, p. 120); CEN to AHC of 25 Apr 1852, NP [bMS Am 1088.8]; for the overture to Emerson, see Turner, *Liberal*, 111.

11. Ripley, "*Latest Form*," 217.

12. CEN's biographical fragment about AN is in NP [bMS Am 1088.5 (Box 4)]; in reprinting this fragment in their biography, Norton's daughter and her co-author, M. A. DeWolfe Howe, soften some of its expressions (cf. *CEN Letters*, 1:84); Richard Henry Dana, Jr., reports an 1855 conversation between two of Andrews' contemporaries: "They agreed Norton was a conscientious & just man, but excessively bigoted to his own creed, & bitter ag[ainst] any who believed a little more or a little less than he, while his creed was one that few persons but himself agreed to" (in Dana, *Journal*, p. 682).

13. Norton reviewed *Essays and Reviews* in the *Atlantic Monthly* for November 1860; he ordered Renan's *Vie de Jésus* from his bookseller in 1863, NP [bMS Am 1088.5 (Box 2)].

14. Notation for 6 Oct 1863 in Stephen's journal, quoted in Maitland, *Life and Letters*, 118; for Stephen's religious quandary, see Bicknell, "The Young Mr. Ramsay," 14–15; Norton, "Arthur Hugh Clough," 462; Clough died in 1861 at the age of 42; Howells, "Charles Eliot Norton," 838; CEN to JRL of 26 Nov 1886, JRL Papers, HL [bMS Am 765 (606)]; Arnold, "The Buried Life," ll. 84, 87.

15. Norton, "Goldwin Smith," 538; CEN to GWC of 18 Oct 1864 in *CEN Letters*, 1:281; CEN to JBH of 15 Aug 1865, NP [bMS Am 1088.2 (Box 4)].

16. CW to CEN of 13 June 1867 in Wright, *Letters*, 99; CEN to JS of 15 May 1875 in *CEN Letters*, 2:53; cf. Turner, *Liberal*, 212: "Probably . . . long conversations with Chauncey Wright abetted Norton's drift from Unitarianism more than any other single influence"; seven years after Chauncey's death, Norton told Ansel Wright, "Your brother's loss is still fresh to me. So long as I may live I shall not cease to miss him" (CEN to Ansel Wright of 16 Oct 1882, Chauncey Wright Papers, American Philosophical Society, Philadelphia, PA).

17. The Unitarian clergyman was the Rev. Charles Grinnell of Charlestown in 1870, quoted in Madden, *Chauncey Wright*, 16; Wright's influence on Norton's religious ideas is dramatically visible in an essay on "Religious Liberty" which Norton wrote for the April 1867 *North American Review*. For in defining religion "as a man's devotion—that is, the compete assent and concentration of his will—to any object which he acknowledges to have a right to his entire service, and to supreme control over his life," Norton is in fact quoting Wright. Here and in the long paragraph immediately following this passage, Norton is taking over the exact words of a "brief" or memorandum Wright sent him summing up the philosopher's reflections on their conversation about Norton's upcoming *North American* essay on religion; Norton, "Religious Liberty," 594; for the parallel passage in Wright, see CW to CEN of 18 Feb 1867 in Wright, *Letters*, 97–98.

18. James, "Chauncey Wright," 145.

19. James, "Chauncey Wright," 145; Perry, *Thought and Character*, 1:522.

20. CEN to MG of 14 July 1867, NP [bMS Am 1088.2 (Box 4)].

21. The American minister was Moncure Conway; see his *Thomas Carlyle*, 123; see Ripley, "Philosophic Thought," 300; Beecher, *Autobiography*, 2:37.

22. Hildreth, "A Letter to Andrews," 226; Eliot, quoted in M. A. DeWolfe Howe, C. E. Norton Notes, HL [bMS Am 1826 (417)].

23. See Turner, *Liberal*, 172–74, 178.

24. CEN to ADV of 30 Mar 1862, NP [bMS Am 1088.2 (Box 3)]; CEN to GWC of 8 Apr 1862, NP [bMS Am 1088.2 (Box 2)]; JN to GWC of 24 Mar [1862], NP [bMS Am 1088.2 (Box 13)]; cf. GN to ECG of 18 May 1862, NP [bMS Am 1088.2 (Box 13)]: "Charles does not leave us but Susan comes to us, to make brighter & happier our home which has always been the brightest & happiest place in the world to us. We have known from the first that this would be so, or I do not know that we could have been as *perfectly* glad as we have been. To have lost Charles' daily companionship would have been an irreparable loss to us, however thankful we might have been for the reason *why* we lost it. But our house though not as large as our hearts, is large enough to take in Charles' wife, & to give her & him all the independence & *separateness* of life which individual interests & occupations require."

25. Taylor, *Sources*, 93.

26. For the Victorian "religion of the hearth," see Frank Turner, "Crisis of Faith," 79 and also Welsh, *City of Dickens*, 147, 167–95; CEN to AHC of 4 Feb 1854, NP [bMS Am 1088.2 (Box 11)]; Patmore, *Angel*, 33; CEN to ECG of 7 Feb 1860 in Gaskell, *Letters*, 46.

27. CEN to CN of 19 Nov 1856, NP [bMS Am 1088.2 (Box 10)]; GWC to JN of 27 March 1862, NP [bMS Am 1088.1 (48)]; Oliver Wendell Holmes to CEN of 25 March 1862, NP [bMS Am 1088 (3514)]; here it may be well to point out that the notorious and long-suppressed postscript that Henry James, Sr., wrote about being "shocked at Charles Norton's engagement" ("To think of that prim old snuffers imposing himself upon that pure young flame!") cannot have referred to Susan Sedgwick. If the date of January 1861 commonly assigned by James scholars to this letter from James to Emerson is correct (see Geoffroy-Menoux), Susan Sedgwick had not yet returned from England, and Norton had

not yet met her as an adult (they had earlier met in 1843 when Norton was fifteen and Susan six). Norton proposed on 20 March 1862 (Turner, *Liberal*, 173), so that the earliest Saturday Club members could have discussed their engagement would have been at the meeting of 29 March 1862. If, as seems likely, James, Sr., was reacting to some gossip or rumor about Norton in 1861, his characteristically vehement reaction reveals perhaps more about his own inflamed sexual preoccupations (see Habegger, *The Father, passim*) than anything about Norton; President Eliot contributed the detail about Norton's cousins in M. A. DeWolfe Howe, C. E. Norton Notes, HL [bMS Am 1826 (417)]; for sarcasm, see Sedgwick, "Words," 438; for self-will, see Higginson, "Charles Eliot Norton," 121.

28. Richard Baird Smith to JN of 17 June 1853, NP [bMS Am 1088.1 [89]); Dana, *Journal*, 1:131; James, *Notes of a Son and Brother* in *Autobiography*, 392; CEN to Sarah Cleveland of 16 Sept 1849, NP [bMS Am 1088.2 (Box 1)].

29. Grace Ashburner, MS diary, entry dated 10 July 1842, Sedgwick Family Papers, Historical Room, Stockbridge Library Association, Stockbridge, MA; Susan Sedgwick to Theodore Sedgwick III of 1 Sept [n.y.], Sedgwick Family Papers, Stockbridge Library Association.

30. Theodore Sedgwick III to "My Children" of 21 April 1859, Sedgwick Family Papers, Stockbridge Library Association; the word "Abscess" has been written over the letters "tum" for tumor; GN to ECG of 18 May 1862, NP [bMS Am 1088.2 (Box 13)].

31. JN mentions Susan's "intense remarkable power of sympathy" in a letter to JRL of 25 Feb 1872 [bMS Am 1193 (258)]; Catharine Maria Sedgwick to "My dear Sister" of 22 May 1862, Catharine Maria Sedgwick Papers, Massachusetts Historical Society, Boston, MA; this characterization by Norton of the ideal woman "complete in all sweet feminine gifts and charms" comes from a review for the *Nation* written in the year after Susan's death (see Norton, "Sara Coleridge").

32. Catharine Maria Sedgwick to "My dear Sister" of 22 May 1862, Catharine Maria Sedgwick Papers, Massachusetts Historical Society.

33. CEN to MG of 25 May 1863, NP [bMS Am 1088.2 (Box 4)]; CEN to ADV of 7 Feb 1863, NP [bMS Am 1088.2 (Box 3)]; cf. CEN to JBH of 17 Oct 1888, NP [bMS Am 1088.2 (Box 4)]: "Let me join with your other friends in celebrating this anniversary of your New Life. . . . You have had the greatest blessing that life can afford,—a steady joy that has shaped character, given strength to right purpose, and been the source of help to many"; CEN to ECG of 23 Apr 1863 in Gaskell, *Letters*, 94; CEN to JR of 2 Apr 1873 in *JR/CEN Correspondence*, 286.

34. See Stone, *The Family, Sex and Marriage*, 149–72; for the ideological reliance of bourgeois companionate marriage upon Aristotelian friendship and the Epicurean *otium* ideal, see W. Dowling, *Epistolary*, 45–47, 132–37; Trilling, *Sincerity*, 82.

35. C. M. Sedgwick, *Married or Single?*, 2:79; Clough, *Amours de Voyage* in *Selected Poems*, 119; CEN, "Arthur Hugh," 462.

36. Cf. CEN to JR of 29 Dec 1872 in *JR/CEN Correspondence*, 271–72: "motives to great deeds, wrought under the impulse of faith, died away as the tide ebbs down a shore."

37. George Eliot to Mrs. John Cash of 6 June 1857 in *Letters of George Eliot,* 2:343; Stephen, "Forgotten," 254; LS to CEN of 1 Apr 1896 in Stephen, *Selected Letters,* 2:462; CEN to LS of 26 Apr 1896, NP [bMS Am 1088.2 (Box 11)].

38. In the *Examination* Mill famously expressed his anger at the orthodox religious notion, as expressed by the Anglican theologian Henry Mansel, of a humanly incomprehensible God demanding of humanity adoration under the threat of eternal damnation: "I will call no being good, who is not what I mean when I apply that epithet to my fellow-creatures; and if such a being can sentence me to hell for not so calling him, to hell I will go" (*Examination,* p. 103); in the *Subjection* Mill objected to the barbaric spectacle—in a progressive age—of one-half of humankind brought under social and legal subjection to the other, calling it "a single relic of an old world of thought and practice exploded in everything else, but retained in the one thing of most universal interest; as if a gigantic dolmen, or a vast temple of Jupiter Olympius, occupied the site of St. Paul's and received daily worship, while the surrounding Christian churches were only resorted to on fasts and festivals" (*Subjection,* p. 275); James, "Mill's *Subjection,*" 561–62; Mill, *Subjection,* 336 (my emphasis).

39. Norton, "Sanitary," 150.

40. Cf. JSM to CEN of 23 June 1869: "It is a great satisfaction that you not only agree so completely with the little book, but think so highly as you do of its probable influence" (*JSM Collected Works,* 17:1618). Georgiana Burne-Jones to SSN of 28 July 1869, NP [bMS Am 1088.1 (331)], makes clear that Susan Norton's recent "thinking & reading" has included Mill's *Subjection of Women*; earlier that spring, Susan and Charles had dined with Mill, Susan telling Chauncey Wright in a letter of 14 July 1868, "He does not talk much, but always in a way to command your attention and excite your extreme respect and admiration," NP [bMS Am 1088.5 (Box 15)]; see also CW to GN of 13 Jan 1870 in Wright, *Letters,* 157–64; first appearing in May 1869, Mill's book had just achieved a second edition in June; JSM to CEN of 24 Nov 1865 in *JSM Collected Works,* 16:1119; in 1866, Mill introduced a petition in the House of Commons that would have amended the pending Reform Bill to permit female suffrage; the measure failed to pass, although it did garner 73 votes; in July 1867 Curtis, quoting Mill throughout his speech ("the most sagacious of living political philosophers"), made an identical move at the New York State constitutional convention; this initiative, too, failed; Norton, "Female Suffrage," 152.

41. Turner, *Liberal,* 222; surviving Ruskin letters suggest that Norton became sick with a violent "chill" shortly after his return from France, where he had gone at Ruskin's repeated entreaty to see the critic at Abbeville, in the following week traveling with Ruskin to Paris and Amiens (see JR to SSN of 22 Oct 1868, NP [bMS Am 1088.1 (442)]. Ruskin himself, possessing more vigorous health than Norton, was stricken with what he called "a wearisome little feverish cold" at about the same time that was serious enough to prevent him from working for more than a week (JR to CEN of 21 Oct 1868 in *JR/CEN Correspondence,* p. 120); Turner indicates that there were fears at this time for Norton's life (*Liberal,* p. 225).

42. Royston, *Sir John Simon,* 553; copy of an extract from the journal of Mary L. (Acland) Hart Davis, dated 28 Apr 1869, NP [bMS Am 1088.5 (Box 10)].

43. Pater's "Poems By William Morris" appeared in the October 1868 number of the Millite journal, the *Westminster Review*; for the affiliations of Aestheticism to political liberalism, see L. Dowling, "Aestheticism," 32–37 and *Vulgarization*, 75–81.

44. Cf. Goldwin Smith to CEN of 30 Aug 1869: "[B]oth you and Mrs Norton seem to have enjoyed yourselves, and you have certainly made as strong an impression as it was possible to make on the rather hard though bright mind of London" NP [bMS Am 1088 (6722)]; CEN to GWC of 8 July 1869, NP [bMS Am 1088.2 (Box 2)].

45. CEN to GWC of 20 June 1869 in *CEN Letters*, 1:344; CEN to GWC of 8 July 1869, NP [bMS Am 1088.2 (Box 2)].

46. William Morris to CEN of 13 May 1869, NP [Nor 2217.2*]; Norton, "Nicolas' *Quatrains*," 576, 577 (Norton is reviewing the second edition of 1868, hence the somewhat less familiar version of this quatrain); Susan Norton's copy of the *Rubáiyát* is preserved in NP [*94N–295].

47. JS to SSN of 16 Oct [1869], NP [bMS Am 1088.1 (498)]; CEN to JRL of 16 Jan 1870, JRL Papers [bMS Am 765 (590)]; cf. also CEN to MG of 16 Jan 1870, NP [bMS Am 1088.2 (Box 4)]: "It is a great relief to have the long period of weariness & discomfort happily at end,—& no longer to be burdened with the solicitude which weighs inevitably on one's spirits & heart. Perhaps such solicitudes deepen the sense of joy, and quicken gratitude for the greatest blessings; but while they press on one they overweight [deleted: take away] the spring of life"; still weakened from his severe illness in England, Norton himself promised Dr. Simon he would give up his cigar habit of twenty-five years and become "indolent"; CEN to JS of 28 Mar 1870, NP [bMS Am 1088.2 (Box 6)].

48. CEN to HJ of 21 March 1870, James Family Papers, HL [bMS Am 1094 (374)]; Appleton, "The Whip of the Sky" in Stearns, *Cambridge* <authorama .com/cambridge-sketches-8.html>; for Norton's social conscience interfering with his self-cultivation, cf. this passage from the same letter to Henry James: "Italy has crooned her old songs of enchantment to me, and has said, as if she were playing the old child's game with me, 'Hold still, hold fast, see what I give you.' And she has given me enough.—If one could but feel that it was enough to get what was precious for oneself,—and that the world had no right to ask, 'What have you got, or what are you getting for me?'"; CEN to JR of 31 March 1870 in *JR/CEN Correspondence*, 187; CEN to MG of 12 July 1870, NP [bMS Am 1088.2 (Box 4)]; CEN to Elizabeth Child of 7 Mar 1903, HL [bMS Am 1922 (368)]; Ruskin, *Praeterita*, 562; Ruskin was not exaggerating the effect of the Italian fireflies: cf. Charles Dickens' description of them near Genoa in 1844: 'Walking there, on a dark night, I have seen it made one sparkling firmament by these beautiful insects: so that the distant stars were pale against the flash and glitter that spangled every olive wood and hill-side, and pervaded the whole air" (Dickens, *Pictures*, p. 94).

49. CEN to JRL of 25 Dec 1870, JRL Papers, HL [bMS Am 765 (590)]; CEN to HJ of 5 Dec 1873, James Family Papers, HL [bMS Am 1094 (379)]; CEN to Sally Norton of 22 Nov 1891 in *CEN Letters*, 2:208; here as elsewhere in his writings, Norton's reference to imaginative "thirst" alludes to Dante's *Divine Comedy*,

Paradiso, Canto II, v. 20: "The concreate and perpetual thirst for the deiform realm," as Norton renders it in his own prose translation (*Paradise,* p. 11).

50. CEN to HJ of 28 Mar 1872, James Family Papers, HL [bMS Am 1094 (375)]; CEN to JS of before 15 Dec 1869, NP [bMS Am 1088.2 (Box 6)]; CEN to FJC of 1 Apr 1872, NP [bMS Am 1088.2 (Box 11)].

51. CEN to MG of 27 May 1866 [bMS Am 1088.2 (Box 4)]; CEN to ELG of 22 Oct 1867, ELG Papers, HL [bMS Am 1083 (707)]; CEN to JRL of 26 Nov 1886 in *CEN Letters,* 2:177.

52. CEN to JR of 19 Sept 1868 in *JR/CEN Correspondence,* 117; copy of an un-dated, unsigned and incomplete letter preserved (apparently accidentally) in a compilation of extracts from CEN's correspondence made at the behest of Sally Norton in NP [bMS Am 1088.5 (Box 15)]; references in this fragment to a din-ner party at the Stephens' described in a letter by CEN to JRL of 1 Jan 1869 (see *CEN Letters,* pp. 1:313–14) make its attribution to Susan Norton certain, and the identification of Chauncey Wright as its recipient highly likely; Minnie Thack-eray Stephen, Stephen's first wife, would die in 1875.

53. Rawdon Brown to CEN of 1 May 1870, NP [Nor 5259.13]; Italian phrase copied into a notebook kept during CEN's Italian travels of 1869–71, NP [bMS Am 1088.5 (Box 2)]; cf. CEN to GWC of 3 Apr 1874, NP [bMS Am 1088.2 (Box 2)]: "Three years ago to-day I was entering Venice" and CEN to Isabella Stew-art Gardner of 20 July 1888, Isabella Stewart Gardner Museum Archives, Bos-ton, MA: "Seventeen years ago yesterday I saw Venice for the last time"; CEN to JRL of 20 Apr 1873, JRL Papers, HL [bMS Am 765 (593)]; cf. CEN to SGW of 9 Mar 1872, Ward Papers, HL [bMS Am 1465 (916J)]: "She had never en-joyed life more than during the months we passed last spring and summer in Venice" and CEN to HJ of 28 Mar 1872, James Family Papers, HL [bMS Am 1094 (375)]: "The happiest months of her life, I think, were the months we passed in Venice"; CEN to CN of 29 June 1871, NP [bMS Am 1088.2 (Box 10)]; Norton is alluding to the "in such a night" exchange between Shylock's daughter Jessica and her lover Lorenzo in *The Merchant of Venice,* Act 5, scene i; Turner, *Liberal,* 243: "In early May she became pregnant once more but re-mained 'uncommonly well'"; CEN to CN of 16 July 1871, NP [bMS Am 1088.2 (Box 10)].

54. CEN to LS of 8 July 1895 in *CEN Letters,* 2:228.

55. JS to CEN of 31 March 1872, NP [bMS Am 1088 (6615)]; Donald MacKay to CEN of 20 Feb 1872, NP [bMS Am 1088 (5675)]; John Morley to CEN of 23 Feb 1872, NP [bMS Am 1088 (4862)]; Henry James, Sr., to CEN of 11 Mar 1872, NP [bMS Am 1088 (3833)]; WJS to CEN of 25 Apr 1872, NP [bMS Am 1088 (7131)].

56. CEN to GWC of 2 Apr 1872, NP [bMS Am 1088.2 (Box 2)]; CEN's notes for a new edition of *Notes of Travel and Study* are preserved in NP [bMS Am 1088.5 (Box 15)], but the project came to nothing; FJC to CEN of 18 and 19 May 1872, NP [bMS Am 1088 (1176)]: "Theodora [Sedgwick, Susan's young-est sister] gives me the impression that it is a question of returning to your own home or none"; Norton's unwilling exile from his home is a point worth stress-ing because in recent years it has become common for critics to assert that his five years' absence abroad is to be taken as a measure of Norton's alienation

from America. Such an interpretation, however, is untrue even of the Nortons' original decision to live abroad, which was dictated by health concerns (especially Susan's and his mother's, then 74), economic pressures (postwar inflation and taxes) and educational considerations, Norton telling Meta Gaskell, "We prefer to go now rather than later on our children's account also; we do not want them to be Europeanised, & we should wish to be at home with them as they grew old enough to be much affected by their surrounding & by influences other than the domestic ones" (CEN to MG of 25 Mar 1868, NP [bMS Am 1088.2 (Box 4)]); cf. also CEN to MG of 2 Oct 1865, NP [bMS Am 1088.2 (Box 4)]: "Too much Europe does not answer for an American. It is the island of Calypso if not of Circe" (Norton was alluding to William Wetmore Story, an American sculptor long resident in Rome who had become "McClellanized" and "has not recovered").

57. JRL to GN of 19 Aug 1872 in *JRL Letters*, 2:94–95; cf. CEN to LS of 8 July 1895, when CEN, counseling LS to guard his health after Julia Stephen's death, says, "In this matter one must strive against one's own desires,—for one would like to die" (*CEN Letters*, 2:228); CEN to JR of 17 Nov 1873 in *JR/CEN Correspondence*, 299; deleted passages from CEN 1872–73 journal, entries for 10 Nov and 18–20 Nov 1872, NP [bMS Am 1088.5 (Box 13)]; the Friar's speech about Hero is from Act IV, scene I of *Much Ado About Nothing*.

58. Cf. William Dean Howells, "Charles Eliot Norton": "I remember that when he came home after that long absence in Europe, with his life broken in two, and the half only left him to make of it what he could on earth, there was a distinct change in his religious belief" (p. 841); entry of 17 Nov 1872, CEN 1872–73 journal, NP [bMS Am 1088.5 (Box 13)]; "Carlyle does not take to Omar Khayyam,—whom he calls 'an old Mahommedan blackguard,' his scepticism is too blank, his solution of life in drink too mean. I quarreled with this as the view of a Philistine, but Carlyle stuck to it" in Norton's MS notes of Carlyle's talk, Oct 1872–Apr 1873, NP [bMS Am 1088.5 (Box 4)]; cf. LS to CEN of 5 Mar 1876, after Minnie Stephen's death, "I read . . . or repeated, for I know him by heart, our old friend Omar" (*LS Selected Letters*, 1:170) and Edward FitzGerald, letter of 15 Sept 1876: "I was told the other Day that Mr. Leslie Stephen, who lately lost his Wife . . . positively found Consolation in Wordsworth's Excursion, and Omar K! And he who told me—an American Professor [i. e. Norton]—said the same thing had happened to him" (*EFG Letters*. 3:704n); I have quoted the 1859 version of this quatrain.

59. CEN to CW of 23 Oct 1872, Chauncey Wright Papers, American Philosophical Society, Philadelphia, PA; CEN to HJ of 23 Mar 1873, James Family Papers, HL [bMS Am 1094 (375)]; CEN to JS of 9 July 1873, NP [bMS Am 1088.2 (Box 6)]; CEN to LS of 8 July 1895 in *CEN Letters*, 2:228.

60. Froude, *Life of Carlyle*, 697n32, 595.

61. Howe, *Life and Letters of George Bancroft*, 2:276.

62. HWL to Clara Crowninshield of 28 July 1838 in *HWL Letters*, 2:86–87; CEN to E. C. Cleveland of 7 June 1869 in *CEN Letters*, 1:336; cf. RWE to CEN of 23 Feb 1870: "I see no bar to the design [of donating the books to Harvard], which is lovely and redeeming in Carlyle, and will make us all affectionate again" (in *CEN Letters*, 1:341).

63. CEN to HJ of 19 Jan 1873, James Family Papers, HL [bMS Am 1094 (376)]; cf. entry of 11 Nov 1872 in CEN's 1872–73 journal: "went to lunch with the Burne Joneses. . . . They were sweet & cordial as ever; [deleted: but the laughing & (illegible word) oppressed me]", NP [bMS Am 1088.5 (Box 13)]; CEN to JRL of 23 Jan 1873 in *CEN Letters*, 1:460; CEN's MS Notes of TC's talk, NP [bMS Am 1088.5 (Box 4)]; entry of 13 Dec 1872, CEN 1872–73 journal: "Carlyle brought me a copy of 'Sartor Resartus'" (in *CEN Letters*, 1:442).

64. *"Morte villana, di pieta nemica / Di dolor madre antica"*; cf. CEN's translation of *The New Life of Dante Alighieri*: "This sonnet is divided into four parts. In the first I call Death by certain names proper to her" (p. 13); JS to CEN of 21 Feb 1873, NP [bMS Am 1088 (6616)].

65. Entry of 21 Mar 1873, CEN's MS Notes of TC's Talk, NP [bMS Am 1088.5 (Box 4)]; CEN to JRL of 23 Jan 1873 in *CEN Letters*, 1:460.

66. CEN to HJ of 19 Jan 1873, James Family Papers, HL [bMS Am 1094 (376)]; CEN to TC of 7 May 1874 in *CEN Letters*, 2:41; TC to CEN of 3 Nov 1873, NP [bMS Am 1088 (999)].

67. CEN to HJ of 5 Dec 1873, James Family Papers, HL [bMS Am 1094 (379)]; CEN to ADV of 1 Jan 1878, NP [bMS Am 1088.2 (Box 3)]; CEN to JRL of 27 June 1880, JRL Papers, HL [bMS Am 765 (600)]; CEN to Horace Howard Furness of 5 Nov 1907, H. H. Furness Papers, Rare Book & Manuscript Library, Univ. of Pennsylvania. That Norton's mourning fidelity to his wife's memory paralleled Dante's idealization of Beatrice quickly became clear to his friends: cf. Lowell, ca. 1876–77: "We can watch among our friends the growth of their own Beatrices that such as have the happiness to know them make amid the agonies of bereavement, each for himself" (quoted in Wendell, "Mr. Lowell as a Teacher," p. 214); by contrast, Alice James spent years in obsessive gossip about Norton's supposed plans for remarriage to one or another of Susan Norton's sisters (see Moore, "Letters of Alice James").

68. HJ to WJ of 22 Sept [1872] in Perry, *Thought and Character*, 1:328; Posnock, *Trial*, 197; Donald MacKay to CEN of 26 May 1872, NP [bMS Am 1088 (5678)].

69. Entry of 31 Jan 1873, CEN's 1872–73 journal, NP [bMS Am 1088.5 (Box 13)]; cf. *CEN Letters*, 1:462; letters concerning the Norton burial plot indicate that none of the family graves was marked before the twentieth century (Lot #712 correspondence file, Historical Dept., Mount Auburn Cemetery, Cambridge, MA). Charles's funerary arrangements during this period deeply shocked and pained his friends. After Jane Norton's death in 1877, he insisted on placing his sister's body in an above-ground charnel; see FJC to JRL of 28 Sept 1879 in Child, *Scholar-Friends*, 41.

70. CEN to HJ of 5 Dec 1873, James Family Papers, HL [bMS Am 1094 (379)]; CEN to JRL of 13 Nov 1872 in *CEN Letters*, 1:428; entry of 15 May 1873, CEN 1872–73 journal in *CEN Letters*, 1:502; CEN to HJ of 5 Dec 1873; in the summer of 1883 CEN would venture far enough across the Swiss border to see the Italian lakes and the touristic towns of Lugano and Bellagio, but he never again saw Venice, Florence or Siena—"your long and heroic privation," as Henry James would later call it (HJ to CEN of 26 Dec 1898, in *HJ Letters*, p. 497).

Chapter 5: The Darker Day

1. CEN to GWC of 10 June 1868, NP [bMS Am 1088.2 (Box 2)]; CEN to MG of 22 May 1868, NP [bMS Am 1088.2 (Box 4)].

2. For the cows, see Turner, *Liberal*, 232; Adams, "Chapter," 104; Lowell, "Tempora Mutantur" in *Poetical Works*, 491; Lowell, "An Epistle to George William Curtis" in *Poetical Works*, 454.

3. CEN to HWL of 21 Jan 1872, NP [bMS Am 1088.13 (Box 5)]; CEN to GWC of 8 June 1870, NP [bMS Am 1088.2 (Box 2)]; CEN to MG of 12 July 1870 in *CEN Letters*, 1:395; CEN to GWC of 8 June 1870, NP.

4. CEN to SGW of 29 June 1873, Ward Papers, HL [bMS Am 1465 (916K)]; Whitman, *Democratic Vistas*, 12; for this central dynamic of postwar American life, see Keller, *Affairs*, 35ff.; "The Revival of Business," *Nation* (28 May 1874), 343.

5. Cf. "Speeches at Ashfield," *Springfield Republican* (23 Aug 1901): "The last speaker was Eliot Norton of New York, whom his father, the professor, announced as the revealed secret,—the power that originally brought him to Ashfield, a little less than 36 years ago, when as an infant the son needed the air of the hills" (p. 3); Ephraim W. Gurney to SSN of 6 July 1868, NP [bMS Am 1088.1 (388)]; T. W. Parsons to Mary A. Heard of 30 July [1866], Rare Book Room, Boston Public Library.

6. CEN to Constance Hilliard of 15 Oct 1873 in *CEN Letters*, 2:17.

7. Tax records preserved in the Cambridge Public Library indicate that taxes on Shady Hill in 1868 were 34.3 percent higher than those paid in 1860; Fanny Kemble to Harriet St. Leger of 9 Feb 1876 in Kemble, *Records*, 2:238; cf. CEN to JGP of 24 June 1867, HL [bMS Am 1704 (639)]: "[Olmsted's] ruling idea is to make an arrangement by which my land and yours may be brought into the most immediate and effective connection with the more settled parts of the town"; Palfrey's extensive property lay to the north of Norton's; Olmsted's design is reproduced in *FLO Papers*, 6:258–59; FLO to CEN of 11 Jan [1867] in *FLO Papers*, 6:163; for this episode, see Turner, *Liberal*, 211; CEN to JRL of 24 Nov 1873 in *CEN Letters*, 2:22, 21.

8. Andrews Norton, "Inaugural," 47; CEN to JRL of 24 Nov 1873 in *CEN Letters*, 2:21; CEN to JR of 10 Feb 1874 in *JR/CEN Correspondence*, 305; cf. CEN to JR of 13 Nov [1873]: "Poor mechanical, material creatures we are,—and yet only a little lower than the angels! What must the angels be!" (*JR/CEN Correspondence*, 298); cf. also this Omaresque stanza Norton copied into his Syllabus of Lectures, 1874–75, NP [bMS Am 1088.5 (Box 2)]: "While we poor puppets jerk'd by unseen wires / With all our pasteboard passions & desires, / Loves, Hates, Ambitions & immortal fires, / Are toss'd pell mell together in the grave."

9. On the eve of the second anniversary of his wife's death, Norton translated a poem by Giacomino Pugliese of Prato, "Death, why hast thou so great war made on me?" NP [bMS Am 1088.2 (Box 2)]; CEN to JR of 10 Jan 1874 in *JR/CEN Correspondence*, 303; William Dean Howells to HJ of 5 Dec 1873 in Anesko, *Letters, Fictions*, p. 91.

10. CEN to CN of 9 Aug 1868 in *CEN Letters*, 1:303; entry of 16 Nov 1872 in

CEN's 1872–73 journal, NP [bMS Am 1088.5 (Box 13)]; entry of 5 Dec 1872 in CEN's 1872–73 journal, NP.

11. Characterization of Norton's lecture style by a reporter for the *Boston Advertiser*, 30 Oct 1867 (clipping in NP, [Nor 5257.25f*]); Emerson who heard this same earlier lecture (variously titled "Thought in America" or "American Culture") noted with regret Norton's "omission, (perhaps the scorn,) of emphasis" (*RWE Journals*, 16:86); CEN to JR of 4 May 1874 in *JR/CEN Correspondence*, 315; Norton, Turner and His Works MS, lecture 2, HL [bMS Am 1732]; Turner and His Works MS, lecture 1, HL.

12. CEN to GWC of 11 May 1874, NP [bMS Am 1088.2 (Box 2)]; Norton, Turner and His Works MS, lecture 2, HL [bMS Am 1732].

13. CEN's 1872–73 journal in *CEN Letters*, 1:506, 503.

14. JRL to CEN of 10 Dec 1869 in *JRL Letters*, 2:59; CEN to SGW of 29 June 1873, Ward Papers, HL [bMS Am 1465 (916K)]; cf. Norton, *Historical Studies*, 110n: "The *carroccio*, or 'great car,' that bore the standard of the commune, was a symbol of independence widely in use among the free cities of Italy"; cf. President Eliot's defense of the new elective system in "Liberty in Education" (1885); for Eliot's hiring policy, cf. G. H. Palmer, "No personal inclination ever diverted him from an approved end. . . . He like to surround himself with strong men, and this the more if such associates were critical of his policies" (Palmer, *Autobiography*, p. 65).

15. Mill, "Inaugural Address," 251–56.

16. In her 1992 dissertation, Carol K. Roemer has argued for the centrality of Mill's Inaugural to Norton's fine arts teaching; CEN to Charles William Eliot of 15 Jan 1874 (copy), HL [bMS Am 1826 (389)]; in this letter, which was plainly written for more eyes than Eliot's, Norton presses for the establishment of a full professorship in the fine arts by indicating that he might not accept a position merely as an annual lecturer. After an preliminary year as lecturer, Norton's appointment as Professor was confirmed in May 1875; for opposition to Norton's appointment, see Turner, *Liberal*, 259–66; JR to CEN of 24 June 1869 in *JR/CEN Correspondence*, 142; Norton's personal copy of Letter I of Ruskin's *Fors Clavigera*, with its inscription by Ruskin, is preserved in NP; JR to CEN of 14 Mar 1877 in *JR/CEN Correspondence*, 391; JR to CEN of 12 Oct 1874 in *JR/CEN Correspondence*, 341; Ruskin, *Praeterita*, 523.

17. Ruskin made the "loathsome cretin" remark about Mill at this time in a letter to Frederic Harrison (quoted in Wright, *Religion*, p. 134), but it may be taken as representative of the sort of abuse of Mill that Ruskin was sending to Norton in letters that Norton later destroyed; Ruskin, "Oxford Inaugural," 34; Moore taught Fine Arts I in so determinedly a Pre-Raphaelite fashion as to arouse the hostility of a *Crimson* reporter, who complained "It seems hardly consistent with the broad and liberal policy of the College that any one branch of knowledge should be looked at from a single standpoint"; Casteras' assumption (see *English Pre-Raphaelitism*, p. 28) that the *Crimson* reporter was referring to Norton is mistaken; Ruskin, "Oxford Inaugural Lecture," 39; Brown and Wiggin, *Lecture Notes in Fine Arts III*, 11; Norton, "A Definition," 39.

18. Chapman, *Memories*, 139–40.

19. Pater, *Renaissance*, 189.

20. Whistler, "Ten O'Clock," 136, 157, 156.

21. Cf. CEN to GEW of 12 May 1884: "I have always had a fondness for the old-style Virginian life. Doubtless a Yankee does more; but I believe in salvation by grace" NP [bMS Am 1088.2 (Box 8)]; Lears discusses Norton' s republican aestheticism in *No Place*, 66–67, 243–47, 258–60; John Jay Chapman, who was his student in the 1870s, insisted that Norton was "a citizen of the Franklin type rather than the Ruskin type . . . a puritan turned aesthete. He retained the battling qualities of his origin," concluding that both Norton and his sister Grace were "tough as boxers," quoted in Howe, *John Jay Chapman*, 191, 192; Norton quoted in W. E. Weaver's stenographic "Notes on Fine Arts III," NP [Nor 5260.12f*]; Whistler, "Ten O'Clock," 143; Wilde, "Decay of Lying," 163, 164, 184–85; cf. also Norton's annotations, made about 1866–68, to Chap. 10, sect. 3 of Ruskin's *Modern Painters*, Vol. 3: "Art and nature are not & ought never to be supposed to be in competition. Each has its own right & domain," NP [*94N–61].

22. EBJ to CEN of 23 Dec 1881, NP [Nor 5259.13, vol. 2]; EBJ to CEN of 9 Jan 1882, NP [bMS Am 1088 (778)]; OW to CEN of [15 July 1882], NP [bMS Am 1088 (8105)].

23. CEN to GEW of 1 June 1882, NP [bMS Am 1088.2 (Box 8)].

24. GEW to CEN of 25 Apr 1882, quoted in Wimberly, "Oscar Wilde," 115; Woodberry, unsigned review of *Marius the Epicurean* in Seiler, *Walter Pater*, 149.

25. CEN to GEW of 12 May 1884, NP [bMS Am 1088.2 (Box 8)]; CEN to GEW of 30 Oct 1885, NP [bMS Am 1088.2 (Box 8)]; Smith, "On Re-Reading Pater," 74–75; Greenslet, *Walter Pater*, 83; Howells, "Recent Literature," 497; Hovey, "Aestheticism," 295.

26. Norton, Dante lecture 3, NP [bMS Am 1088.5 (Box 13)] p. 9; Bernhard [*sic*] Berenson to CEN of 23 Dec 1886, NP [bMS Am 1088 (449)]; the sort of aesthete Berenson was to become may be suggested by his diary entry for 20 Dec 1941: "The part of me that is a relatively dispassionate student of history and politics is as pleased with the Japanese attack on the U.S.A. as a chemist may be who is eager to see how two elements will behave whose reciprocal reactions are not fully known" (*Rumor and Reflection*, p. 50).

27. Mason, "Harvard in the 1890s," 64; "Notes of Ethical Points" taken by a student in Norton's Fine Arts IV, NP [bMS Am 1088.5 (Box 4)]; Wendell, "Charles Eliot Norton," 83; it is perhaps worth noting that Wendell's story ends this way: "Years afterward, though, I met [my friend] at a Roman goldsmith's, choosing some trifle for his wife. The horseshoe still gleamed not very far from his heart, where it belonged; but, as he showed me two pieces of delicate workmanship between which he was hesitating, he asked me, seriously and simply, which I thought Norton would prefer"; Norton, "Harvard," 38; Howe, *John Jay Chapman*, 191; Brown, "Self-Indulgent," 194; Copeland, "Norton in His Letters," 86; for the overcoat, see Edward Revere Little's caricature of Norton in *Harvard Celebrities*, unpaginated.

28. Peabody, *Diary and Letters*, 73; Lovett, *All Our Years*, 38 (my emphasis); Savage, *Poems*, 91.

29. JR to CEN of 18 Aug 1886 in *JR/CEN Correspondence*, 494; Alice James, who detested Norton, was convinced of his baleful effect on women; see

A. James, *Death and Letters*, 74; "You ask about the favoritism that Professor Norton showed toward his eldest daughter, Sara. I was brought up to believe this was true, possibly because she had mercifully inherited something of her mother's beauty," Harold Bend Sedgwick, letter to the author, 15 Oct 1995; Esther Marshall, a friend of Norton's daughter Lily, noted "this story has come to me from so many sources that one is forced to credit it," Marshall, Biographical Sketch TS, 16; see also Turner, *Liberal*, 323; Wharton, *Backward*, 127; Hapgood, *Changing*, 56–57.

30. Brooks, *Scenes and Portraits*, 116; Chapman, "Charles Eliot Norton," 4; H. James, "An American Art-Scholar," 127; Edith Wharton uses the phrase "tiptoe malices" about Henry James in *Backward*, 178; WJ to HJ of 24 Jan 1909 in *WJ Correspondence*, 3:376–77.

31. Howells, "Charles Eliot Norton," 840; Russell Sturgis to CEN of 29 Jan 1881, NP [bMS Am 1088 (7253)]; cf. Norton, "Definition of Fine Arts," 36: "There is among us little of the spirit of noble discontent that stimulates to emulation of greatness, quickens generous ambitions, and is the source of steadfast effort to attain to better things" and Norton's Fine Arts III lecture: "A man who becomes thoroughly imbued with a sense of the beauty of the Greek work, and of the power which it indicates, will live forever with a noble discontent, inciting him to improve himself and the generation to which he belongs,— a discontent which will keep him from that foolish, spread-eagle Fourth-of-July optimism which characterizes the American people in general" (quoted in Brown and Wiggin, *History of Ancient Art*, 2:91); this Socratic theme of a constructive discontent had been powerfully reaffirmed by Mill: "[N]othing is more certain, than that improvement in human affairs is wholly the work of the uncontented characters" (Mill, *Considerations on Representative*, 407).

32. CEN to MG of 2 Jan 1871, NP [bMS Am 1088.2 (Box 4)]; CEN to JBH of 23 July 1882 in *CEN Letters*, 2:135.

33. Norton, *Historical Studies*, 6, 10, 253.

34. CEN to JR of 17 July 1873 in *JR/CEN Correspondence*, 296.

35. Howes, *History of . . . Ashfield*, 378; Lizzie Curtis in 1909, quoted in Howes, *History of . . . Ashfield*, 386.

36. Congressman George P. Ikirt of Ohio, quoted in Blake, "Background of Cleveland's," 272; CEN to LS of 8 Jan 1896 in *CEN Letters*, 2:236.

37. TR to HCL of 20 Dec 1895 in *TR/HCL Selections*, 1:200; TR to HCL of 27 Dec 1895 in *TR/HCL Selections*, 1:204.

38. CEN to William Lloyd Garrison II of 1 Jan 1896 (copy), Garrison Family Papers, Sophia Smith Collection, Smith College, Northampton, MA; WJ to Frederick Myers of 1 Jan 1896 in Perry, *Life and Character*, 2:305; Norton, "Some Aspects": "Such exhibitions as we have lately had—as we are now having—of public men of note making deliberate appeal to the most brutal instincts of the populace by advocacy of a policy of national aggression and of war, afford the plainest evidence of the low estimate which these spurious patriots set upon the public intelligence and morality. . . . But these political swaggerers . . . who disparage the virtue of peace and good will among men, are the worst of criminals, for they aim their blows at civilization itself" (p. 648); for a lynching done laughingly, see Edward J. Pringle to CEN of 16 Oct 1860, NP [bMS Am 1088

(5576)]; Norton quotes Roosevelt in his 1902 Academy Dinner speech, see "August Breezes at Ashfield," *Springfield Republican*, 22 Aug 1902, p. 5.

39. CEN, "Some Aspects," 649; Dunne, *Mr. Dooley*, 43; A. B. Farquahar to Mrs. Cleveland of 20 Dec 1895, quoted in Blake, "Background of Cleveland's," 276; Norton, "Some Aspects," 649.

40. Norton, Address at Bryn Mawr Commencement, June 1896, NP [bMS Am 1088.5 (Box 1)]; Norton, lecture notes for History of Ancient Art, NP [bMS Am 1088.5 (Box 3)].

41. Norton, "Some Aspects" 651; Lodge, quoted in May, *Imperial Democracy*, 77.

42. Emerson, "Heroism," 155; Norton quoted in Wendell, "Charles Eliot Norton," 84.

43. "Charles Eliot Norton," *New York Tribune*, 6 Mar 1898, clipping in NP [bMS Am 1088.5 (Box 5)]; cf. "Anti-Imperialism," a publication of the New England Anti-Imperialist League (to which Norton belonged): "RESOLVED, That our first duty is to cure the evils in our own country, the corrupt government, . . . the disturbed relations between labor and capital, our disordered currency, our unjust system of taxation, the debasing influence of money at elections and on legislation, the use of offices as spoils; then when we have shown that we can protect the rights of men within our own borders like the colored race at the south and Indians in the west, and that we can govern great cities . . . it will be time to consider whether we can wisely invite distant populations of alien race and language and of traditions unlike our own to become our subjects and accept our rule or our fellow-citizens and take part in governing us," NP, Records of the Hour, Vol. 2, a scrapbook of newspaper clippings relating to the Spanish-American War controversy and Norton's part in it collected by his daughter Sally [bMS Am 1088.3]; for Norton's knowledge of McKinley's rejection of last-minute concessions by Spain, see CEN to Lyman Abbott of 6 Aug 1898, NP [bMS Am 1088.2 (Box 8)]; "Fine Arts Toryism," in Records of the Hour, Vol 1.

44. Norton, Syllabus of Lectures, 1874–75, NP [bMS Am 1088.5 (Box 2)]; in the MS, Norton has careted in the phrase "to delicacy but not effeminacy" above the line of text; cf. Thucydides, *Peloponnesian War*, 2:40: "We cultivate refinement without extravagance and knowledge without effeminacy" (*Landmark Thucydides*, p. 113) and Pocock, *Machiavellian*, 500: "[I]t was only in nineteenth-century liberal England, when culture finally replaced property as the qualifying characteristic of the civic elite, that the Funeral Oration of Pericles was ranked among the sacred writings of liberal civilization."

45. "Fine Arts Toryism" in Records of the Hour, Vol. 1; cf. CEN to G[eorge] G[rantham] Bain of 13 May 1898: "I regret to find that I was mistaken in trusting to your virtual pledge not to bring me in any way before the public. I told you that I should be glad to see you again. I must now withdraw these words," NP [bMS Am 1088.2 (Box 8)]; Norton's "True Patriotism," delivered to the Men's Club of the Prospect Street Congregational Church on 7 June 1898, is reprinted in *CEN Letters*, 2:261–69; Hoar's attack and the ensuing exchange of letters between the two men are reprinted in Hoar, *Quality of Our Honor*; see also Turner, *Liberal*, 395; Hale quoted in *Philadelphia Public Ledger* of 28 May 1898 (clipping in Records of the Hour, Vol. 1); cf. also "A Cambridge View of

the War," *New York Times*, 10 June 1898: "The little circle of men without hope, without a country, and therefore without patriotism, of whom Prof. CHARLES ELIOT NORTON is one of the chief members, are already punished and virtually suppressed by a total loss of influence and public respect. They talk and they publish, but nobody any longer attends to them" (clipping in Records of the Hour, Vol. 1 [bMS Am 1088.3].

46. CEN to Lyman Abbott of 6 Aug 1898 (MS draft of letter), NP [bMS Am 1088.2 (Box 8)]; cf. the explanation given for U.S. inaction in the face of the 1994 Rwandan genocide by George Moose, Assistant Secretary of State for African affairs: "We were psychologically and imaginatively too limited" (quoted in Power, "Bystanders," p. 92); HCL to Elihu B. Hayes of 18 May 1898, quoted in Garraty, *Henry Cabot Lodge*, 204.

47. Proctor, quoted in Linderman, *Mirror of War*, 59; for the influence of this journalistic revolution, see Wilkerson, *Public Opinion*, pp. 1–6; "In Review," *Boston Herald* clipping in Records of the Hour, Vol. 2, NP [bMS Am 1088.3]; cf. May: "A frightened elite retreated from resistance to acquiescence. Politicians in one party, the Democratic, prepared to make capital of the issue, while those in the other, the Republican, more terrified of the opposition than of Spain, begged the administration to capitulate and make war for the sake of party survival and domestic peace" (*Imperial Democracy*, p. 147).

48. Editorial in *Springfield Republican*, 25 Aug 1898, clipping in Records of the Hour, Vol. 2, NP [bMS Am 1088.3]; "The Blunder of Last Spring," *Boston Herald* editorial of 19 Sept 1898 in Records of the Hour, Vol. 2.

49. CEN to Sally Norton of 8 Feb 1899 in *CEN Letters*, 2:281; cf. McKinley's famous account, given to a group of clergymen, of his conversion to the policy of Philippine annexation: "I walked the floor of the White House night after night until midnight; and I am not ashamed to tell you gentlemen, that I went down on my knees and prayed almighty God for light and guidance more than one night. And one night it came to me this way—I don't know how it was, but it came: (1) That we could not give them back to Spain—that would cowardly and dishonorable; (2) that we could not turn them over to France or Germany—our commercial rivals in the Orient—that would be bad business and discreditable; (3) that we could not leave them to themselves—they were unfit for self-government—and they would soon have anarchy and misrule over there worse than Spain's was; and (4) that there was nothing left for us to do but to take them all, and to educate the Filipinos, and uplift and Christianize them, and by God's grace do the very best we could by them, as our fellow-men for whom Christ also died" (quoted in May, *Imperial Democracy*, pp. 252–53; cf. CEN to A. L. Conger of 18 Nov 1899: "There is certainly a considerable portion of the people of Manila and of other important places on the island of Luzon who possess such a degree of intelligence, such an acquaintance with the world, and such knowledge of the requirements of civilization, who have, in a word, attained to such a degree of civilization, that it seems unfortunate that they should not have been allowed to endeavor to establish such a government for the island as might be within their power, and adapted to the needs of the people," NP [bMS Am 1088.2 (Box 11)]; E. L. Godkin in the *Nation* of 9 Mar 1899, quoted in Beisner, *Twelve Against Empire*, 78; Mark Twain described the "action"

on Mt. Dajo of 9 Mar 1906 this way: "The enemy numbered six hundred—including women and children—and we abolished them utterly, leaving not even a baby alive to cry for its dead mother. *This is incomparably the greatest victory that was ever achieved by the Christian soldiers of the United States*" ("Comments on the Moro Massacre," in *Mark Twain's Weapons*, p. 172 [Twain's emphasis]); William Vaughn Moody, "On a Soldier Fallen in the Philippines," in *Poems and Plays*, 1:30; CEN to William Vaughn Moody of 28 Jan 1901, General MSS, Rare Books and Special Collections, Princeton Univ. Libraries.

50. CEN to JBH of 13 Mar 1894 in *CEN Letters*, 2:220.

51. CEN to WJS of 26 June 1898, Special Collections, Schaffer Library, Union College, Schenectady, NY.

52. CEN to WJS of 26 June, Union College Library; cf. the account of Ruskin given by Norton's son Rupert, a physician, who visited him in May 1899: "He sits in his bed-room all the time, looking out of the window over across the lake. There he sat at a small table drawn close up to him, with his small shrunken hands in thick wool mits. He asked no questions and I don't know how well he understood who I was but I talked to him of you, and he smiled a little. He seems and is absolutely childish or worse than that" (Rupert Norton to CEN of 28 May 1899, NP [bMS Am 1088 (5087)]).

53. Cf. CEN to Elizabeth Ellery Child of 11 May 1905: "It quite grieved me that the good should have to suffer because of the evil when the fence was put round these acres which had so long been open to all,—but that you should fancy that the exclusion was to apply to you could never have crossed my mind. The grass, the trees are all at your disposal; it is *tierra de usted*. The policeman shall not vex you, and the mosquito has already learned that he must follow the loafers and be gone" (HL [bMS Am 1922 (369)]); Henry Ware Eliot, "Beyond the Vulgar Current of Events" in *Harvard Celebrities*, unpaginated; McKim, quoted in Moore, *Life and Times*, 100, 111; for Norton's criticism of McKim's fence and his admiration for Pisa's Campo Santo, see "A Criticism of Harvard Architecture" and *Notes of Travel*, 9–11; cf. Russell Sturgis' reaction to the barren classicism of McKim, Mead & White, expressed in an 1897 letter to his old SATA colleague, Peter Bonnet Wight: "That firm is deliberately working—and has been for three years working—in the direction of mere blank, bare, square, unvaried, unmodified boxes with square holes cut in them" (quoted in Wight, "Reminiscences of Russell," p. 127).

54. "Annual Ashfield Dinner," *Springfield Republican*, 26 Aug 1898, p. 4; Dr. Philip Moxom of Springfield, quoted in *Springfield Republican*, 26 Aug 1898, p. 4; in the battle of El Caney on 1 July 1898, U.S. forces captured a heavily fortified blockhouse three miles to the north of the San Juan Heights at about the same time as other U.S. soldiers, including Roosevelt, were capturing the Heights.

55. Norton, quoted in "Philippine War Arraigned at Ashfield," *Springfield Republican*, 18 Aug 1899, p. 5; Norton, quoted in "Speeches at Ashfield," *Springfield Republican*, 24 Aug 1900, p. 3; cf. Norton's remarks to the Harvard Board of Overseers, as recorded on a slip of paper preserved in one of his commonplace books: "Shall we give our highest honors [to] the chief author of these crimes? . . . For my part I do not understand this honoring of an official without regard

to the manner of his conduct of his office. This is no [R]epublican doctrine; it may be pressed to dangerous length[s]; its root is in the same soil as that of the Divine Right of Kings. It is urged, indeed, that the policy of Pres. McKinley has been approved by the nation in his reelection, and that he should therefor[e] be exempt from criticism," NP [bMS Am 1088.5 (Box 3)]; cf. CEN to F. B. Sanborn of 5 June 1901, Papers of Charles Eliot Norton, MSS 8371, -a, -b. Clifton Waller Barrett Library of American Library, Special Collections, Univ. of Virginia Library: "I do not mean to be present at Commencement whether or not the President is there. I think far better of Harvard men & Harvard principles than you profess to, but I do not sympathize with its actual temper"; "Ashfield Annual Dinner," *Springfield Republican*, 23 Aug 1901, p. 3.

56. Cf. "Some of the stanch adherents of the administration, who disliked the tone of some of the speeches last year, have signified their intention to boycott the dinner this year" in "August Breeze at Ashfield," *Springfield Republican*, 21 Aug 1902, p. 5; Norton, quoted in "August Breeze at Ashfield," p. 5; Norton had also refused to attend the Harvard Commencement ceremony bestowing an honorary degree on Roosevelt, later declaring to a friend, "It was an occasion of much self-glorification on both sides, in which the University gave itself over to the celebration of the ideals of barbarism in place of those of civilization" (CEN to SGW of 8 July 1902, NP [bMS Am 1088.2 (Box 7)]; for Norton's letter to his unnamed Ashfield critic, see Appendix C in *CEN Letters*, 2:455–56; cf. Norton, "some others who, perhaps, I can hardly call my friends, have gone so far as to suggest that in some regions of the country, where they seem to believe that a healthier tone of sentiment exists than in this peaceful neighborhood, we who have uttered objectionable opinions should be taken out by our indignant fellow-citizens and treated to a coat of tar and feathers" (quoted in "August Breeze at Ashfield," p. 5).

57. Norton, quoted in "August Breeze at Ashfield," *Springfield Republican*, 22 Aug 1902, p. 5.

58. Edwin Burritt Smith, quoted in "August Breeze at Ashfield," *Springfield Republican*, 22 Aug 1902, p. 5; Hall, quoted in "August Breeze at Ashfield," p. 5; Norton used the phrase "his bitter and elaborate rebuke of me" about Hall's speech in a letter to WJ of 1 Sept 1902, James Family Papers, HL [bMS Am 1092 (630)]; after this incident, relations between Norton and Hall were coldly civil; when Hall sought to buy a pasture from Norton in 1905 ("My dear Professor Norton"), the older man informed him ("Dear President Hall") that he had transferred all of his Ashfield holdings the year before to his children who were not inclined to sell (GSH to CEN of 29 Sept 1905 and CEN to GSH of 4 Oct 1905, Archives and Special Collections, Goddard Library, Clark University, Worcester, MA); cf. Hall on Norton in his 1923 autobiography: "in very many ways and for many years he broadened and refined my views of life, although I fear in later years there was less sympathy of standpoint and opinion between us" (Hall, *Life and Confessions*, p. 171); the Colorado anti-silverite speaker was Louis R. Ehrich.

59. "When the Ashfield dinners were first proposed they were received with acquiescent indifference," a remark made by Frederick G. Howes, quoted in "The Dinner at Ashfield," *Springfield Republican*, 21 Aug 1903, p. 5; Lowell was

an Ashfield speaker in 1885, Warner in 1881, 1887, 1894 and 1899; Booker T. Washington spoke in 1898, and was invited to speak on at least two other occasions; in 1903, when Washington had to cancel his appearance at the farewell Dinner, his wife attended and read his speech in his place; "The Philippine War Arraigned at Ashfield," *Springfield Republican*, 18 Aug 1899, p. 5; cf. Hungerford, "Our Summer": "The sight of numbers of apparent idlers or pleasure-seekers is not inspiring to those who are tied to toil, and we may well believe that discontent with the country, and a restless desire to taste the imagined ease of city life, have been aroused by the sight" (p. 575).

60. "'We should respect every vigorous race, however rude and undeveloped, for any such may be chosen by the God of History to be an organ of a new dispensation of culture and civilization. The same principle applies here today,' said President Hall, in closing, 'where the sentiment of the Ashfield community should be expressed and not repressed, still less offended,'" quoted in "August Breeze at Ashfield," *Springfield Republican*, 22 Aug 1902, p. 5; although traces of the 1902 Norton/Hall contretemps have disappeared from NP, they may be found in WJ's correspondence (see also note 58 above), cf. WJ to CEN of late August 1902: "'I wish to say right here' that I thank you from the bottom of my heart for organizing that rebellious dinner at Ashfield, which, I hear indirectly, has caused local bad blood and tribulation. The more the better! May the wound never heal till decent acknowledgement of sin is made" (quoted in Perry, *WJ Life and Character*, 2:314); Hall, *Adolescence: Its Psychology and Its Relations to Physiology, Anthropology, Sociology, Sex, Crime, Religion and Education*, quoted in Ross, *G. Stanley Hall*, 332.

61. Norton's farewell speech, quoted in "The Dinner at Ashfield," *Springfield Republican*, 20 Aug 1903, p. 5: "Once more the benignant presence of Curtis is with us. He and Lowell lead the procession of the immortals. Howells and Warner, [the Rev. John W.] Chadwick and [George Washington] Cable, come close behind. [Joseph H.] Choate and [Edward J.] Phelps, Moorfield Storey and [Wayne] MacVeagh, Gov. [William E.] Russell [of Massachusetts] and Gov. [Daniel H.] Chamberlain [of South Carolina] and many other men of high distinction follow on, while Booker T. Washington, the wise leader of his race, calm, steadfast, sagacious, takes his place where he will, honored by all, equal to the best."

62. Charles Macomb Flandrau, quoted in Mason, "Harvard," 46; Norton, typescript of a lecture "On Imagination," given 1898–1900, NP [bMS Am 1088.5 (Box 1)].

Works Cited

Acton, John Emerich Edward Dalberg. *Acton in America: The American Journal of Sir John Acton.* Ed. S. W. Jackman. Shepherdstown: Patmos, 1979.

Adams, Charles Francis, Jr. *Autobiography.* Boston: Houghton Mifflin, 1916.

———. "A Chapter of Erie," *NAR* 109 (July 1869): 30–106.

Anesko, Michael. *Letters, Fictions, Lives: Henry James and William Dean Howells.* NY: Oxford Univ. Press, 1997.

Arnold, Matthew. "The Function of Criticism at the Present Time" in *Complete Prose Works.* Ed. R. H. Super. 11 vols. Ann Arbor: Univ. of Michigan Press, 1960–77. 3:258–85.

"Art and Art-Life in New York." *Lippincott's Monthly Magazine* 29 (Jan 1882): 597–605.

"Arts Electives, The." *Crimson* 1 (30 Sept 1875): 6–7.

Bagehot, Walter. "Adam Smith as a Person" in *Biographical Studies.* Ed. Richard Holt Hutton. London: Longmans, Green, 1889. 247–81.

Barringer, Tim. *Reading the Pre-Raphaelites.* New Haven and London: Yale Univ. Press, 1998.

Beecher, Lyman. *The Autobiography of Lyman Beecher.* 2 vols. Ed. Barbara M. Cross. Cambridge: Harvard Univ. Press, 1961.

Berenson, Bernard. *Rumor and Reflection.* NY: Simon and Schuster, 1952.

Beisner, Robert L. *Twelve Against Empire: The Anti-Imperialists, 1898–1900.* NY: McGraw-Hill, 1968.

Bellows, Henry W. "The Sanitary Commission." *NAR* 98 (Jan 1864): 153–94.

Berkowitz, Peter. *Virtue and the Making of Modern Liberalism.* Princeton: Princeton Univ. Press, 1999.

Bicknell, John W. "The Young Mr. Ramsay" in *Selected Letters of Leslie Stephen.* 2 vols. Ed. John W. Bicknell. Columbus: Ohio State Univ. Press, 1996. 1:11–19.

Biswas, Robindra Kumar. *Arthur Hugh Clough: Towards a Reconsideration.* Oxford: Clarendon, 1972.

Blake, Nelson M. "Background of Cleveland's Venezuelan Policy." *American Historical Review* 47 (1942): 259–77.

Blau, Eve. *Ruskinian Gothic: The Architecture of Deane and Woodward, 1845–1861.* Princeton: Princeton Univ. Press, 1982.

Boswell, James. *Life of Johnson.* 6 vols. Ed. George Birkbeck Hill and L. F. Powell. Oxford: Clarendon, 1971.

Breisach, Ernest A. *American Progressive History*. Chicago: Univ. of Chicago Press, 1993.

"British Gallery in New York, The." *AtMo* 1 (Feb 1858): 501–507.

Brodhead, Richard H. *Cultures of Letters: Scenes of Reading and Writing in Nineteenth-Century America*. Chicago and London: Univ. of Chicago Press, 1993.

———. *The School of Hawthorne*. NY: Oxford Univ. Press, 1986.

Brooks, Van Wyck. *The Dream of Arcadia: American Writers and Artists in Italy, 1760–1915*. NY: E. P. Dutton, 1958.

———. *The Flowering of New England*. NY: E. P. Dutton, 1940.

———. *Scenes and Portraits: Memories of Childhood and Youth*. NY: E. P. Dutton, 1954.

Brown, H. F. and W. H. Wiggin. *Lecture Notes in Fine Arts III*. Boston: Alfred Mudge, 1891.

Brown, Rollo W. "A Self-Indulgent Apostle" in *Lonely Americans*. NY: Howard-McCann, 1929. 165–96.

Bruce, George A. *The Twentieth Regiment of Massachusetts Volunteer Infantry, 1861–1865*. Boston and NY: Houghton Mifflin, 1906; rptd. Salem, MA: Higginson, 1998.

Bryce, James. *The American Commonwealth*. 2 vols. NY: Macmillan, 1895.

Buchan, Alastair. *The Spare Chancellor: The Life of Walter Bagehot*. Lansing: Michigan State Univ. Press, 1960.

Bundy, Carol. *The Nature of Sacrifice: A Biography of Charles Russell Lowell, Jr., 1835–64*. NY: Farrar, Straus and Giroux, 2005.

Burne-Jones, Georgiana. *Memorials of Edward Burne-Jones*. 2 vols. London: Macmillan, 1906.

Burrow, J. W. *Whigs and Liberals: Continuity and Change in English Political Thought*. Oxford: Clarendon, 1988.

Bushnell, Horace. *Barbarism the First Danger*. NY: printed for the American Home Missionary Society, 1847.

Butler, Leslie. "The Mugwump Dilemma: Democracy and Cultural Authority in Victorian America." Ph.D. diss., Yale, 1997.

Camfield, Gregg. "The Moral Aesthetics of Sentimentality: A Missing Key to *Uncle Tom's Cabin*." *Nineteenth-Century Literature* 43 (1988): 319–45.

Carlyle, Thomas. *The Correspondence of Thomas Carlyle and Ralph Waldo Emerson*. 2 vols. Ed. C. E. Norton. Boston: Ticknor, 1888.

———. "On History" (1830) in *Critical and Miscellaneous Essays*. 4 vols. Boston: Brown and Tapgard, 1860. 2:228–40.

———. "On History Again" (1833) in *Critical and Miscellaneous Essays*. 4 vols. Boston: Brown and Tapgard, 1860. 3:247–56.

———. *Past and Present*. Ed. Richard D. Altick. NY: New York Univ. Press, 1965.

Carr, Comyns. "Edward Burne-Jones" in *Some Eminent Victorians*. London: Duckworth, 1908. 71–84.

Cary, Edward. *George William Curtis*. Boston and New York: Houghton Mifflin, 1894.

Casteras, Susan P. *English Pre-Raphaelitism and Its Reception in America*. Rutherford, NJ: Fairleigh Dickinson Univ. Press, 1990.

———. "The 1857–58 Exhibition of English Art in America: Critical Responses to Pre-Raphaelitism" in *The New Path: Ruskin and the Pre-Raphaelites*. Ed. Linda S. Ferber and William H. Gerdts. NY: Brooklyn Museum, 1985. 108–33.

Catalogue of the Library of the Boston Athenaeum, 1807–1871. 5 vols. Boston: n. p., 1874–82.

Chapman, John Jay. "Charles Eliot Norton" in *Memories and Milestones*. NY: Moffat, Yard, 1915. 129–45.

———. "Charles Eliot Norton." *The Nursery* 2, iv (June 1898): 4.

Chesnut, Mary. *A Diary from Dixie*. Ed. Isabella D. Martin and Myrta Lockett Avary. NY: Gramarcy, 1997.

———. *Mary Chesnut's Civil War*. New Haven: Yale Univ. Press, 1981.

———. *The Private Mary Chesnut: The Unpublished Civil War Diaries*. Ed. C. Vann Woodward and Elisabeth Muhlenfield. NY: Oxford UP, 1984.

Child, Francis James. *The Scholar-Friends: Letters of Francis James Child and James Russell Lowell*. Ed. M. A. DeWolfe Howe and G. W. Cottrell, Jr. Westport, CT: Greenwood, 1970.

Clough, Arthur Hugh. *The Correspondence of Arthur Hugh Clough*. 2 vols. Ed. F. L. Mulhauser. Oxford: Clarendon, 1957.

———. *Selected Poems*. Ed. Jim McCue. London: Penguin, 1991.

Collini, Stefan. *Public Moralists: Political Thought and Intellectual Life in Britain, 1830–1930*. Oxford: Clarendon, 1993.

Conway, Moncure D. *Thomas Carlyle*. NY: Harpers, 1881.

Copeland, Charles T. "Norton in his Letters." *Harvard Alumni Bulletin* (29 Oct 1913): 84–86.

Curtis, George William. "Emerson" (1854) in *Literary and Social Essays*. NY: Harpers, 1895. 3–29.

———. "Eulogy of Sumner" in *A Memorial of Charles Sumner . . . 16 March 1874*. Boston: n. p., 1874. 107–76.

———. "The Good Fight" in *Orations and Addresses of George William Curtis*. 3 vols. Ed. Charles Eliot Norton. NY: Harpers, 1894. 1:149–77.

———. *Lotus-Eating: A Summer Book*. NY: Harper, 1852.

———. *The Potiphar Papers*. NY: G. P. Putnam, 1853.

———. "The Public Duty of Educated Men" (1877) in *Orations and Addresses of George William Curtis*. 3 vols. Ed. Charles Eliot Norton. NY: Harpers, 1894. 1:263–85.

Dana, Richard Henry, Jr. *Journal of Richard Henry Dana, Jr.* 3 vols. Ed. Robert Lucid. Cambridge: Harvard Univ. Press, 1968.

Davis, Burke. *Sherman's March*. NY: Vintage, 1988.

De Forest, John W. "The 'High-Toned Gentleman'" *Nation* 6 (12 Mar 1868): 206–208.

———. *Miss Ravenel's Conversion From Secession to Loyalty*. Ed. Gordon S. Haight. NY: Rinehart, 1955.

Dew, Thomas R. "Review of the Debate in the Virginia Legislature, 1831–32" in *The Pro-Slavery Argument, as Maintained by the Most Distinguished Writers of the Southern States*. Philadelphia: Lippincott, Grambo, 1853. 286–489.

Dicey, Edward. *Spectator in America*. Ed. Herbert Mitgang. Athens: Univ. of Georgia Press, 1989.

Dickens, Charles. *Pictures from Italy*. NY: Ecco, 1988.

"D'Israeli's *Tancred, or the New Crusade.*" *NAR* 65 (July 1847): 201–47.

Donald, David. *Charles Sumner and the Rights of Man.* NY: Alfred A. Knopf, 1970.

Donner, Wendy. *The Liberal Self: John Stuart Mill's Moral and Political Philosophy.* Ithaca: Cornell Univ. Press, 1991.

Dowling, Linda. "Aestheticism." *Encyclopedia of Aesthetics.* 4 vols. Ed. Michael Kelly. NY: Oxford Univ. Press, 1998. 1:32–37.

———. *The Vulgarization of Art: the Victorians and Aesthetic Democracy.* Charlottesville: Univ. of Virginia Press, 1996.

Dowling, William C. *The Epistolary Moment: The Poetics of the Eighteenth-Century Verse Epistle.* Princeton: Princeton Univ. Press, 1991.

Duffy, Timothy P. "The Gender of Letters: Charles Eliot Norton and the Decline of the Amateur Intellectual Tradition." *New England Quarterly* 69 (1996): 91–109.

Dunne, Finley Peter. *Mr. Dooley in Peace and War.* Boston: Small, Maynard, 1898.

Eliot, Charles William. "Liberty in Education" (1885) in *Educational Reform: Essays and Addresses.* NY: Century, 1898. 125–48.

Eliot, George. "A Natural History of German Life" (1856) in *A George Eliot Miscellany.* Ed. F. B. Pinion. Totowa, NJ: Barnes and Noble, 1982. 11–14.

———. *George Eliot Letters.* 9 vols. Ed. Gordon S. Haight. New Haven: Yale Univ. Press, 1954–78.

Emerson, Edward Waldo. *The Early Years of the Saturday Club, 1855–1870.* Boston and NY: Houghton Mifflin, 1918.

———. *Life and Letters of Charles Russell Lowell.* Boston and NY: Houghton Mifflin, 1907.

Emerson, Ralph Waldo. "American Civilization." *AtMo* 9 (Apr 1862): 502–11.

———. *English Traits* (1856). Boston: Houghton Mifflin, 1884.

———. "The Fortune of the Republic" in *Complete Works of Ralph Waldo Emerson.* 12 vols. Ed. Edward Waldo Emerson. Boston: Houghton Mifflin, 1903–1904. 11:395–25.

———. "Heroism" in *The Collected Works of Ralph Waldo Emerson.* Ed. Alfred R. Ferguson *et al.* Cambridge: Harvard Univ. Press, 1979. Vol. 2: *Essays, First Series.* 143–56.

———. "History" in *The Collected Works of Ralph Waldo Emerson.* Ed. Alfred R. Ferguson *et al.* Cambridge: Harvard Univ. Press, 1979. Vol. 2: *Essays, First Series.* 3–23.

———. *Journals and Miscellaneous Notebooks.* 16 vols. Ed. William H. Gilman *et al.* Cambridge: Harvard Univ. Press, 1960–82.

———. "New England Reformers" in *The Collected Works of Ralph Waldo Emerson.* Ed. Alfred R. Ferguson et al. Cambridge: Harvard Univ. Press, 1983. Vol. 3: *Essays, Second Series.* 149–67.

———. "The Problem" in *Ralph Waldo Emerson.* Ed. Richard Poirier. NY: Oxford Univ. Press, 1990. 495–97.

———. "The Progress of Culture" (1867) in *Complete Works of Ralph Waldo Emerson.* 12 vols. Ed. Edward Waldo Emerson. Boston: Houghton Mifflin, 1903–1904. 8:197–222.

Emerson, W. Eric. *Sons of Privilege: The Charleston Light Dragoons in the Civil War.* Columbia: Univ. of South Carolina Press, 2005.

Ferber, Linda S. "'The Clearest Lens': William J. Stillman and American Landscape Painting" in *Poetic Localities: William J. Stillman.* N.p.: International Center of Photography, n. d. 91–102.

———. "'Determined Realists': The American Pre-Raphaelites and the Association for the Advancement of Truth in Art" in *The New Path: Ruskin and the American Pre-Raphaelites.* Ed. Linda S. Ferber and William H. Gerdts. NY: Brooklyn Museum, 1985. 11–37.

Ferguson, Adam. *An Essay on Civil Society* (1767). New Brunswick: Transaction, 1995.

Fields, Annie. *Authors and Friends.* Boston: Houghton Mifflin, 1897.

Fite, Emerson David. *Social and Industrial Conditions in the North During the Civil War.* NY: Macmillan, 1910.

FitzGerald, Edward. *The Letters of Edward FitzGerald.* 4 vols. Ed. Alfred McKinley Terhune and Annabelle Burdick Terhune. Princeton: Princeton Univ. Press, 1980.

———. *Rubáiyát of Omar Khayyám: A Critical Edition.* Ed. Christopher Decker. Charlottesville: Univ. Press of Virginia, 1997.

"Fortieth Exhibition of the National Academy of Design." *Nation* 1 (6 July 1865): 26–28.

Fox, Richard Wightman. *Trials of Intimacy: Love and Loss in the Beecher-Tilton Scandal.* Chicago: Univ. of Chicago Press, 1999.

Fraser, Hilary. *The Victorians and Renaissance Italy.* Oxford: Basil Blackwell, 1992.

Fredrickson, George M. *The Inner Civil War: Northern Intellectuals and the Crisis of the Union.* Urbana: Univ. of Illinois Press, 1993.

Freedman, Jonathan. *Professions of Taste: Henry James, British Aestheticism, and Commodity Culture.* Stanford: Stanford Univ. Press, 1990.

Froude, James Anthony. *Froude's Life of Carlyle.* Abridged and edited by John Clubbe. Columbus: Ohio State Univ. Press, 1979.

Garraty, John A. *Henry Cabot Lodge: A Biography.* NY: Alfred A. Knopf, 1953.

Gaskell, Elizabeth. *Letters of Mrs. Gaskell and Charles Eliot Norton, 1855–1865.* Ed. Jane Whitehill. Hildesheim: Georg Olms, 1973.

Geoffroy-Menoux, Sophie. "Henry James and Family: Eleven Unpublished Letters" <www.paradigme.com/sources/SOURCES-PDF/Sources14-2.pdf>.

Gray, Wood. *The Hidden Civil War: The Story of the Copperheads.* NY: Viking, 1964.

Green, Martin. *The Problem of Boston: Some Readings in Cultural History.* NY: W. W. Norton, 1966.

Greenough, Horatio. *The Travels, Observations and Experience of a Yankee Stonecutter* (1852). Gainesville, FL: Scholars, 1958.

Greenslet, Ferris. *Walter Pater.* London: William Heinemann, 1904.

Gurstein, Rochelle. *The Repeal of Reticence: A History of America's Cultural and Legal Struggles Over Free Speech, Obscenity, Sexual Liberation, and Modern Art.* NY: Hill and Wang, 1996.

Habegger, Alfred. *The Father: A Life of Henry James, Sr.* NY: Farrar, Straus, 1994.

Hall, David. "The Victorian Connection." *American Quarterly* 27 (1975): 561–74.

Hall, G. Stanley. *Life and Confessions of a Psychologist.* NY: Appleton, 1923.

Hapgood, Norman. *The Changing Years.* NY: Farrar, 1930.

Harper, William. *Memoir on Slavery* in *The Pro-Slavery Argument, as Maintained by the Most Distinguished Writers of the Southern States.* Philadelphia: Lippincott, Grambo, 1853. 1–98.

Harrison, Eliza Cope, ed. *Best Companions: Letters of Eliza Middleton Fisher and Her Mother, Mary Hering Middleton from Charleston, Philadelphia and Newport, 1839–1846.* Columbia: Univ. of South Carolina Press, 2001.

Harvard Celebrities: A Book of Caricatures and Decorative Drawings. Cambridge: University Press, 1901.

Hawthorne, Nathaniel. *The English Notebooks.* NY: Modern Language Association, 1941.

Hersey, George L. *High Victorian Gothic: A Study in Associationism.* Baltimore: Johns Hopkins Univ. Press, 1972.

Hess, Earl J. *The Union Soldier in Battle: Enduring the Ordeal of Combat.* Lawrence: Univ. Press of Kansas, 1997.

Higginson, Thomas Wentworth. "Charles Eliot Norton" in *Carlyle's Laugh and Other Surprises.* Boston: Houghton Mifflin, 1909. 121–36.

Hildreth, Richard. "A Letter to Andrews Norton on Miracles as the Foundation of Religious Belief" in *The Transcendentalists: An Anthology.* Ed. Perry Miller. Cambridge: Harvard Univ. Press, 1950. 220–26.

Hoar, George Frisbie. *Quality of Our Honor: Senator Hoar Speaks Eloquently of Real Americanism.* NY: Bonell, Silver, 1898.

Hofstadter, Richard. *The Age of Reform: From Bryan to F. D. R.* NY: Vintage, 1955.

Hollis, Christopher. *The Oxford Union.* London: Evans, 1965.

Holmes, Oliver Wendell. "Bread and the Newspaper." *AtMo* 8 (Sept 1861): 346–52.

———. "The Inevitable Trial: An Oration delivered before the City Authorities of Boston on the 4th of July 1863" in *Pages from an Old Volume of Life.* Boston: Houghton Mifflin, 1884. 78–120.

Hoogenboom, Ari. *Outlawing the Spoils: A History of the Civil Service Reform Movement, 1865–1883.* Urbana: Univ. of Illinois Press, 1961.

Hovey, Richard. "Aestheticism." *Dartmouth* 4 (30 Mar 1883): 294–95.

Howe, M. A. DeWolfe. *John Jay Chapman and His Letters.* Boston: Houghton Mifflin, 1937.

———. *Life and Letters of George Bancroft.* NY: Da Capo, 1970.

Howells, William Dean. "Charles Eliot Norton: A Reminiscence." *NAR* 198 (1913): 836–48.

———. *A Hazard of New Fortunes.* 2 vols. NY: Harper, 1889.

———. "Recent Literature." *AtMo* 32 (Oct 1873): 496–98.

Howes, Frederick G. *History of the Town of Ashfield, Franklin County, Massachusetts, From Its Settlement in 1742 to 1910.* Ashfield: published by the Town, 1985.

Hungerford, Edward. "Our Summer Migration." *Century Magazine* 42 (Aug 1891): 569–76.

James, Henry. "An American Art-Scholar: Charles Eliot Norton" (1909) in *Henry James: The American Essays*. Ed. Leon Edel. Princeton: Princeton Univ. Press, 1989. 118–28.

———. *The American Scene* in *Collected Travel Writing: Great Britain and America*. NY: Library of America, 1993. 353–736.

———. *The Letters of Henry James*. 4 vols. Ed. Leon Edel. Cambridge: Harvard Univ. Press, 1974–84.

———. *Notes of a Son and Brother* in *Autobiography*. Ed. Frederick W. Dupee. NY: Criterion, 1956. 239–544.

———. *William Wetmore Story and His Friends*. Boston: Houghton Mifflin, 1903.

James, William. "Chauncey Wright" in *The Philosophical Writings of Chauncey Wright: Representative Selections*. Ed. Edward H. Madden. NY: Liberal Arts, 1958. 143–45.

———. *The Correspondence of William James*. 3 vols. Ed. Ignas K. Skrupskelis and Elizabeth M. Berkley. Charlottesville: Univ. of Virginia Press, 1992–94.

———. "Mill's *Subjection of Women*." *NAR* 109 (Oct 1869): 556–65.

Jenkyns, Richard. "The Legacy of Rome" in *The Legacy of Rome: A New Appraisal*. Ed. Richard Jenkyns. Oxford and NY: Oxford Univ. Press, 1992. 1–35.

Keller, Morton. *Affairs of State: Public Life in Late Nineteenth-Century America*. Cambridge: Harvard Univ. Press, 1977.

Kemble, Fanny. *Records of Later Life*. 3 vols. NY: Henry Holt, 1882.

Kent, Christopher. *Brains and Numbers: Elitism, Comtism, and Democracy in Mid-Victorian England*. Toronto: Univ. of Toronto Press, 1978.

Lambert, Royston. *Sir John Simon, 1816–1094, and English Social Administration*. London: MacGibbon and Kee, 1963.

Lears, T. J. Jackson. *No Place of Grace: Antimodernism and the Transformation of American Culture 1880–1920*. Chicago: Univ. of Chicago Press,1981.

Lee, J. Edward and Ron Chepesiuk, eds. *South Carolina in the Civil War: The Confederate Experience in Letters and Diaries*. Jefferson, NC and London: McFarland, n. d.

Liddell Hart, Basil H. *Sherman: Soldier, Realist, American*. NY: Da Capo, 1993.

Linderman, Gerald F. *The Mirror of War: American Society and the Spanish-American War*. Ann Arbor: Univ. of Michigan Press, 1974.

Longfellow, Frances. *Mrs. Longfellow: Selected Letters and Journals of Fanny Appleton Longfellow*. Ed. Edward Wagenknecht. NY: Longmans, Green, 1956.

Longfellow, Henry Wadsworth. *The Letters of Henry Wadsworth Longfellow*. 6 vols. Ed. Andrew Hilen. Cambridge: Harvard Univ. Press, 1966–82.

Lovett, Robert Morss. *All Our Years*. NY: Viking, 1948.

Lowell, James Russell. "The Causes and Consequences of the Rebellion." *NAR* 99 (July 1864): 246–69.

———. "Democracy" in *Democracy and Other Papers*. Ed. Max J. Herzberg. Boston: Houghton Mifflin, 1931. 3–32.

———. "An Epistle to George William Curtis" (1874) in *The Poetical Works of James Russell Lowell*. Boston and NY: Houghton Mifflin, 1899. 451–54.

———. *Letters of James Russell Lowell*. 2 vols. Ed. Charles Eliot Norton. London: Osgood, McIlvaine, 1894.

———. "Ode Recited at the Harvard Commemoration, July 21, 1865" in *The*

Poetical Works of James Russell Lowell. Boston and NY: Houghton Mifflin, 1899. 398–404.

———. "Tempora Mutantur" (1872) in *The Poetical Works of James Russell Lowell.* Boston and NY: Houghton Mifflin, 1899. 491–92.

McLachlan, James. "American Colleges and the Transmission of Culture: The Case of the Mugwumps" in *The Hofstadter Aegis.* Ed. Stanley Elkins and Eric McKitrick. NY: Alfred A. Knopf, 1974. 184–206.

McPherson, James M. *Battle Cry of Freedom: The Civil War Era.* NY: Ballantine, 1989.

———. *The Struggle for Equality: Abolitionists and the Negro in the Civil War and Reconstruction.* Princeton: Princeton Univ. Press, 1964.

———. *What They Fought For, 1861–1865.* Baton Rouge: Louisiana State Univ. Press, 1994.

Madden, Edward H. *Chauncey Wright and the Foundations of Pragmatism.* Seattle: Univ. of Washington Press, 1963.

Maitland, Frederic William. *The Life and Letters of Leslie Stephen.* London: Duckworth, 1906.

Marshall, Esther S. Biographical Sketch of the Life of Elizabeth Gaskell Norton TS. Historical Room, Stockbridge Library Association, Stockbridge, MA.

Martineau, Harriet. *Retrospect of Western Travel.* 2 vols. London: Saunders and Otley; NY: Harper, 1838.

Mason, Daniel Gregory. "Harvard in the 1890s." *New England Quarterly* 9 (1936): 43–70.

Mather, Frank Jewett, Jr. *Charles Herbert Moore: Landscape Painter.* Princeton: Princeton Univ. Press, 1957.

Max, D. T. "Two Cheers for Darwin." *American Scholar* 72 (2003): 67–75.

May, Ernest R. *Imperial Democracy: The Emergence of America as a Great Power.* NY: Harcourt, Brace and World, 1961.

Memorials of Two Friends: J. R. Lowell, 1819–1891; George William Curtis, 1824–1892. NY: privately printed, 1902.

Menand, Louis. *The Metaphysical Club: A Story of Ideas in America.* NY: Farrar, Straus and Giroux, 2001.

Middleton, Alicia Hopton. *Life in Carolina and New England During the Nineteenth Century.* Bristol, RI: privately printed, 1929.

Mill, John Stuart. "Bentham" in *Collected Works of John Stuart Mill.* 33 vols. Ed. J. M. Robson. Toronto: Univ. of Toronto Press, 1963–91. 10:77–115.

———. *Considerations on Representative Government* in *Collected Works of John Stuart Mill.* 33 vols. Ed. J. M. Robson. Toronto: Univ. of Toronto Press, 1963–91. 19:373–613.

———. "The Contest in America" in *Collected Works of John Stuart Mill.* 33 vols. Ed. J. M. Robson. Toronto: Univ. of Toronto Press, 1963–91. 21:127–42.

———. *An Examination of Sir William Hamilton's Philosophy* in *Collected Works of John Stuart Mill.* 33 vols. Ed. J. M. Robson. Toronto: Univ. of Toronto Press, 1979. Vol. 9.

———. "Inaugural Address Delivered to the University of St. Andrews" (1 Feb 1867) in *Collected Works of John Stuart Mill.* 33 vols. Ed. J. M. Robson. Toronto: Univ. of Toronto Press, 1963–91. 21:217–57.

———. *On Liberty* in *Collected Works of John Stuart Mill.* 33 vols. Ed. J. M. Robson. Toronto: Univ. of Toronto Press, 1963–91. 18:213–310.

———. "The Slave Power" in *Collected Works of John Stuart Mill.* 33 vols. Ed. J. M. Robson. Toronto: Univ. of Toronto Press, 1963–91. 21:145–64.

———. *The Subjection of Women* in *Collected Works of John Stuart Mill.* 33 vols. Ed. J. M. Robson. Toronto: Univ. of Toronto Press, 1963–91. 21:261–340.

———. *Utilitarianism* in *Collected Works of John Stuart Mill.* 33 vols. Ed. J. M. Robson. Toronto: Univ. of Toronto Press, 1963–91. 10:203–59.

Miller, Perry. *American Thought: Civil War to World War I.* NY: Holt, 1954.

Miller, Richard F. *Harvard's Civil War: A History of the Twentieth Massachusetts Volunteer Infantry.* Hanover and London: Univ. Press of New England, 2005.

———. "The Trouble with Brahmins: Class and Ethnic Tensions in Massachusetts' 'Harvard Regiment'." *New England Quarterly* 76 (2003): 38–72.

Moody, William Vaughn. *The Poems and Plays of William Vaughn Moody.* 2 vols. Boston: Houghton Mifflin, 1912.

Moore, Charles. *The Life and Times of Charles Follen McKim.* Boston: Houghton Mifflin, 1929.

Moore, Rayburn S. "The Letters of Alice James to Anne Ashburner, 1873–78." *Resources for American Literary Study* 27 (2001): 17–64, 196–236.

Moorhead, James H. *American Apocalypse: Yankee Protestants and the Civil War, 1860–1869.* New Haven: Yale Univ. Press, 1978.

Morison, Samuel Eliot. "Reminiscences of Charles Eliot Norton." *New England Quarterly* 33 (1960): 364–68.

———, Henry Steel Commager, and William E. Leuchtenburg. *A Concise History of the American Republic.* 2nd ed. NY: Oxford Univ. Press, 1983.

Morley, John. "The Death of Mr. Mill." *Fortnightly Review* 13 (June 1873): 669–76.

Motley, John Lothrop. *The Correspondence of John Lothrop Motley.* 2 vols. Ed. George William Curtis. NY: Harper, 1889.

Murdock, Kenneth B. *A Leaf of Grass From Shady Hill.* Cambridge: Harvard Univ. Press, 1928.

Neely, Mark E., Jr. "Politics Purified: Religion and the Growth of Antislavery Idealism in Republican Ideology During the Civil War" in *The Birth of the Grand Old Party: The Republican First Generation.* Ed. Robert F. Engs and Randall M. Miller. Phila.: Univ. of Pennsylvania Press, 2002. 103–27.

———. *The Union Divided: Party Conflict in the Civil War North.* Cambridge: Harvard Univ. Press, 2002.

Norton, Andrews. "Hamilton's *Men and Manners in America.*" *Select Journal of Foreign Periodical Literature* 3 (Jan 1834): 81–99.

———. *Inaugural Discourse, Delivered Before the University, in Cambridge, August 10, 1819.* Cambridge: printed by Hilliard and Metcalf, 1819.

———. "On the Duty of Continual Improvement (Philippians iii: 13, 14)." *Christian Examiner and Theological Review* 2 (Jan–Feb 1825): 412–19.

Norton, Charles Eliot. "The Advantages of Defeat." *AtMo* 8 (Sept 1861): 350–65.

———. "American Political Ideas." *NAR* 101 (Oct 1865): 550–66.

———. "Arthur Hugh Clough." *AtMo* 9 (Apr 1862): 462–69.

———. "Beadle's Dime Books." *NAR* 99 (July 1864): 303–309.

———. "The Church and Religion." *NAR* 106 (Apr 1868): 376–96.

———. *The Common Objects of the Seashore* by J. G. Wood." *AtMo* 2 (July 1858): 253–55.

———. *Considerations on Some Recent Social Theories*. Boston: Little, Brown, 1853.

———. "A Criticism of Harvard Architecture Made to the Board of Overseers." *Harvard Graduates' Magazine* 12 (1904): 359–62.

———. "A Definition of the Fine Arts." *Forum* 7 (Mar 1889): 30–40.

———. "Draper's *Civil Policy of America*." *Nation* 1 (28 Sept 1865): 407–409.

———. "Dwellings and Schools for the Poor." *NAR* 75 (Apr 1852): 464–89.

———. *"Essays and Reviews*." *AtMo* 6 (Nov 1860): 633–35.

———. "Female Suffrage and Education." *Nation* 5 (22 Aug 1867): 152.

———. "Francis James Child." *Harvard Graduates' Magazine* 6 (Dec 1897): 161–69.

———. "Goldwin Smith." *NAR* 99 (Oct 1864): 523–29.

———. "Good Manners." *Nation* 2 (4 May 1866): 571.

———. "Harvard" in *Four American Universities: Harvard, Yale, Princeton, Columbia*. NY: Harper, 1895. 3–43.

———. "The Harvard and Yale Memorial Buildings." *Nation* 5 (11 July 1867): 34–35.

———. "Harvard Memorial Biographies." *NAR* 103 (Oct 1866): 498–509.

———. *Historical Studies of Church-Building in the Middle Ages: Venice, Siena, Florence*. NY: Harper, 1880.

———. *"A History of New England*." *NAR* 102 (Apr 1866): 638–40.

———. "International Policy." *NAR* 103 (Oct 1866): 608–609.

———. "Introduction" to *A Joy For Ever*. Brantwood edition. NY: Charles E. Merrill, [1890]. v–xv.

———. "Introduction" to *The Seven Lamps of Architecture*. Brantwood edition. NY: Charles E. Merrill, [1890]. xi–xiv.

———. *"The Laws of Race as Connected with Slavery*." *AtMo* 7 (Feb 1861): 252–54.

———. *Letters of Charles Eliot Norton*. 2 vols. Ed. Sara Norton and M. A. DeWolfe Howe. Boston: Houghton Mifflin, 1913.

———. "The Life and Character of George William Curtis" in *Memorials of Two Friends: J. R. Lowell, 1819–1892; George William Curtis, 1824–1892*. NY: privately printed, 1902. 73–103.

———. "The Manchester Exhibition." *AtMo* 1 (Nov 1857): 33–46.

———. " 'The New Life' of Dante." *AtMo* 3 (Jan 1859): 62–69.

———. *The New Life of Dante Alighieri*. Boston and NY: Houghton Mifflin, 1895.

———. *"The New Path*." *NAR* 98 (Jan 1864): 303–304.

———. "Nicolas' *Quatrains de Kheyam*." *NAR* 109 (Oct 1869): 565–84.

———. *Notes of Travel and Study in Italy* (1859). Boston: Houghton Mifflin, 1887.

———. "Notices of Gillett's *Huss*." *NAR* 99 (July 1864): 269–74.

———. "Our Soldiers." *NAR* 99 (July 1864): 172–204.

———. "The Oxford Museum." *AtMo* 4 (Dec 1859): 767–70.

———. "The Paradise of Mediocrities." *Nation* 1 (13 July 1865): 43–44.

———. *Paradise* in *The Divine Comedy of Dante Alighieri*. Trans. Charles Eliot Norton. Rev. ed. Boston: Houghton Mifflin, 1920.

————. "Partridge's *Making of the American Nation*." *NAR* 104 (Jan 1867): 247–52.

————. "Religious Liberty." *NAR* 104 (Apr 1867): 586–97.

————. "The St. Nicholas and the Five Points." *Putnam's Magazine* 1 (May 1853): 509–12.

————. "Sir Alexander Grant's *Ethics of Aristotle*." *Nation* 3 (9 August 1866): 106–107.

————. "Some Aspects of Civilization in America." *Forum* 20 (Feb 1896): 641–51.

————. "Waste." *Nation* 2 (8 Mar 1866): 301–302.

————. "Wight's National Academy of Design." *NAR* 103 (Oct 1866): 586–89.

————. "Wilson's *Anti-Slavery Legislation*." *NAR* 100 (Jan 1865): 238–41.

————. "The Work of the Sanitary Commission." *NAR* 104 (Jan 1867): 142–55.

Ogden, Rollo. *Life and Letters of Edwin Lawrence Godkin*. 2 vols. NY: Macmillan, 1907.

Olmsted, Frederick Law. *The Cotton Kingdom: A Traveller's Observations on Cotton and Slavery in the American Slave States* (1861). Ed Arthur M. Schlesinger. NY: Da Capo, 1996.

————. *The Papers of Frederick Law Olmsted*. 6 vols. Ed. Charles Capen McLaughlin *et al*. Baltimore: Johns Hopkins Univ. Press, 1977–92.

Orlowski, Mark B. "Frank Furness: Architecture and the Heroic Ideal." D. Arch. diss., Univ. of Michigan, 1986.

Palfrey, Francis Winthrop. "The Ambulance System." *NAR* 98 (Jan 1864): 74–86.

Palmer, George Herbert. *Autobiography of a Philosopher*. Boston: Houghton Mifflin, 1930.

Pater, Walter. *The Renaissance: Studies in Art and Poetry: The 1893 Text*. Ed. Donald L. Hill. Berkeley: Univ. of California Press, 1980.

Patmore, Coventry. Book 1: "The Betrothals" of *The Angel in the House*. 2nd ed. London: J. W. Parker, 1858.

"Patriotic Young Men." *Boston Evening Transcript* (4 Jan 1864), col. 1.

Peabody, Josephine Preston. *Diary and Letters of Josephine Preston Peabody*. Ed. Christina Hopkinson Baker. Boston: Houghton Mifflin, 1925.

Perry, Ralph Barton. *Thought and Character of William James*. 2 vols. Boston: Little, Brown, 1935.

Persons, Stow. *The Decline of American Gentility*. NY: Columbia Univ. Press, 1973.

"Peter Bonnet Wight." *Dictionary of American Biography*. 20 vols. NY: Scribners, 1928–58. 20:195–96.

Pocock, J. G. A. "Josiah Tucker on Burke, Locke, and Price: A Study in the Varieties of Eighteenth-Century Conservatism" in *Virtue, Commerce and History: Essays on Political Thought and History, Chiefly in the Eighteenth Century*. Cambridge: Cambridge Univ. Press, 1985. 157–91.

————. *The Machiavellian Moment: Florentine Political Thought and the Atlantic Republican Tradition*. Princeton: Princeton Univ. Press, 1975.

Posnock, Ross. *The Trial of Curiosity: Henry James, William James and the Challenge of Modernity*. NY: Oxford Univ. Press, 1991.

Power, Samantha. "Bystanders to Genocide." *AtMo* 288 (2001): 84–108.

Rable, George C. "Hearth, Home, and Family in the Fredericksburg Campaign" in *The War Was You and Me: Civilians in the American Civil War*. Ed. Joan E. Cashin. Princeton: Princeton Univ. Press, 2002. 85–111.

Rand, Benjamin. "Philosophical Instruction in Harvard University from 1636 to 1906—Part II." *Harvard Graduates' Magazine* 37 (1928): 193–97.

Richardson, Heather Cox. *The Death of Reconstruction: Race, Labor, and Politics in the Post–Civil War North, 1865–1901*. Cambridge: Harvard Univ. Press, 2001.

Riddleberger, Patrick W. *1866: The Critical Year Revisited*. Lanham, MD: Univ. Press of America, 1984.

Ripley, George. "*The Latest Form of Infidelity* Examined" in *The Transcendentalists: An Anthology*. Ed. Perry Miller. Cambridge: Harvard Univ. Press, 1950. 213–20.

———. "Philosophic Thought in Boston" in Justin Winsor, *Memorial History of Boston*. 4 vols. Boston: James R. Osgood, 1880. 4:299–301.

Roemer, Carol K. "The Bread of Angels: Charles Eliot Norton's Art History." Ed.D. diss., Claremont Graduate School, 1992.

Roosevelt, Theodore and Henry Cabot Lodge. *Selections from the Correspondence of Theodore Roosevelt and Henry Cabot Lodge, 1884–1918*. 2 vols. NY: Charles Scribner's Sons, 1925.

Rosenberg, John D. *The Darkening Glass: A Portrait of Ruskin's Genius*. NY: Columbia Univ. Press, 1980.

Ross, Dorothy. *G. Stanley Hall: The Psychologist as Prophet*. Chicago: Univ. of Chicago Press, 1972.

Rossetti, William Michael. *Ruskin: Rossetti: Pre-Raphaelitism*. London: George Allen, 1899.

Royce, Josiah. *The Letters of Josiah Royce*. Ed. John Clendenning. Chicago: Univ. of Chicago Press, 1970.

Ruskin, John. "Academy Notes, 1855" in *The Works of John Ruskin*. 39 vols. Ed. E. T. Cook and Alexander Wedderburn. London: George Allen, 1903–12. 14:5–39.

———. "Academy Notes, 1858" in *The Works of John Ruskin*. 39 vols. Ed. E. T. Cook and Alexander Wedderburn. London: George Allen, 1903–12. 14:147–72.

———. "Cambridge School of Art" (1858) in *The Works of John Ruskin*. 39 vols. Ed. E. T. Cook and Alexander Wedderburn. London: George Allen, 1903–12. 16:177–201.

———. *The Correspondence of John Ruskin and Charles Eliot Norton*. Ed. John Lewis Bradley and Ian Ousby. Cambridge: Cambridge Univ. Press, 1987.

———. "Essay on Literature" (1836) in *The Works of John Ruskin*. 39 vols. Ed. E. T. Cook and Alexander Wedderburn. London: George Allen, 1903–12. 1:357–75.

———. "Oxford Inaugural Lecture" in *The Works of John Ruskin*. 39 vols. Ed. E. T. Cook and Alexander Wedderburn. London: George Allen, 1903–12. 20:17–44.

———. *A Joy For Ever* in *The Works of John Ruskin*. 39 vols. Ed. E. T. Cook and Alexander Wedderburn. London: George Allen, 1903–12. 16:9–139.

———. *Modern Painters—Vol. 1* in *The Works of John Ruskin*. 39 vols. Ed. E. T. Cook and Alexander Wedderburn. London: George Allen, 1903–12. Vol. 3.

———. *Modern Painters—Vol. 2* in *The Works of John Ruskin*. 39 vols. Ed. E. T. Cook and Alexander Wedderburn. London: George Allen, 1903–12. Vol. 4.

———. *Modern Painters—Vol. 5* in *The Works of John Ruskin*. 39 vols. Ed. E. T. Cook and Alexander Wedderburn. London: George Allen, 1903–12. Vol. 7.

———. *Praeterita* in *The Works of John Ruskin*. 39 vols. Ed. E. T. Cook and Alexander Wedderburn. London: George Allen, 1903–12. Vol. 35.

———. *The Seven Lamps of Architecture* in *The Works of John Ruskin*. 39 vols. Ed. E. T. Cook and Alexander Wedderburn. London: George Allen, 1903–12. Vol. 8.

———. "The Study of Art" (1858) in *The Works of John Ruskin*. 39 vols. Ed. E. T. Cook and Alexander Wedderburn. London: George Allen, 1903–12. 16:455–60.

———. *The Stones of Venice—Vol. 2* in *The Works of John Ruskin*. 39 vols. Ed. E. T. Cook and Alexander Wedderburn. London: George Allen, 1903–12. Vol. 10.

———. *The Two Paths* in *The Works of John Ruskin*. 39 vols. Ed. E. T. Cook and Alexander Wedderburn. London: George Allen, 1903–12. 16:259–411.

Santayana, George. "The Genteel Tradition in American Philosophy" (1911) in *The Genteel Tradition: Nine Essays*. Ed. Douglas L. Wilson. Cambridge: Harvard Univ. Press, 1967. 37–64.

———. "Materialism and Idealism in American Life" in *Character and Opinion in the United States*. NY: Scribners, 1920. 165–91.

Savage, Philip Henry. *Poems*. Boston: Small, Maynard, 1901.

Sedgwick, Arthur. "Words of a Contemporary" in *Letters of Charles Eliot Norton*. 2 vols. Ed. Sara Norton and M. A. DeWolfe Howe. Boston: Houghton Mifflin, 1913. 2:425–444.

Sedgwick, Catharine Maria. *Married or Single?* 2 vols. NY: Harper, 1857.

Shaffer, Robert B. "Ruskin, Norton and Memorial Hall." *Harvard Library Bulletin* 3 (1949): 213–31.

Shaw, Robert Gould. *Blue-Eyed Child of Fortune: The Civil War Letters of Colonel Robert Gould Shaw*. Ed. Russell Duncan. Athens: Univ. of Georgia Press, 1999.

Sherman, William T. *Memoirs*. NY: Library of America, 1990.

Shklar, Judith N. "Emerson and the Inhibitions of Democracy." *Political Theory* 18 (1990): 601–14.

Simms, William Gilmore. "The Morals of Slavery" in *The Pro-Slavery Argument, as Maintained by the Most Distinguished Writers of the Southern States*. Phila.: Lippincott, Grambo, 1853. 175–285.

———. *The Sack and Destruction of the City of Columbia, S. C.* Ed. A. S. Salley. 2nd ed. Atlanta: Oglethorpe Univ. Press, 1937.

Smith, Adam. *The Theory of Moral Sentiments*. Ed. D. D. Raphael and A. L. Macfie. Indianapolis: Liberty, 1976.

Smith, George W. and Charles Judah, eds. *Life in the North During the Civil War*. Albuquerque: Univ. of New Mexico Press, 1966.

Smith, Goldwin. "The Experience of the American Commonwealth" in *Essays on Reform*. London: Macmillan, 1867. 217–37.

Smith, Logan Pearsall. "On Re-Reading Pater" in *Re-perusals and Re-collections*. London: Constable, 1936. 66–75.

Solomon, Barbara Miller. *Ancestors and Immigrants: A Changing New England Tradition.* NY: John Wiley, 1965.

Spring Rice, Cecil. *Letters and Friendships of Sir Cecil Spring Rice.* 3 vols. Ed. Stephen Gwynn. Boston: Houghton Mifflin, 1929.

Sproat, John G. *"The Best Men": Liberal Reformers in the Gilded Age.* NY: Oxford Univ. Press, 1968.

Stein, Roger B. "A Flower's Saving Grace: The American Pre-Raphaelites." *Artnews* 85 (1985): 85–90.

Stearns, Frank Preston. *Cambridge Sketches.* Philadelphia: Lippincott, 1905.

Stephen, Leslie. "Forgotten Benefactors" in *Social Rights and Duties.* 2 vols. London: Swan Sonnenschein, 1896. 2:252–67.

———. *Selected Letters of Leslie Stephen.* 2 vols. Ed. John Bicknell. Columbus: Ohio State Univ. Press, 1996.

———. *Some Early Impressions.* London: Hogarth, 1914.

Stewart, Dugald. *Elements of the Philosophy of the Human Mind.* Boston: Wells and Lilly, 1818.

Stillman, W. J. "*Modern Painters*, Vol. 5 by J. Ruskin." *AtMo* 6 (Aug 1860): 239–42.

Stone, Lawrence. *The Family, Sex and Marriage in England 1500–1800.* NY: Harper, 1979.

Stowe, Harriet Beecher. "Introduction" to *The Works of Charlotte Elizabeth [Tonna].* 6th ed. 2 vols. NY: M. W. Dodd, 1848. ii–iv.

Strong, George Templeton. *The Diary of George Templeton Strong.* 4 vols. Ed. Allan Nevins and Milton Halsey Thomas. NY: Macmillan, 1952.

Sturgis, Russell. "The Condition of Art in America—2." *NAR* 210 (Jan 1866): 1–24.

———. "The 45th Exhibition of the National Academy of Design." *Nation* 8 (29 Apr 1869): 340–41.

———. "The Pre-Raphaelites and Their Influence—I." *Independent* 52 (18 Jan 1900): 181–83.

Summers, Mark Wahlgren. *The Era of Good Stealings.* NY: Oxford Univ. Press, 1993.

Sumner, Charles. "The Barbarism of Slavery." *Complete Works of Charles Sumner.* 20 vols. Boston: Lee and Shepard, 1900. 6:113–238.

———. *The Selected Letters of Charles Sumner.* Ed. Beverly Wilson Palmer. 2 vols. Boston: Northeastern Univ. Press, 1990.

Taylor, Charles. *Sources of the Self: The Making of Modern Identity.* Cambridge: Harvard Univ. Press, 1989.

Terry, Rose. "The New Sangréal." *AtMo* 12 (Sept 1863): 343–44.

Thompson, Henry Yates. *An Englishman in the American Civil War: Diaries of Henry Yates Thompson, 1863.* Ed. Christopher Chancellor. NY: New York Univ. Press, 1971.

Thucydides. "Funeral Oration of Pericles" in *The Landmark Thucydides: A Comprehensive Guide to "The Peloponnesian War."* Trans. Richard Crawley. Ed. Robert B. Strassler. NY: Free Press, 1996. 111–18.

Timrod, Henry. "The Cotton Boll" in *An American Anthology 1787–1900.* Ed. E. C. Stedman. Boston: Houghton Mifflin, 1900. 314–16.

Tocqueville, Alexis de. *Voyages en Angleterre et en Irlande*. Paris: Gallimard, 1967.

Tomsich, John. *A Genteel Endeavor: American Culture and Politics in the Gilded Age*. Stanford: Stanford Univ. Press, 1971.

Trachtenberg, Alan. *The Incorporation of America: Culture and Society in the Gilded Age*. NY: Hill and Wang, 1982.

Trent, William P. *William Gilmore Simms*. NY: Haskell House, 1968.

Trilling, Lionel. *Sincerity and Authenticity*. Cambridge: Harvard Univ. Press, 1972.

Trollope, Frances. *Domestic Manners of the Americans*. London: Whitaker, Treacher, 1832.

Tucker, David M. *Mugwumps: Public Moralists of the Gilded Age*. Columbia: Univ. of Missouri Press, 1998.

Turner, Frank. "The Victorian Crisis of Faith and the Faith that was Lost" in *Victorian Faith in Crisis: Essays on Continuity and Change in Nineteenth-Century Religious Belief*. Ed. Richard Helmstadter and Bernard Lightman. Stanford: Stanford Univ. Press, 1990. 9–38.

Turner, James. *The Liberal Education of Charles Eliot Norton*. Baltimore: Johns Hopkins University Press, 1999.

Twain, Mark. *Mark Twain's Weapons of Satire: Anti-Imperialist Writings on the Philippine-American War*. Ed. Jim Zwick. Syracuse: Syracuse Univ. Press, 1992.

Vanderbilt, Kermit. *Charles Eliot Norton: Apostle of Culture in a Democracy*. Cambridge: Harvard Univ. Press, 1959.

Ware, John. *Memoir of the Life of John Henry Ware, Jr.* Boston: J. Monroe, 1846.

Wells, Edward L. *A Sketch of the Charleston Light Dragoons From the Earliest Formation of the Corps*. Charleston: Lucas, Richardson, 1888.

Welsh, Alexander. *The City of Dickens*. London: Oxford Univ. Press, 1971.

Wendell, Barrett. "Charles Eliot Norton." *AtMo* 103 (1909): 82–88.

———. "Mr. Lowell as a Teacher" in *Stelligeri*. NY: Charles Scribners, 1893. 205–17.

Werner, Morris R. *It Happened in New York*. NY: Coward, McCann, 1957.

Whistler, James A. M. "The Ten O'Clock Lecture" in *The Gentle Art of Making Enemies*. NY: Dover, 1967. 135–59.

Whitman, Walt. *Democratic Vistas and Other Papers*. London: Walter Scott, 1888. 1–83.

Whittier, John Greenleaf. "In War-Time." *AtMo* 10 (Aug 1862): 235–36.

Whittredge, Worthington. *Autobiography*. Ed. I. H. Baur. NY: Arno, 1969.

Wight, Peter Bonnet. "Reminiscences of the Building of the Academy of Design." *New York Times* (22 Apr 1900): 25.

———. "Reminiscences of Russell Sturgis." *Architectural Record* 26 (1909): 123–31.

Wilde, Oscar. "The Decay of Lying" in *The Soul of Man Under Socialism and Selected Critical Prose*. Ed. Linda Dowling. London: Penguin, 2001. 163–92.

Wilkerson, Marcus M. *Public Opinion and the Spanish-American War: A Study in War Propaganda*. NY: Russell and Russell, 1932.

Wimberly, Lowry Charles. "Oscar Wilde Meets Woodberry." *Prairie Schooner* 21 (1947): 108–16.

Wimsatt, Mary Ann. *The Major Fiction of William Gilmore Simms*. Baton Rouge: Louisiana State Univ. Press, 1989.

Wood, Christopher. *The Pre-Raphaelites*. NY: Crescent, 1994.

Wood, Gray. *The Hidden Civil War: The Story of the Copperheads*. NY: Viking, 1964.

Woodberry, George E. Unsigned review of Walter Pater's *Marius the Epicurean* (1885) in *Walter Pater: The Critical Heritage*. Ed. R. M. Seiler. London: Routledge and Kegan Paul, 1980. 144–51.

Woodward, C. Vann. "Introduction." *Mary Chesnut's Civil War*. New Haven: Yale Univ. Press, 1981. xv–xlv.

Woodworth, Steven E. *While God is Marching On: The Religious World of Civil War Soldiers*. Lawrence: Univ. Press of Kansas, 2001.

Wright, Chauncey. *Letters of Chauncey Wright, with Some Account of His Life*. Ed. James Bradley Thayer. Cambridge: privately printed, 1878.

Wright, Terence. *The Religion of Humanity: The Impact of Comtean Positivism in Victorian Britain*. Cambridge: Cambridge Univ. Press, 1986.

"Yale College Art Building and Exhibition." *Nation* 5 (8 Aug 1867): 115–16.

Young, Edward. *Pre-Raffaelitism or, A Popular Enquiry into Some Newly-Asserted Principles Connected with the Philosophy, Poetry, Religion, and Revolution of Art*. London: Longman, Brown, Green, Longmans and Roberts, 1857.

Index

Acton, John Emerich Edward Dalberg, 35
Adams, Abigail, 110
Adams, Charles Francis, Jr., 86, 128
Adams, Henry, 21, 23–24, 119
Adams, John, xii, 82, 110
Adams, Marian Hooper (Clover), 119
Aestheticism, 137–41, 185n43
Agassiz, Alexander, 120
Agassiz, Jean Louis Rodolphe, 18
Akers, Benjamin Paul, 32
Albert, Prince Consort of England, 1
Allston, George Washington, 96, 179n50
Andrew, John Albion, 48
Appleton, Thomas Gold, 74–75, 107, 116
Arnold, Matthew, 89, 103, 111
Arnold, Thomas, 23
Ashfield Academy Dinners, ix–xii, 145, 154–58, 196n59, 197n60
Ashfield, Mass., ix–x. *See also* Charles Eliot Norton
"Atmosphere." *See* Civic liberalism
Austen, Jane, 110

Bagehot, Walter, 70–71, 86
Ball's Bluff. *See* Civil War
Bancroft, George, 122
Barbarism: as analyzed in Scottish "4-stage" theory, 71–72; as opposed to civilization, 70, 175n6, 196n56; in North, 79–82, 91, 93; in South, 72–73, 84–85. *See also* Civilization
Beard, Charles, xii–xiii
Beisner, Robert L., 162n8
Bellows, Henry W., 54, 58, 61
Bentham, Jeremy, 8, 90

Berenson, Bernard, 140, 191n26
Berkowitz, Peter, xv
"Best, the." *See* Charles Eliot Norton
"Best men," xv, 88–92, 94–97, 144, 153–54
Bicknell, John W., 181n14
Blaine, James Gillespie, 146
Blanc, Jean Joseph Charles Louis, 3
Boston Athenaeum, 58, 83, 173n52
Breisach, Ernest, xii
Brodhead, Richard H., 162n8
Brooks, Phillips, 37
Brooks, Preston, 73
Brooks, Van Wyck, xiii, 2, 7, 30, 65, 142
Brown, Ford Madox, 25
Brown, John, xii, 36, 101
Brown, Rawdon, 118
Browning, Elizabeth Barrett, 20
Bullard, William S., 20, 40, 58, 173n52, 180n5
Bundy, Carol, 168n6
Burke, Edmund, 163n18
Burne-Jones, Edward Coley, xvii, xix, 19, 24, 31, 115, 138, 166n53
Burne-Jones, Georgiana, 115
Burton, William Shakespeare, 18
Bushnell, Horace, 71–72, 74
Butler, Leslie, 161n7

Cabet, Étienne, 5
Cairnes, John Elliott, 72
Carlyle, Jane Welsh, 122–23
Carlyle, Thomas, 23–25, 90, 105; dislikes *Rubáiyát*, 121, 187n58; as spiritual guide, 98–99, 122–26, 131; and U.S. Civil War, 42–43, 187n62. See also *Sartor Resartus*
Casteras, Susan P., 190n17

215

Catholic Church, 4, 35, 102, 104, 110
Cedar Creek. *See* Civil War
Chamberlain, Daniel H., xi, 155
Chapman, John Jay, 142–43, 191n21
Chase, William Merritt, 167n62
Chesnut, Mary Boykin, 43, 68, 76–77
Child, Francis James, 46
Civic liberalism, 92–95, 149; and
  "atmosphere," 88–91, 179n50
Civil War, U.S., xi, 40–46, 48–52, 147–
  48; battle of Ball's Bluff, 45–46;
  Bull Run, first, 43, 51, 53, 79,
  173n49; Bull Run, second, 51;
  Cedar Creek, 45; Chancellorsville,
  48; Chattanooga, 52; Cold Harbor,
  78; Fort Wagner, 45; Fredericksburg,
  41, 45, 79; Gettysburg, 48, 64;
  Glendale, 45–46; Matadequin
  Creek, 78; Murfreesboro, 51; New
  Berne, 45; Petersburg "Crater," 45;
  Vicksburg, 41; Winchester, 45; as
  commemorated at Harvard, 37–39;
  suffering in, 43–50, 169n15
Civilization, as opposed to "barbarism,"
  70; in South, 73–74, 78, 84–85, 148,
  175n6
Clarke, Sir James (CEN's doctor), 32
Classical republicanism, 82–83, 92
Cleveland, Grover, 143, 146–47
Clough, Arthur Hugh, 28, 98–103, 107,
  154; and companionate love, 111
Cold Harbor. *See* Civil War
Companionate marriage, ideal of,
  110–19, 183n34
Compromise, 88; Crittenden (1861), 47
Comte, Auguste, 86–87, 95
Conway, Moncure Daniel, 182n21
Cook, Clarence, 59
Cox, Samuel Sullivan ("Sunset"), 93
Crédit Mobilier, 82
Cromwell, Oliver, 43, 78
Cuba, ix, 148, 151–52, 155
Culture, ideal of, xv, 137, 141; and J. S.
  Mill, 85–86, 91–97, 114–15
Curtis, Anna Shaw, 170n20, 170n21
Curtis, George William, xi, xviii, 3–5,
  21, 75, 102–103, 145, 176n19; and
  CEN's engagement, 107; and Civil
  War, 42, 45–46, 68, 92–93; on Mill,

178n42, 184n40; as orator, 154; and
  women's suffrage, 113, 147
Curtis, Joseph Bridgham, 45, 170n20

Dana, Richard Henry, Jr., 100, 181n12
Dante Alighieri, 19, 21; *Divine Comedy*,
  185n49, 188n67; *La Vita Nuova* (The
  New Life), 33–34, 114, 124
Darwin, Erasmus, 105
Darwin, Charles, 17–18, 22, 103, 106
Davis, Jefferson, 78
Davis, Admiral Charles Henry, 37
De Forest, John William, 73, 77, 84–85
De Vere, Aubrey, 57
Dew, Thomas R., 74
Dicey, Edward, 87
Dickens, Charles, 6, 10–12
Dix, Dorothea, xviii
Donatello, 144, 154
Donner, Wendy, 179n52
Dowling, William C., 183n34
Duane, William, xiii
Duffy, Timothy P., 162n8

Eliot, George, 9–10, 111, 115
Eliot, Charles William, 106, 131,
  134–35, 183n27, 190n14
Emancipation Proclamation, 40, 41,
  48–49, 56
Emerson, Edward Waldo, 169n6
Emerson, Ralph Waldo, xix, 23, 37,
  56, 86–87; and Andrews Norton,
  101; and Carlyle, 42, 123, 187n62;
  and CEN, 134; and culture, 85,
  95–96; on heroism, 148; "The
  Problem"(poem), 66; dislikes
  Rubáiyát, 121; on weeds, 60
"Emersonian June," 38, 56, 67, 95, 134
Essays and Reviews (1860), 102, 181n13

Farrer, Thomas, 59–60
Ferguson, Adam, 9, 70–71, 83
Field, John W., 145
Fifty-fourth Mass. Volunteers, 45
Fisher, Sidney George, 171n25
Fisk, Jim, 128–29
FitzGerald, Edward, 162n15, 187n58
Florence. *See* Italy
Forbes, John Murray, 40, 45, 48, 170n19

Fraser, Hilary, 165n41
Fredericksburg. *See* Civil War
Fredrickson, George M., 162n8, 171n25
Freedman, Jonathan, 162n8
Froude, James Anthony, 21, 24, 98–99
Fuller, Margaret, 101
Furness, Frank, 174n65

Gardner, Isabella Stewart, 136
Garrison, William Lloyd, 47, 171n24
Gaskell, Elizabeth Cleghorn, 1, 9–13,
  28–29, 77
Gaskell, Meta, 105
Geoffroy-Menoux, Sophie, 182n27
Giotto, 17, 30, 33, 62
Gladstone, William Ewart, 87, 114
Glendale. *See* Civil War
Godkin, Edwin Lawrence, 87, 129,
  152–53
Goodhue, Bertram Grosvenor, xix
Gosse, Philip, 18
Gothic and neo-Gothic architecture,
  20–21, 25–27, 31–35, 57, 61–67
Gould, Jay, 82
Grant, Ulysses S., 41, 50, 93, 128–29
Green, Martin, 164n11
Greenough, Horatio, 96
Gurstein, Rochelle, 162n8

Habegger, Alfred, 183n27
Hale, Edward Everett, 150
Hall, David D., 86
Hall, G. Stanley, ix–xi, 154–57, 161n2,
  196n58, 196n60
Hamilton, Sir William, 90, 112
Harper, William, 93
Harvard College, 37–39, 123, 168n1;
  as "our 'carroccio,'" 134, 142,
  190n14
Harvard, Memorial Biographies, 52–53
Harvard Memorial Hall, 38, 64–67,
  131, 140
Hawthorne, Nathaniel, 1, 16–18
Hay, John Milton, x
Hearst, William Randolph, 146, 151
Helps, Arthur, 101
Hess, Earl, 49
Hildreth, Richard, 105
Hill, Thomas, 37

History: expanded scale of, 21–23; as
  human sublime, 22–25, 30
Hoar, George Frisbie, xiv, 150, 193n45
Hofstadter, Richard, xiii, 161n7
Holmes, Dr. Oliver Wendell, 37, 44–45,
  50, 81, 107
Holmes, Oliver Wendell, Jr., 43–44, 49,
  52
Hoogenboom, Ari, 161n7
Howe, Julia Ward, 37
Howe, Samuel Gridley, xviii
Howells, William Dean, 82, 139; on
  CEN, 6, 103, 132, 142, 163n19
Hunt, Richard Morris, 140
Hunt, William Holman, 16, 18, 20

Imagination, as social power, xiv, xviii,
  7–13, 30, 136, 147, 151–52, 164n17
Imperialism, U.S., ix–xi, 193n43
Italy, 44, 117, 125, 185n48, 188n70;
  Florence, 34–36, 66, 116, 127,
  144; Orvieto, 33–35; Pisa, 35, 154,
  195n53; *Risorgimento*, 21, 33, 36,
  168n72; Rome, 35–36; Siena, 35,
  116–17, 127, 145; Venice, 35, 116,
  118–19; Verona, 35

James, Alice, xvii, 188n67, 191n29
James, Henry, xvii, 17, 31, 37–38, 108;
  on CEN, 126, 132, 142
James, Henry, Sr., 119, 182n27
James, William, 31, 104–105, 112, 146;
  on CEN, xvii–xviii, 142, 162n15;
  and Spanish-American War, 152–53,
  197n60
Jameson, Anna Brownell, 96
Johnson, Andrew, 69, 128, 175n3

Keller, Morton, 189n3
Kemble, Frances (Fanny), 62, 130
Kensett, John Frederick, 32, 176n19
Khayyám, Omar, 115, 141, 162n15,
  187n58. See also *Rubáiyát*
Kingsley, Charles, 9
Kossuth, Louis, 3, 5, 164n10

Lears, T. J. Jackson, 162n8, 191n21
Lee, Col. William Raymond, 46,
  171n22
Lee, Gen. Robert E., 43, 78

Index   217

Terry, Rose, 51
The Angel in the House, 107
Thompson, Henry Yates, 87, 168n6
Thoreau, Henry David, 4
Ticknor, George, 2, 122–23, 163n2
Timrod, Henry, 79
Tocqueville, Alexis de, 4, 89
Tonna, Charlotte Elizabeth, 9, 11, 29
Trachtenberg, Alan, 162n8
Transcendentalism, 38, 101–2, 105–6
Trilling, Lionel, 183n34
Tucker, David M., 161n7
Turner, James, xvii, 39, 106, 164n17,
    165n43, 181n10, 184n41
Turner, Joseph Mallord William, 15–16,
    28, 132–34
Twain, Mark, 194n49
Tweed, William Magear (Boss Tweed),
    82, 129
Twentieth Mass. Volunteers ("Harvard
    regiment"), 44–46, 64–65
"Two Nations," problem of the, 6, 11–12

Unitarianism, xii, xiv, 28, 85, 100–101,
    104–6, 181n7, 181n16
Utilitarianism. *See* Jeremy Bentham

Vallandigham, Clement, 41–42
Van Brunt, Henry, 65, 175n69
Vanderbilt, Kermit, xiii, 174n58, 180n4
Vasari, Giorgio, 144

Venezuelan crisis of 1895–1896, xv,
    143, 145–48
Venice. *See* Italy
Vicksburg. *See* Civil War
Victoria, Queen of England, 1

Ware, W. R., 65
Ware, Henry, 85
Warner, Charles Dudley, xi, 197n59
Washington, Booker Taliaferro, xi,
    161n4, 197n59, 197n61
Wendell, Barrett, xix, 32, 140, 191n27
Wharton, Edith, 17, 141
Whistler, James Abbott McNeill,
    137–38
Whitman, Walt, 25, 129
Whitney, William Dwight, 94
Whittier, John Greenleaf, 85
Wight, Peter Bonnet, 59–64. *See also*
    National Academy of Design
Wilde, Oscar, 137–39
Williams, Raymond, 164n11
Winchester. *See* Civil War
Wister, Owen, 77
Women's suffrage, 113, 147, 184n40
Wood, Fernando, 42
Woodberry, George Edward, 139
Woodward, Benjamin, 27, 63
Wordsworth, William, 133–34
Wright, Chauncey, 103–5, 108, 162n15,
    181n16, 182n17, 186n52